2843

5

A.

KU-995-289

Frances Butler

The Star-Crossed Renaissance

The
Star-Crossed Renaissance

*The Quarrel about Astrology
and Its Influence in England*

D ON C AMERON A LLEN

1966
OCTAGON BOOKS, INC.
New York

Reprinted 1966
by special arrangement with Duke University Press

OCTAGON BOOKS, INC.
175 FIFTH AVENUE
NEW YORK, N.Y. 10010

LIBRARY OF CONGRESS CATALOG CARD NUMBER: 66-17500

Printed in U.S.A. by
NOBLE OFFSET PRINTERS, INC.
NEW YORK 3, N.Y.

p 30
32
38
45
47
48
78 note re Eudoxus also ps 128, 133
astronomy not much used against also p. 99
90
93
* 103 medieval classif of sciences resucked in
106 summary confusion of astronomy & astrology —
108 medieval notion of
      limitability of the knowable
109 beliefs vs symbols
110 arguments re naming & transfer
120 - again cubl. - no prediction
143 - same
145-146 - continue to thrive after rejection
148 - Aristotelian cosmology
155 new science
159

PREFACE

LIKE MOST other students of the culture of the English Renaissance, I have often been puzzled by the attitude of the men of that age toward astrology. The studies of this subject published during the last fifty years dissatisfied me. Nobody, I found, had attempted to take into consideration all of the evidence. No truly comprehensive account of the problem had ever been written. This essay about Shakespeare's use of astrology made him out a believer, that essay made him out an unbeliever; but in all cases, it seemed to me that scholars had worked with insufficient material and had based their conclusions on a very narrow investigation of the question. As a consequence of both my interest and ignorance, I resolved to study the matter for myself, and I quickly realized why I had found all previous studies incomplete, and why I could hope to do only a little better than my predecessors. The problem is too large.

The literature of astrology is as vast as the history of man. No one scholar can possibly hope to untangle all of its intricately woven strands; in the course of his life, he cannot read the extant works on the subject, let alone resolve its intricate patterns of thought. In this wilderness of printed words, I found the first obstacle to the realization of my all-embracing plans. This difficulty accounts for the abrupt beginning of my first chapter. For this abruptness I must apologize, however ineffectually, by pointing out that the English and continental writers on the subject obtained their arguments and attitudes from the Italians of the late fifteenth century; for even when they refer to medieval authorities, they usually do so because these writers are cited by Pico della Mirandola or one of his contemporaries. Having to start somewhere, I decided to make Pico and his fellows my point of departure.

[v]

The second obstacle in my way was a bibliographical one. Gardner's bibliography[1] provided me with an excellent start, but I soon found that it was not exact enough for the modern student. To the titles listed in this book, I added many culled from Watt,[2] Caillet,[3] and Peddie;[4] I found other useful bibliographical material in the first volume of J. C. Houzeau and A. Lancaster, *Bibliographie générale de l'astronomie.*[5] In addition to this, I read through the *Short Title Catalogue* and checked my bibliography against the index of *The Catalogue of the Thomason Tracts, 1640-1641.* Finally, I obtained the titles of numerous modern works on astrology from the *Subject Index of the Modern Books Acquired by the British Museum,*[6] and when I was able, I studied the bibliographies compiled by the authors of these books. I regret that the studies of Henseling[7] and of Saintyves,[8] which contain important bibliographies, appeared too late to be of much use to me. Perhaps the most useful of all bibliographies that I came upon is the catalogue of William Lilly's personal library. This list occupies the eleven concluding pages of the astrologer's *An Easie and Plain Method Teaching How to Judge Upon Nativities* and records the titles of one hundred and ninety-five books.[9] In spite of all these aids, I have had to compile my

[1] F. Leigh Gardner, *A Catalogue Raisonné of Works on the Occult Science.* Vol. II, *Astrological Books* (London, 1911).

[2] Robert Watt, *Bibliotheca Britannica, or A General Index to British and Foreign Literature* (4 vols.; Edinburgh, 1824).

[3] A. L. Caillet, *Manuel Bibliographique des Sciences Psychiques ou Occultes* (3 vols.; Paris, 1912).

[4] R. A. Peddie, *Subject Index of Books before 1880* (London, 1933); *Subject Index of Books to 1880. Second Series* (London, 1935); *Subject Index of Books to 1880. Third Series* (London, 1939).

[5] 3 vols.; Bruxelles, 1882-89.

[6] 9 vols.; London, 1881-1935.

[7] Robert Henseling, *Umstrittenes Weltbild. Astrologie. Welteislehre. Um Erdgestalt und Weltmitte* (Leipzig, 1939).

[8] P. Saintyves, *L'Astrologie populaire étudiée spécialement dans les doctrines et les traditions relatives à l'influence de la lune* (Paris, 1937).

[9] Because of the irregularities of capitalization, I have followed the A. L. A. method of reducing all early foreign titles, save for the first word, to lower case letters. I have not followed this practice with English titles because of the infrequent reprintings of these works and a more regular system of capitals.

own bibliography largely from the references given in books by Renaissance writers. This method, though blind in some ways, has its merits also; but I should be the last to claim that definitiveness can be reached by following it. I expect to be told that I have overlooked just about as many works as I have included. Some of these oversights are conscious, for I discovered that some books with promising titles contributed nothing important to the history of the astrological controversy. Other omissions are the result of my inability to find the volumes in the libraries at which I worked.

Another problem, not unrelated, was the question of what to include. Besides the statements about astrology in formal treatises, there are countless other sources of information about the attitude of the age to astrology. Historians pause to express their opinions; compilers of *lectios* devote a few paragraphs to the question; preachers and theologians express their ideas in sermons or commentaries. I have permitted some of these views to leak into the book, but, in the main, I have limited myself, both for the reader's sake and my own peace of mind, to a discussion of the formal treatises on both sides of the question. The student will find little in the asides of laymen that the professionals have not mentioned. I have followed this same principle in the fourth chapter, where I discuss the occurrence of astrological attitudes and usages among English men of letters; I have discarded ten reference slips for each one I have used. The word *exhaustive* has many meanings, and one of these meanings strikes two ways.

The incessant and interminable repetition of arguments for and against astrology was a definite problem when I came to organize the book. Should I inflict my ennui upon the reader? Having read several scholarly books, I had imposing precedents, to be sure; but I had also learned how weary the flesh can become when it is subjected to learned reiterations. First, I planned two introductory chapters. In one, I sketched an ideal defense of astrology; in the other, I summarized a typical attack. But the task of integration was great; the annotations extravagant; and the presentation of development impossible. Finally, for lack of a better scheme, I fell back on the chronological method, hoping that its advantages would compensate for its disadvantages.

My inference now is that everybody who lived during the Renaissance believed to some extent in astrology. This is but to say that I have gone on a long journey and arrived at my starting point, but it has been a journey undertaken and pursued with good faith. On the way I have seen a good deal of flat land and a few mountains, and I trust that my description of the plains has not tired the reader so much that he is asleep when we pass the less ordinary scenes.

I began this study in 1935-36, when, thanks to a grant from the American Council of Learned Societies, I was given a year of freedom from the round of academic duties. At this time I completed the research for Chapters II, III, and V. During the years 1936-38, my study lay dormant because my university post was in an isolated part of the West, and I was unable to obtain materials necessary to complete it. Since 1938, I have been able to proceed with my investigations and prepare my manuscript for the press.

In the course of my labors I have incurred many obligations. My thanks go first to the American Council of Learned Societies, which made the inauguration of this study possible, and to the Research Council of Duke University, which, by a grant for photostats and by a partial subsidy for publication, provided for the completion and printing of my work. I must acknowledge also the aid and courtesies that I received from the officials of the British Museum, the Bodleian Library, the Sion College Library, the Henry E. Huntington Library, the Folger Shakespeare Library, and the Library of Congress. I have not spared my friends; and I am grateful to Professor W. C. Curry of Vanderbilt University, Professor Merritt Y. Hughes of Wisconsin University, Professor John W. Spargo of

Northwestern University, and Professors Allan H. Gilbert and Paull F. Baum of Duke University, who have read my manuscript in whole or in part and have suggested many ways to improve it. Finally, I must express my gratitude to Professor F. C. Brown and the other members of the Duke Committee on Publications, and to Mr. David K. Jackson, the assistant editor of the Duke Press, for innumerable kindnesses and efforts in my behalf.

D. C. A.

Durham, North Carolina
October 1, 1940.

CONTENTS

CHAPTER   PAGE

 I. Ficino, Pico della Mirandola, Pontano, and the Astrologers' Doctrine   3

 II. Some Continental Attitudes   47

III. Attack and Defense in Renaissance England   101

IV. Some Aspects of the Dispute about Astrology among Elizabethan and Jacobean Men of Letters   147

 V. Elizabethan and Jacobean Satires on the Almanack and Prognostication   190

Appendix. Some Astrological Physicians and Their Works   247

Bibliography   256

Index   269

The Star-Crossed Renaissance

CHAPTER I

FICINO, PICO DELLA MIRANDOLA, PONTANO, AND THE ASTROLOGERS' DOCTRINE

ASTROLOGY, which was born as a twin to religion in the East, spread over the Western world as the eagles and the superstitions of the Empire advanced. Though it was scorned by some emperors and denounced by many of the fathers of the Church, few wearers of the imperial purple were without their colleges of astrologers and few priests were unmindful of the stars of Genesis and the fate of Sisera. After the Antonines vanished, the doctrine of the ministry of planets became an integral part of the creed by which men lived, but like most doctrines it was not accepted with complete unanimity. There were many believers and a few doubters; there were many orthodox and a few heterodox; there were even martyrs. But the career of astrology in the ancient and medieval world has already been charted by faithful and careful observers;[1] hence we shall take up the course of its history in the Italian peninsula during the latter part of the fifteenth century.

In 1459, Marsilio Ficino, who had been studying medicine at Bologna, returned to Florence and accepted the patronage of Cosimo de' Medici so that he might devote the remainder of his life to the translation and elucidation of the Platonic and Neoplatonic writings. The translations and commentaries that were the fruit of the long and quiet years at the Villa di Careggi are too well known to inventory. Equally well known are the lamp that burned continually before the bust of Plato

---

[1] L.-F. Alfred Maury, *La Magie et l'astrologie dans l'antiquité et au moyen âge* (Paris, 1877); A. Bouché-Leclerq, *L'astrologie Grecque* (Paris, 1899); L. Thorndike, *History of Magic and Experimental Science* (4 vols.; New York, 1929-34).

and the title "pater Platonicae familiae" that Pico della Mirandola bestowed upon Ficino. One knows—thanks to the labors
of Della Torre[2]—of the erudite gatherings that were patterned
on the anniversaries celebrated by the disciples of Plato. At
these gatherings the learned of Florence refurbished in their
own way the prestige of ancient Greece. Here under the eyes
of Ficino, who could style himself "dilectissimus in veritatis
venatione,"[3] and at times under those of Lorenzo, the philosopher prince, scholars expounded the *Phaedrus* or read lectures
on Aristophanes. But most of these men felt that they were
future citizens of the *Civitas Dei* as well as current residents
of the Neo-akademeia, and Ficino's realization of this takes
emphatic shape in the *Theologia Platonica*.

In this book, Ficino expresses his conception of Man's relation to God and the cosmos and provides us with a philosophic
basis for the understanding of his notions about astrology. The
world of Ficino rests on the Neoplatonic ladder of being and
becoming. At the apex of all things is God, who is absolute
goodness, truth, and immobility; in God are the archetypes and
there the multiple is made one and all contraries are reconciled.
From God emanate the Angels, an immobile multitude of pure
intellects, and from the Angels one descends to the rational
soul. The soul is pure form; it is perfect and immortal; in
contrast to the Angels, it is a mobile many. From the soul
emanate the qualities or forms of bodies and from thence there
is a declination to the bodies and to matter, a passive and infinitely divisible substance. The key to Ficino's philosophy is
his concept of the rational soul, which is the bridge between
the material and spiritual worlds. The rational soul shares in
the nature of Angels and by its mobility participates in the
nature of the forms. It can ascend to a higher grade without
losing its inferior nature and descend to a lower grade without
shedding its superiority. The rational soul is, then, the nexus

[2] *Storia dell' Accademia Platonica di Firenze* (Firenze, 1902).
[3] *Opera* (Basel, 1561), I, 889.

between the higher and lower spheres.[4] The cosmogony of Ficino is, of course, clearly Neoplatonic and of Proclean rather than of Plotinian provenance. It represents a definite advance over the older systems because of certain popular theses that the members of the Florentine group were quick to question.

The first of these theses was the microcosmic hypothesis which Bruno and Leibnitz were later to modify and develop. This doctrine had descended from antiquity and had made a place for itself in the Middle Ages. By its tenets man was chained to the operations of the great world of which he was little more than a replica. Ficino is not uncharmed by this notion, for he is quite capable of saying that man is a terrestrial star sheathed in a cloud and that a star is a heavenly man.[5] His doctrine of the independent nature of the rational soul suggests, however, that he would not vote with this school. The other theses which rob the soul of its essential independence were those maintained by the followers of Averroes and Alexander. To the demolition of these doctrines, which were especially cherished by the advanced thinkers of Padua, Ficino devotes the early books of the *Theologica Platonica.* We need not recount Ficino's attempt to erase Averroes' theory of the unity of the intellect or Alexander's doctrine of the impotence of providence; it is only necessary to remember that Ficino constantly opposed, both in his formal treatise and his epistles,[6] any philosophy that fettered the freedom of the rational soul.

Against most of these ideas Ficino opposed his notion of the circular movement of the rational soul, a doctrine somewhat contrary to that of Plotinus, who held that the movement was rectilinear. The normal mode of thought in later Platonism had been to conceive of the ego as concreted to the soul as a medium between being and becoming. Nicholas of Cusa had, however, attacked this notion and argued that the soul was not enclosed in the body as in a jar but expressed itself through the body *qua* medium. This idea was accepted by

[4] *Ibid.,* I, 119-121.   [5] *Ibid.,* I, 659.   [6] *Ibid.,* I, 628, 803, 872.

Ficino, who holds that the soul and its immortality are not based on conceptual cognition but on will or, as Cassirer has so lucidly demonstrated,[7] on eros. This eros, like that of the *Symposium,* causes the spirit to descend to the sensible body and elevate it to the celestial regions not by external compulsion but by free effort.

In delineating Ficino's attitude toward astrology, we must keep in mind the individuality of his cosmology and its essential conflict with orthodox Platonism and the theses of the Neoperipatetics of Padua. The best authority for the doctrines of astrology is the cosmic philosophy of the *Timaeus;* but the moment one admits the concept of eros into the pattern, it becomes hopelessly distorted. In similar wise, Ficino inclines toward the macrocosmic-microcosmic hypothesis and struggles against it. In the early pages of the *De vita,* he insists that the universe is no collection of dead elements and that all things are vitalized and interacting, but he is also inclined to provide evidence like that previously mentioned which suggests that he was basically uncertain. The notion of a free-acting rational soul renders the essential tenets of astrology nugatory; the same idea is likewise unfriendly to the theory of the microcosm. This conflict between the microcosm and the autarchy became in Elizabethan England one of the most jarring of philosophic disputes.[8] It must be remembered, then, that Ficino's fluctuating attitude toward astrology is not, as many have held, the sign of a superstitious and credulous pedant, but the outward manifestation of the doubts of a road-breaking philosopher with an inclination toward eclecticism. With this caveat, we turn to a consideration of Ficino's astrological attitudes.

Like all physicians of his day, Ficino was versed in the doctrine of the stars. As a small boy in Figline, he had un-

---

[7] *Individuum und Kosmos in der Philosophie der Renaissance* (Leipzig and Berlin, 1927), pp. 68-69.

[8] Hans Leube, *Reformation und Humanismus in England* (Leipzig, 1930), pp. 12-26.

doubtedly seen his father consulting the heavens before treating a patient or fashioning a medical amulet in the moment of an auspicious conjunction. These childhood experiences were without doubt emphasized by the medical curriculum of Bologna, for a long training in the art of astrology is apparent not only in Ficino's principal tractates but in his many letters to his friends.

The problem of astrology receives its earliest extended treatment at the hands of Ficino in the *Theologia Platonica,* a work consistently overlooked by commentators, who have preferred to base their discussions of Ficino's astrological notions on the *De vita* and the *Epistolae.* In the course of this work, Ficino considers the three orders of force which govern ratiocination. These orders are providence, fate, and nature. Providence is the radiation of the Divine Mind into the intellect of Angels or even lower rational forms; fate is a mutual share in the eidolons. In Ficino's definition of nature, we get the basis of his theory and a possible clue to his attitude. There are twelve natures attached to the twelve spheres, and these essentially superior natures may be transferred to inferior things. Through providence, says Ficino, the soul is above fate; but through nature, the body is subordinate to fate.[9] This is an early adumbration of Ficino's position. Matter is subject to fate and the complexions are bound to the spheres, but the rational soul, through the offices of providence, is superior to its universe. He recognizes, nevertheless, that the *corpus* has a power, but not a necessitated power, over the *animus.*[10] Thus far one can see only order and reason in Ficino's thinking. The macro-

---

[9] *Op. cit.,* I, 288-289.

[10] The relation of the *animus* to the *corpus* is explained in the first book of the *Theologia Platonica.* "Mens ipsa, quia per intelligentiam et voluntatem, non necessario dependet a corpore, et naturaliter formas separat, atque circa separatas versatur, et quiete potius quam motu proficit, per naturam est a corpore motuque libera" (I, 87). Though the mind is freed from the body by these various agents and qualities, yet the body as it is affected by the planets can affect the mind. Saturn, says Ficino, can modify the seed of the parent, and the fetid, melancholy vapors produced by the planet can produce a Saturnine cast of mind. Similarly, Mars can stir the bile in old men and produce in them a bitter and irascible character (I, 300).

cosm may have an influence on the matter of the microcosm
and this influence may color the rational flame, but the mind
is delivered from matter in the variety of ways that an assumption of free election makes possible. This notion flows through
the three parts of the *De vita,* a work favorable to astrology,
but its stream is often narrow and shallow.

The first section of the *De vita* is devoted to a consideration of the health of the studious and how it should be
guarded. Much of the book is concerned with the Saturnine
melancholic, a section of mankind in which Ficino found
himself enrolled. The children of Mercury and Saturn, cold
and dry planets,[11] are, he says, often people of genius who are
driven by Saturn, the highest of planets, to the study of the
highest things.[12] For these melancholics, Ficino recommends
a certain astrological time for study and creative work and
supplies the formulae for their medicines, which must be com-
pounded under Venus and Jove.[13] The second section of the
book is devoted to a consideration of how life is prolonged.
A long life, says Ficino, is not only the gift of the fates but a
reward for our own care. The astrologer with his prognostic
and the physician with his regimen share in increasing the
span of life.[14] Old people should remember that Saturn is
their star and that Venus, the planet of youth, is of all stars
most malign to them; therefore, the children of Saturn should
fly the things of Venus.[15] For the elderly, Ficino offers a large
number of medicines for the composition of which a knowledge of astrology is essential;[16] he sees, in fact, a connection
between these astrological pharmaceuticals and the gifts of the
Magi.[17] He recommends amulets made during an auspicious
conjunction, but feels that the old man who follows a diet and
keeps his eye on his benign stars will fare well.[18]

The third section of this work, the *De vita coelitus,* is the

[11] *Ibid.,* I, 496.
[13] *Ibid.,* I, 501-505.
[15] *Ibid.,* I, 516, 523.
[17] *Ibid.,* I, 527.

[12] *Ibid.,* I, 498.
[14] *Ibid.,* I, 510.
[16] *Ibid.,* I, 518-519.
[18] *Ibid.,* I, 528.

most astrological of the three sections and the one to which critics of Ficino have referred readily. In the beginning of this section, Ficino addresses a preface to the reader in which he states that he will be charged with credulity for citing astrological formulae and invites the reader to recall that he is simply narrating this matter and not approving it. "Ego non tam probo quam narro."[19] He sees himself simply as a good physician, who offers all that is known about his subject, although he is perfectly sure that much of it has not been proved.

For the student of astrological thought, the most important parts of this section are those given over to the discussion of stellar influences, which Ficino considers in the manner of an adherent to the microcosmic hypothesis. He likes to repeat the figure of the struck harp which set the strings of the unstruck harp vibrating;[20] and, in a way, this figure sets the text for his theory. In the stars, says Ficino, all the species and properties of inferior objects are stored. When the mind produces special forms or begets special powers, it does so by the aid of the stars and the celestial forms. When men are possessed of such admirable gifts that they seem unique among their fellows, this is not so much the result of the celestial forms as of the position of the planets, or their motion, or their relation to other planets.[21] We, and all that is about us, can be claimed by the heavens because of certain preparations that it has made and because all is made and ruled by the heavens. Here one notices that Ficino inclines to the ancient notion that the stars were God's agents during the week of creation, but the notion is immediately shown to be Platonic and quite consonant with Ficino's essential cosmology. As in man the most excellent members move and impart their qualities to the others, so the most perfect things in the universe move and control the inferior things.[22]

With this notion in mind, Ficino considers the stones and

[19] Ibid., I, 530.
[20] Ibid., I, 532-533.
[21] Ibid., I, 531-532.
[22] Ibid., I, 533.

herbs related to the various stars and lists the talents, dispositions, and characters granted by the planets. He repeats his
cithara figure and bases his argument on the Arab theory that
the vibrations of the world soul are transmitted to the souls
of individuals by means of the stellar rays. The spirit of man
may drink these vibrations from the world spirit if his nature
is ready to receive them, if he is ready to rise to the heavens.
"One may arise to the sky," he says, "if one will free oneself
from all that is sordid, from all that is dissimilar to the celestial."[23] The good influence of the stars becomes then a reward
for a form of ethical gymnastics. In this respect Ficino differs
markedly from the conventional astrologer. The rest of the
book swerves from the theoretical to the practical.

The sixth chapter of the book contains a complete survey
of the virtues of the planets; the seventh chapter, a discussion of
the relations between the planets and the bodily organs; the
eighth, an account of the powers of the fixed stars; the tenth
and eleventh, accounts of the uses of astrology in medicine;
and the twelfth, an exhaustive treatment of terrestrial objects
that have celestial virtues. In the thirteenth chapter Ficino
informs his reader about astrological amulets. He says that
he does not use them in his medical practice because when a
stone or metal is inscribed, it gets a new form and not new
qualities. He points out that an amulet does not receive a
celestial influxion in the course of its fashioning as medicine
does in the course of digestion; hence, he will put his entire
faith in medicine.[24] In spite of his doubts, Ficino gives complete directions for the making of amulets.

In the latter part of this section, he turns aside from astrological medicine to consider man's relation to the stars. Whoever is born with a sane mind is destined by the heavens to
some honest work and to a natural life; consequently, each
man should discover for what the heavens have fitted him and
direct himself toward that end. An unfortunate man is one

---

[23] *Ibid.*, I, 535, 544.   [24] *Ibid.*, I, 552, 561-564.

who selects a profession that is inimical to his star or who
resides in a place in which his star has no virtue.[25] In his later
writings, Ficino attacks these ideas; however, he never approaches any closer to the position of the astrological funda-
mentalist. He says that he has no patience with those who
trust the stars instead of God, but in some forms of business it
is wise to consult the heavens. Should his opponents say that
he is doing little more than making life a perpetual servitude,
he would reply that they are the foolish slaves of wealth and
honors, unless, by a little diligence in medicine, they are able to
add a few more days to their credit.[26]

When he composed the *De vita,* Ficino without doubt
thought of himself as a physician writing a handbook for other
physicians; as a consequence of this attitude, he included all
the material that members of his profession would expect to
find in such a book. He believed that the stars had some influence over matter; such a belief was compatible with his essential
cosmology. There is, however, no evidence that he believed
that the stellar rays affected in any way the *animus,* which
according to his basic thought was free in action and capable
of its own elections. There is then no reason to believe that
he subscribed at all to that form of astrology that his contemporaries called "judicial astrology." In his remarks about
astrological amulets he gives one the impression of a man

[25] *Ibid.,* I, 566-567.

[26] *Ibid.,* I, 569. That the *De vita's* astrological coloring brought criticism is evi-
denced by the *Apologia* that Ficino wrote shortly after its publication and addressed
to his friends Nero, Soderino, and Guicciardini. He says that his opponents have
criticized him for dabbling in astrology because he is a priest and a Christian; they
have also denied that the sky is a living thing. He asks his friends to defend him
and puts the arguments in their mouths. Nero is to tell of the historical relationship
between the priest and the physician; Christ ordered his disciples to heal the sick.
If one cannot do this by the word, one must use herbs, minerals, and even the
heavens. Guicciardini is to say that Ficino did not approve of amulets but simply
discussed them. He is to prove that the best type of magic unites medicine and
astrology. Soderino is to show that the heavens are alive. Why should one consider
the vilest plants and animals alive when one insists that the perfect heavens are
dead? Can there be life in the parts and not in the whole; the heavens procreate
on the earth; can the power that grants life be lifeless? (I, 572-573).

fleeing from suspicion but caught by a convention that demanded of each medical writer a section or two on this phase of healing. In some of his epistles, however, we discover that Ficino was at times intrigued by the more superstitious aspects of astrology.

The letters of Ficino abound in astrological allusions. Some of these allusions are of a general nature and indicate the extent of Ficino's astronomical and astrological learning; other allusions are brought in for stylistic reasons, for Ficino was charmed by the astrological witticism. Once he borrowed a book on astrology from Benivieni and returned it after some delay with the excuse that since he is so prompt, the tardiness must have been caused by the stars.[27] He writes to Cavalcanti and apologizes for the stiffness of his style; Saturn has imparted his rigidity to Ficino's pen.[28] At other times, he uses astrological material for literary ornament or for the pointing of ideas. He compares the splendor of the joint magistracy of Niccolini and Valori to a conjunction of the sun and Jupiter.[29] Writing to his friend Barbaro, he tells him that civil ambitions interfere with scholarship, and emphasizes his idea by saying that the planets favorable to study and to politics are hostile to each other.[30] Often he uses illustrations of this sort to give weight to a moral notion; he writes, for example, to Lorenzo de' Medici that as the planets temper each other, so one may be blessed by tempering oneself in a similar fashion. Each has a sky within: a moon symbolizing the continued motion of body and soul, a Mars signifying swiftness and a Saturn slowness, and a Venus for humanity. Learn, Ficino admonishes, to temper this inward sky.[31] In other epistles, Ficino shows that he accepted the basic doctrines of astrologers.

Like most of the men of his age, Ficino believed in portents, and such a philosophy carries one quickly to a belief in judicial

[27] *Ibid.*, I, 801.   [28] *Ibid.*, I, 785.
[29] *Ibid.*, I, 919.   [30] *Ibid.*, I, 892; see also I, 844, 846.
[31] *Ibid.*, I, 805; see also I, 723, 911, 946.

astrology.[32] Ficino is chiefly obsessed by his own lot as a child of Saturn. He likes to mention the position of the stars on his birthday;[33] he sees the influence of the stars in his studies and in his writing;[34] he accounts for his friendship with Bembo[35] and Pico della Mirandola[36] by references to the planets; and he ascribes his lassitudes and his failures to the position of his ruling constellations.[37] At other times, he studied the heavens so that he might give advice to his friends.[38] On one occasion, he saw a warning in the stars for Lorenzo de' Medici;[39] at another time, he predicted Barbaro's fitness for the priesthood.[40] Before he began to write the *De vita,* he consulted the stars to see if the season was auspicious.[41] He narrates the death of Bonatti, who was thrown from his horse according to the prediction of the stars.[42] At another time, Ficino predicts that within two years Italy will be ruled by pious men, because at that time Jupiter will displace Mars as the dominant planet.[43] Finally, we find him writing to Sixtus IV in an excited manner. The coming year looks black; the end of the world is threatened; a supreme calamity of war, pestilence, or famine menaces the whole race; a new false prophet will preach a new heresy and the barbarians will ravage all Italy. This disaster the Pope must avert with a miracle.[44]

We cannot gloss over these allusions; they are exactly the

[32] *Ibid.,* I, 931. Prodigies, he writes to Valori, are not the products of nature or chance; they contain a sublime mystery and arise from forces surpassing man's understanding. They originate from the personal genius, the genius of the place, or the choir of Angels or demons. The angelic choir produces comets, thunder, and lightning; the genius of the place shakes and overturns houses; the personal genius causes dreams and makes dogs howl. These portents show that superior souls do not die but rule with their equals after death; that a great man is about to join his colleagues; and that the dying man is not really dying but being reborn.

[33] *Ibid.,* I, 901.   [34] *Ibid.,* I, 948, 952.

[35] *Ibid.,* I, 821.   [36] *Ibid.,* I, 888.

[37] *Ibid.,* I, 644, 726, 760, 731. The last reference is to a letter to Cavalcanti in which Ficino complains of Saturn. Cavalcanti replies that the stars can neither wish nor do evil. "Beware that you do not transfer your faults to a star that has done you innumerable favors."   [38] *Ibid.,* I, 783, 948.

[39] *Ibid.,* I, 831.   [40] *Ibid.,* I, 920.

[41] *Ibid.,* I, 901.   [42] *Ibid.,* I, 894.

[43] *Ibid.,* I, 861.   [44] *Ibid.,* I, 813.

type of reference that we find in the works of the judicial astrologer. They do not, however, show that Ficino was definitely committed to the notion that the stars governed and predicted everything that happened in the realm below the moon. In the first place, his cosmology prohibited him from believing such a theory; in the second place, we can find as many remarks against judicial astrology in Ficino's writings as we have found for it. In one letter, Ficino says that when one can be mistaken about things near at hand, one can err greatly when one consults objects as distant as the stars. He asks his reader to remember that human affairs depend on a variety of things, such as ancestry, food, and rearing. He remarks that he has noticed that people born under the same constellations have very different characters.[45] In an epistle to Cavalcanti, he observes that though his stars are unfavorable, Saturn is hostile, yet he is untouched.[46] When an astrologer friend wrote Ficino to tell him that his horoscope predicted a man who would restore ancient learning, Ficino replied that such things are the work of God's ministers and come about only when the human mind strives to reach the eternal. The stars did not cause him to labor at his career.[47]

In addition to these scattered objections to judicial astrology, there are in letters written during the 1470's references to a book against astrology that Ficino is in the course of writing. He tells Poliziano that among the books that he has written is a "Disputationes contra Astrologorum iudicia."[48] At nearly the same time, Ficino wrote to Bembo, indicating that the book was not completed but in the course of composition and suggesting that he was going to defend providence and free will against the arguments of the astrologers.[49] The

[45] *Ibid.*, I, 857.   [46] *Ibid.*, I, 724.
[47] *Ibid.*, I, 872.   [48] *Ibid.*, I, 619.
[49] *Ibid.*, I, 771. "Compono librum de providentia Dei atque humani arbitrii libertate, in quo illa Astrologorum iudicia, quae providentiae libertatique detrahunt, pro ingenii facultate redarguo. Nempe quam diligenter coelestia vere metiuntur Astronomi, tam multum circa humana inanes Astrologi mentiuntur." The puns on *metor* and *mentior* suggest Ficino's attitude toward astrology and astronomy.

same information is conveyed to Francisco Marescalco in a
letter that has some additional remarks about providence and
fate.[50] Finally, Ficino sends the proem of the book to Gazolti
and promises in a letter to send the complete book as soon as
the scribe can write out a fair copy.[51] All of these letters are
prior to the publication of Pico della Mirandola's polemic
against astrologers, and the last letter suggests that sometime
before 1480 Ficino had finished a draft of his book. The
treatise against astrology was never published, but there is
good reason to believe that it was not lost.

In 1494, Ficino wrote a letter to Poliziano in which he
discussed his personal attitude toward astrology. Like Pico
and Poliziano, he writes, he, too, has always been an enemy
of astrologers. The Platonists accept the signs of the zodiac
as convenient images, but Plotinus makes sport of them; and
like Plotinus, he has made them laughable in his commentary
on the works of that philosopher.[52] There is in this letter no

[50] *Ibid.*, I, 776.

[51] *Ibid.*, I, 781. A summary of the proem may indicate the structure of the book.
Those that think all events necessitated by the stars err in three ways: they deprive
God of providence and control; they steal away the justice of the Angels; and they
take away man's free will and tranquillity. If they prophesy good, they do it
obscurely; and if a good prophecy comes true, it makes us seem worthless, for it
comes (as the astrologers say) without effort on our part. If the prophecy is ill—
and this is the usual case—we suffer in anticipation although the evil may never be
realized. If astrologers cannot thwart fate, what good is their prescience; if they
can thwart fate, why do they defend fatal necessity? They say that among things
fated there are some things that can be foretold and avoided, but that is saying that
one of the fatal sisters wishes to strike whereas another desires to protect the victim.
Virtue protects a man, not something fated moving against the fated; for if necessity protected against necessity, necessity would be denied. We are driven by fate
only when we believe in fate; if we consider events with care, we will see that we
are driven mainly by astrologers, champions of fate. They not only predict for
individuals but for whole communities, and they tell so many lies that it is not
surprising that occasionally something comes true. They wish to inform others but
they are ignorant themselves. He concludes by urging philosophers to attack these
rogues and hopes that God will thrust down these stormers of the celestial summits.

[52] *Ibid.*, I, 958. In this letter, Ficino returns to the *De vita* and admits that he
used astrology there. He defends himself by his old argument; he was laboring as
a medical curator and was gathering what was probable as well as what was true.
He put in astrological details as the result of a wish rather than of a hope. If one
will read the book with care, one will see that he did not believe in these matters.
In the *De sole*, he taught by allegories rather than by astronomy, and in all his

mention of the finished polemic against astrology, which proves
that it had never been completed and published; for if it had
been completed, there would have been small need for Ficino
to expound his views on astrology to Poliziano. This letter
indicates, as a matter of fact, what happened to the "Disputationes"; it became part of the commentary on Plotinus.

If we turn to Ficino's commentary on Plotinus, we find
twenty folio pages devoted to an attack on astrology. Ficino
admits that the stars may be signs, but denies that they are
causes.[53] He points out the inconsistencies of the astrologers,[54]
and says that a man's future depends on his heredity, not on
his stars.[55] There are various factors that hinder accurate prediction. Astrologers ascribe different effects to different stars,
but there are between 27,000 and 476,000 stars, and one cannot
tell which one had the observed effect. Then, too, the stars
are always shifting their orbits. What is the moment of
nativity about which the astrologers speak? Is it when the
seed enters the matrix? When the child is conceived? When
the foetus leaves the womb? When the child is born? How
does one determine the exact moment of birth?[56] He observes
that farmers and physicians often fail in their simple prognostications, and inquires how astrologers can be successful in their
more complex predictions.[57] He tells of a friend whose horoscope showed a short life, but who lived to be over eighty-five.[58]
At best the stars influence only the matter,[59] and evil comes
not from the planets but from the motions of the free-working
animus.[60] Most of the things that happen to man, he states,
can be traced far more easily to other things than the stars.[61]
These illustrations enable one to determine the nature of

questioned books, he mingled the poetic with the philosophic. He is especially glad
that Pico della Mirandola has attacked the astrologers.

[53] Plotinus, Operum philosophicorum omnium (Basel, 1580), p. 111.
[54] Ibid., pp. 113-115.   [55] Ibid., pp. 120-121.
[56] Ibid., pp. 121-124.   [57] Ibid., p. 124.
[58] Ibid., p. 125.   [59] Ibid., p. 128.
[60] Ibid., p. 129.   [61] Ibid., p. 130.

Ficino's attack. It is not a logical or well-organized treatise, but rather the jottings of a commentator, who put down comments as they came into his head and sometimes forgot that he was repeating what he had said a few pages earlier.

An unfinished manuscript of Ficino's polemic was discovered by Baron in the Bibliotheca Nazionale Centrale at Florence.[62] This manuscript contains many sections from the *Theologia Platonica* and many arguments and illustrations that had been used in the commentary on Plotinus; it is without doubt a rough sketch of the "Disputationes." As he had done in the letter to Bembo, Ficino devotes a large part of this work to the consideration of providence and free will in the affairs of men. These sections should be studied carefully because many of the subsequent attacks on astrology used the same arguments.

The world secures its inner life from the fact that it is permeated with the spirit of its Creator. When God created the world, says Ficino, he created part of himself in it; and he created from his own matter with the same care that he would use in creating himself. As a consequence of this care, God can find a reflection of some aspect of his nature in everything that he created. This world is continually directed by God, but men are allowed to use their free will.[63] To each thing created God gave a *modus agendi,* and in man this is free election, which God may persuade but never force.[64] That action, says Ficino, is most happy in which the actor is the lord of the action, in which he prescribes the mode, measure, and end of his act.[65] With this as a cosmological first principle, it is impossible to think of the stars as playing a very important part in the affairs of the universe, and Ficino pro-

[62] "Willensfreiheit und Astrologie bei Marsilio Ficino und Pico della Mirandola," *Kultur- und Universalgeschichte* (Leipzig, 1927), pp. 145-170. The text has been reprinted in the *Supplementum Ficinianum,* ed. P. O. Kristeller (Florence, 1937).

[63] *Op. cit.,* II, 12; see also *Opera,* I, 111, which is inserted here; for further matter on providence see Kristeller, II, 44-45.

[64] *Ibid.;* this is substantially *Opera,* I, 114.

[65] *Ibid.;* for further matter on free will see II, 23, 71-73.

ceeds to attack astrology as he had in the commentary on
Plotinus and introduces a great amount of material that is
familiar to the student of medieval polemics against astrology.[66]
At the conclusion of the incomplete essay, Ficino returns again
to the question of free will, to the powers of the rational soul.
This, he says, is moved by no body, by none of the celestial
beings; God alone can sway it.[67]

So in the end Ficino returns to the essential notions of the
Theologia Platonica. The rational soul is ever free and no
power below the sphere of God can enslave it. Like a later
Englishman, Sir Thomas Brown, Ficino would have liked to
believe in the creed of the fundamental astrologer, but the
philosophic system which he had accepted made this impossible. To accept astrology wholeheartedly, Ficino would have
had to surrender all of his beliefs and abandon his great and
harmonious Platonic Christianity. This he could not do. During his middle years, he seems to have found many of the
notions of astrology seductive, and he perhaps never gave up
his belief in the influence of the stars on the *corpus;* but in the
end, he seems to have turned from all these philosophic irregularities, as other men turned from sin, and to have put his faith
in the providence of God and man's saving gift of free choice.

We do not know why Ficino failed to publish his "Disputationes." Perhaps he was never satisfied with it; perhaps he
felt that he had said all that he could say about the subject in
the *Theologia Platonica* and the commentary on Plotinus.
Baron suggests that he abandoned the treatise when he learned
that Pico della Mirandola was composing his polemic. There
is a great possibility that this conjecture is correct, since Ficino,

[66] Evil arises from the will (II, 28-30); astrology not a science (II, 33-34); the
mythology of the zodiac and the planets (II, 33-35); the astrologer's lack of logic
(II, 38-39); the moment of nativity (II, 54-56); laws and customs vitiate astrology
(II, 56-59, 70-71); the two opposed generals who consult the stars at the same
moment (II, 60-61); arguments from personal experience (II, 66-68).

[67] *Ibid.*, II, 74.

like all his contemporaries, was impressed by the learning of the young Pico; there is, however, not a shred of evidence to support this conclusion. Both men used common arguments, but whether or not Ficino deferred to the projected book of the younger man will never be known. It is, however, the polemic of Pico della Mirandola that one must now consider, for it was the first great treatise against astrology in modern times and the pattern and authority for many similar tractates printed during the sixteenth century.

The career of Pico della Mirandola was in his own time the subject of many a legend that recent biographers have found difficult to penetrate.[68] For the purpose of this study, however, we may emphasize the publication of the nine hundred theses in 1486 that brought Pico under the ban of the Pope[69] and did much to shape the latter part of his brief life. As an introduction to the theses, Pico wrote an *Oratio de hominis dignitate* which is of the greatest importance for the comprehension of his cosmology and the determination of the basis on which his philosophical objections to astrology rest. The *Oratio,* written when Pico was twenty-four, supplies the reader with a cabalistic interpretation of the universe and with Pico's conception of the position of man in that universe. We discover the key to Pico's theory in an address to Adam that Pico places in the mouth of God. In this speech, God informs Adam that he has not limited him as he has the other objects of creation: Adam is to make his own decisions by means of the free judgment that God has given him. He has placed Adam in the center of the world so that he may con-

---

[68] For biographical details one may consult G. Semprini, *La Filosofia di Pico della Mirandola* (Milano, 1936), or L. Gautier Vignal, *Pic de la Mirandole* (Paris, 1937).

[69] Pico offered to defend his theses against all at Rome, but the contest was halted when thirteen theses were found to border on heresy. Annoyed, Pico wrote an *Apologia* which caused the Vatican to act. Innocent VIII condemned all the theses and by means of his nuncio blocked Pico's attempt to defend his theses in the north. Pico was arrested and imprisoned in the castle of Phillippe de Savoie. His imprisonment was not long and he soon returned to Florence. Alexander VI absolved him from the taint of heresy, but the condemnation by Innocent colored the rest of Pico's life.

template it more easily; and by not making Adam terrestrial or celestial, mortal or immortal, he has allowed Adam to choose the sphere of his existence. "You may degenerate to inferior things, to the brutes, and you may lift yourself, if you wish, to the supernal spheres, to the Divine."[70] In this section, Pico indicates the gulf between his philosophy and that of Ficino. Ficino is incapable of going beyond the notion of transcendence; Pico frees man from any dependence on the Divine Will. For Ficino, the providence of God looks after man and enables him to rise to the higher spheres; for Pico, man has the force to convert himself from a brute into an angel. Such a hypothesis banishes forever the possibility that man can be controlled by any external forces. But there is another philosophic notion in Pico's writings that would also make the tenets of astrology repugnant to him.

Like Ficino, Pico was attracted by certain aspects of the macrocosmic-microcosmic hypothesis. In the *Oratio*, Pico says that man contains the whole universe in himself, but this is a cabalistic notion, and, as Semprini observes,[71] Pico perceives a perfect correspondence between heaven and earth, between the spheres and the decalogue. This correspondence is, however, not the indication of an interdependence but of a harmony. If man contains the whole universe and is also the possessor of a completely separate mind, it is quite impossible that anything in the cosmos can have an influence on him. Because of this philosophy, it is impossible for Pico to subscribe, as Ficino did, to even the milder doctrines of the astrologers, although one ignorant of these notions might see a connection between his interest in cabalistic magic and astrology. Nevertheless, this philosophy does not account for the production of the *Disputationes adversus astrologiam;* the

---

[70] I have used the *Opera* (Venetiis, 1557), which is so badly paged that it is impossible to give references save to book and chapter as I do in the *Disputationes*. The speech here referred to may be found in Italian translation in Semprini, *op. cit.,* pp. 224-225.   [71] *Op. cit.,* p. 118.

incentive for the writing of this work came from a religious conviction rather than from a philosophic motive.

During the latter years of his short life, Pico, because of the papal ban that his earlier theological errors had brought on him, twisted in spiritual agony. Even when he had been exonerated by Alexander VI from the taint of heresy, he still strained every fiber of his being to vindicate himself from the charges that had been aimed earlier at him. After he had regained his freedom and come under the protection of Lorenzo de' Medici, he devoted himself almost entirely to the composition of religious writings. He wrote a commentary on the Psalms, of which only a fragment remains, and the *Heptaplus de septiformi sex dierum Geneseos enarratione,* the most important work from his pen and the one on which his reputation for vast and recondite learning rests. After the completion of these works, he composed the *De ente et uno,* which he dedicated to Poliziano and which contains his ontological attitude. But before this book was printed, he had come under the influence of the ascetic preacher Girolamo Savonarola.

The intense friar had a tremendous influence on Pico, who was already staggering under self-accusations of heretical guilt, and Savonarola saw at once in the gifted young noble an important recruit for his preaching order. Pico seems to have placed himself in the hands of the monk, who directed him in exercises that would prepare him for full participation in the work of the Dominican order. During this period of training, Pico wrote a *In orationem dominicam expositio* and a *Regulae XII.* In addition to these books, he planned, as an exercise of personal atonement, a great work against the enemies of religion. This magnum opus was to be encyclopedic in scope and to contain seven books; one book was to be against unbelievers, one against pagans, one against Hebrews, one against Mohammedans, one against Laodiceans, one against heretics, and one against astrologers. None of these books was published when Death stepped between Pico and the tonsure. The friar, however, had done his work well. Pico's associates knew of his desire to embrace the monastic life; and in England, a young scholar, Thomas More, who was also considering the life of the cloister, pondered the career of the young Italian genius and was ravished by its sublimity.

Thus we see that the _Disputationes adversus astrologiam_ did not originate from a philosophic belief but from religious compulsion. Pico's philosophic essentials are found in it, for he could hardly divorce himself from himself, but we must remember that he wrote the book not as a servant of philosophy but as a servant of God. The _Disputationes_ is not a well-ordered work; we struggle to clutch a central thread that we eventually discover does not exist. The posthumous publication of the polemic may have something to do with this, for the book, as we have it, was edited from Pico's manuscript by his nephew and biographer, who informs us in an introductory epistle to Cardinal Carafa that the manuscript was crabbed and unreadable. We gather that Pico had never completed the treatise to his own satisfaction; yet we feel that had he done so, it would still lack the unity and coherence that a good confutation should possess.

Professor Baron has emphasized the importance of free will in Pico's attack on astrology. We wish that the will was the center of the argument, for we could then show that the philosophy of Pico joined hands with his religious fervor when he couched his pen against the enemies of his faith. The _Disputationes_ is, to be sure, not void of philosophical touches; in the twenty-seventh chapter of the third book, we come on this grand notion: "The miracles of nature are greater than those of the sky. If you will raise yourself to these, you will lift yourself above the skies." In the eighth and ninth chapters of the fourth book, Pico discusses the attitudes of the philosophers and the astrologers concerning free will and there are references to this problem in other portions of the treatise, but it does not form the basic theme. There is no doubt that the postulate of man's independence of spirit was in the mind of Pico when he wrote this book, but it never became his thesis. In the main, the *Disputationes* gathers together all the conventional material against astrology and adds many new and authoritative arguments. It owes its subsequent popularity to the Pico legend and to the fact that it was an encyclopedia where all the opponents of astrology might delve. Since the work is so loosely constructed, we are forced to analyze it seriately.

The *prooemium* to the work makes the distinction that Ficino made between astrologers and astronomers: the latter measure the size and plot the orbits of stars; the former for mercenary gain attempt to predict the future by consulting the stars. Astrologers are wolves in sheep's clothing, for they try to cloak their evil designs by calling themselves *mathematicians*. There is nothing weighty or balanced in their books; there is nothing reasonable in their reasons. Their writings are, in fact, so silly that we doubt if the authors themselves believe what they say. They intrude everywhere; they corrupt philosophy, adulterate medicine, weaken religion, strengthen idolatry, destroy prudence, pollute customs, blight the heavens, and make men anxious, unquiet, and unfortunate in all things.

The first book of the *Disputationes* is devoted to an inspection of authorities in the medieval fashion. Pico points out that Pythagoras, Democritus, Seneca, Cicero, Plato, Aristotle, and other ancient philosophers had no faith in astrology. Even Averroes and Avicenna condemned it. With these ancients, Henry of Hess and the philosophers of Paris agree; another recent authority, Nicholas Oresme, said that astrology was pestilential to all men and especially to princes. Marliani also agrees with this view. Pico looks among his contemporaries and mentions the story of Ficino's friend who lived to be more than eighty-five in spite of astrological predictions to the contrary. He relates how he and his friends laughed at astrology,

and how violent the laughter became when Poliziano was
present to add his wit. He cites Leo, who said that few astrologers believed what they wrote; and remarks that if astrologers spent their time working at their science, observing
magnitudes and velocities, they would get no rewards from
princes, who are interested only in learning about their heirs,
their own careers, and the prospects of victory and empire.
Pico now denies the authenticity of the pseudo-Aristotelian
De secretis and the pseudo-Platonic *De vacca*. Astrologers use
these authorities, he says, as the Gnostics used the works of
the pseudo-Zoroaster. He lists the titles of various other works
falsely attributed to important authorities. He now turns to
the errors of Ptolemy, which, he declares, move a philosopher
to laughter rather than to refutation. Albumasar, originally
a grammarian who was converted to astrology by reading
history, is next held up to scorn; he was so stupid that he confused Ptolemy the astronomer with the kings of Egypt. The
prophets like Isaiah and the fathers like Ambrose, Augustine,
Basil, and Tertullian are called to witness against astrology
and astrologers. He finds it necessary to consider Albertus
Magnus, who seems to have had a penchant for astrology; he
clears up this difficulty by saying that a great part of Albertus'
writings are the interpolations of others. He attacks Pierre
d'Ailly, who applied astrology to history, but has a good word
for the Frenchman's learning. Finally, he quotes the laws
and cites the penalties for the practice in the code of Justinian;
he points out, however, that before the code was established,
astrologers were expelled from Rome.

Pico introduces the second book of ten chapters by quoting
Ptolemy's reasons for the errors of astrologers. He adds to
these, reasons like those mentioned by Ficino, who had insisted
on the importance of laws, food, education, and various factors
in breeding. He offers reasons derived from a variety of astrological sources to prove that even astrologers are aware that
there is no certainty about their science. Astrologers, he pro-

tests, declare that they enable men to obtain a favorable end and to avoid an unfavorable one. This can be done without astrology. He narrates the histories of various men who scorned astrology and reached their chosen goals by their own efforts; then he tells of others, who followed the advice of astrologers and ended miserably. He gives various reasons to prove that astrologers cannot advise correctly about the embracing or shunning of an action. He contradicts d'Ailly's thesis that the seven great conjunctions since the creation of Adam have had significant religious results, and maintains that d'Ailly's attempted concords show how unskilled he was in those sciences that he attempted to wed to astrology. He contends that the belief in the astrological causes of religious events is a common heresy. Albumasar attributed the rise of the Mohammedan sect to the stars; Macliviensis said that Noah found the pattern for the ark in the heavens; Bonatti had Christ subject to His natal conjunctions and derived His character and His mission from the planets. The sixth and seventh chapters of this book are devoted to a discussion of the disagreements of astrologers and to an account of their ignorance of the essentials of astronomy. Pico notices that contemporary astrologers depend on tables and books that are known to be erroneous; and says that if astrology were true, the astrologer's lack of diligence would make it false. The ninth chapter is a familiar essay in which Pico writes that astrologers have always been ridiculed. Although people are always anxious to know the future and although monuments are erected to physicians, philosophers, poets, and emperors, no one has ever seen a monument to an astrologer or heard of an astrologer being accorded public honors. Pico states that he had checked the weather predictions of the astrologers during the current winter and found their predictions correct for seven of a total of one hundred and thirty days. If they cannot foretell the weather correctly, how can they make predictions about the futures of men? He adds numerous amusing and contemporary examples to show how far the astrologer can miss the mark. Occasionally something happens as it was predicted; but since so much happens that the astrologers do not predict, one must assume that whatever happens according to predictions, happens by chance. There is also a tendency to record Apollo's hits and forget his misses. If the predictions of astrologers are based on science, one should get the same answer from every astrologer. One never does.

The major doctrine of Pico and one that was accepted by continental and English opponents of astrology appears in the third book. The heavenly bodies transmit heat, motion, and light—a largess scattered by all the stars—and nothing more. The stars are the signs and causes of nothing. Pico begins this book by arguing for astrology. Theologians and philosophers agree that the inferior world is governed by the sky; and if we will study the matter, we shall see that there is some truth in this belief. The seasons are governed by the stars and the diurnal revolution produces obvious effects. Physicians know the influence of the moon and so do farmers and mariners; other stars have similar powers. The qualities of hot, cold, dry, and moist arise in the heavens; so do changes in the weather and earthquakes. From this one can pass to a study of the effects of these forces on man's humors and complexions which make his character. The human character, in turn, accounts for wars, changes in government, and other far-reaching events. We also know that there are hidden powers in terrestrial things; the powers in heavenly objects must, as a consequence, be more potent because of the added force of light and motion. Finally, there are so many things that cannot be explained, so many things that apparently have no cause and can only be understood when one takes the influence of the stars into consideration. When one looks at men, says Pico, one discovers that some have high skill and others strange temperaments; this ambiguity in the characters and careers of men indicates a fatal and necessitating force. Having set up this straw man, Pico proceeds to knock him down.

The sky, he insists, is a universal not a particular cause; the more particular and material a thing is, the less universal is its cause. The natures and careers of people born at the same moment in the same degree of latitude and longitude show this to be true. It is obviously matter that determines their differences of character; for if the skies were true causes, these people would be identical. Pico now seeks to prove that the skies act qualitatively through their light and motion. The motion of the skies is the source of inferior motion; the heat of the skies contains all the qualities in perfection of inferior bodies and acts on matter as a seminal agent. The fact that the heat and light of the stars vivifies all living matter does not prove, he says in opposition to Ficino's opinion, that the skies are animate. Earthly things live through their souls; the skies simply aid in propagation. He considers whether or not the planets are hot, dry, cold, and moist; and says that since motion and light are common in the sky, their effects must be common. Pico proves that nothing particular depends upon the motion of the planets; and shows that aside from the light of the sun and moon, the light of the other heavenly bodies must have either the same or no effect on sublunar things. He makes sport of the notion that the stars on the other side of the world can have any effect and that the influence of a star can be altered by a shift in its position. He says that the influence of the stars is either substantial or accidental; the influence is substantial when one is subjected to the heat or light of all the stars and accidental when the light is stronger or weaker as in the case of the phases of the moon. These accidental causes produce some influences, but, in the main, the influence of the sky is widely spread. Many of the influences attributed to various planets are really the result of the sun's light and heat. Astrologers like to point to the influence of the sun when it is in Leo or Aries, but the signs have no share in the potency of the sun, which is at this time simply closer to the earth. The latitude in which man lives will definitely influence his life and career, but so will many other things. Men who are born on the coast usually follow fishing and sailing; those born in fertile lands are often less industrious than other men. Pico believes that the moon has a force similar, but not equal, to that of the sun, and says that its phases should be observed by the sailor, the farmer, and the physician. He does not, however, think that the moon has anything to do with the ebb and flow of the tides, and attacks Galen's theory of the influence of the moon on critical days. He observes that the farmer, navigator, and physician are always more skillful in their predictions than the astrologer. The last five chapters of the book are little more than résumés of Pico's previous remarks about universal causes and his central notion that the sky influences inferior things only by its light, heat, and motion.

The fourth book is consecrated to demonstrating the foolishness of the astrologers' arguments. Pico says that their work is not founded on reason, experiment, or the authority of Plato and Aristotle. We do not fear anything with an obvious cause; it is the hidden cause that frightens. When we make a safe voyage by sea, find a treasure, escape from thieves, or leave a building shortly before it collapses, we speak of our good fortune. The sky, however, can only be a natural cause, and so it has nothing to do with fortuitous happenings. He attacks the notion that events are ordained by God but effected by the stars; this, he says, is absurd because all authority has shown that God directs men through the angels. This discussion evokes the question of providence and free will, which Pico solves in the scholastic fashion. We act freely, because although God foresaw what we would do, he foresaw that we would act according to our own choice. He makes fun of those astrologers who put the efficient cause after the effect and describe the fortunes of the ancestors from the constella-

tions of the child. If they cannot predict the child's sex before
its birth, how can they know all these other matters? He also
ridicules the theory that a woman will conceive only when
her stars are in harmony with her husband's. He laughs at
the astrologers who say that by means of an infused force the
natal constellations take effect later in life; a cause, he declares,
is always strongest at its inception. Pico insists that the stars
can have no effect on man's conduct and scorns the notion that
they have any influence on religion. What constellation lasted
for the five thousand years that the world was pagan? Thus
far Pico has dealt with the stars as causes; he will now show
that they cannot be signs. If the stars are signs, they must
always be signs; they can never be causes. He takes up the
theory that the Mosaic and Christian laws were heralded by
the stars, that the flood was so announced, and that the star
of the Magi was such a sign. These, he asserts, were not true
stars, but temporary miraculous stars created by God for an
express purpose.

Book Five takes up the influence of the stars on religion.
In the first chapter, Pico continues his remarks on the relation
between religion and astrology; in the second, third, and fourth
chapters, he shows how astrologers disagree about the great
conjunctions, the cycle of Saturn, and the ascension of the
planets. In the fifth chapter, he points out the more novel
ideas about the effects of the conjunctions and observes that
among the ancients only the sun and the moon were thought
to have any influence. He promised in the first book to refute
the theories of d'Ailly and he now begins his rebuttal. He
admits that the astrologer can plot the position of the stars in
remote times, but he does not believe that he can interpret the
positions in terms of history. The ninth, tenth, and eleventh
chapters continue the assault on d'Ailly's chronology. In the
twelfth chapter, he demolishes Abraham Judaeus' theory that
certain conjunctions accompanied the birth of Christ and
Moses. He argues that there was nothing in the geniture of

Christ to indicate either his death or his mission. In the fifteenth chapter, he questions Albumasar's attribution of the rise of Mohammedanism to a conjunction of Jupiter and Saturn in Scorpio, and objects to the use of the same method for determining the advent of the Antichrist. He concludes the book by condemning the theory, which he credits to Bacon and d'Ailly, that the conjunction of Jupiter with another planet produces a new religion.

The sixth book is devoted to a discussion of the disagreements of the astrologers. Pico says that the astrologers cannot agree on a number of important things, such as the beginning of the year and the nature of an exaltation. He discusses the various theories of the Great Year and mentions with mirth the idea that the Great Year is what the Jews, Mohammedans, and Christians mean by the final resurrection—a term that their astrologer prophets gave to it. He notices that the astrologers disagree in their theories of the twelve houses. Using Aristotle's theory of *locus* for his point of departure, he challenges the hypothesis that a star can lessen or increase the force of its rays by altering its position. Pico is surprised that some people think that the signs of the zodiac were established by nature when they were obviously set up for the convenience of mathematicians. In the fifth, sixth, and seventh chapters, he assails the theories of aspects and shows how the astrologers disagree among themselves on that problem. In the eighth chapter, he questions the doctrine of *obsessio,* and in the ninth chapter disagrees with the theory that the sun's rays lessen by combustion the influence of an adjacent planet. The rays of the sun, he thinks, should increase the powers of the planets. The rest of the book deals in similar fashion with astrological contradictions on such matters as *antiscia,* trigons, sex of signs, climacteric year, and other technical matters.

Book Seven continues Pico's account of astrological fallacies. He argues that the so-called fatal hour is not when a thing is done, but when it begins to be done. He takes up the old problem of the correct moment for making the horoscope and inquires if the foetus is not alive when its heart begins to beat; then he attacks the notions of Ptolemy and Haly on this question. He turns from the consideration of particular fate to discuss such universals as the fates of cities, kingdoms, and nations. Astrologers disagree on whether or not the horoscope of a king should be taken when he is acclaimed or when he is crowned. They take the horoscope of a city when the first stone is laid, but it would be more reasonable to take it when the city is inhabited and its legal code formulated. Pico returns to the subject of the opening of the year; the disagreement about this, he believes, vitiates a great section of astrological practice. He notices that there is a similar confusion in determining future time. He now makes fun of the astrologers' notions of the powers of the fixed stars; they use some of these stars, but they say that others are too small to be effective. This is like omitting the eighth note in music. Some astrologers like Bonatti say that they use all the stars but do not know their names or specific virtues. If a physician said that there were ten curative herbs, but that the names and powers of only nine were known to him, would he be a physician? Pico remarks that it seems absurd to rule out a fixed star because it is too small, when Mercury, which is the smallest of planets, is considered very important in determining genitures.

The eighth book begins with a discussion of the lacunae in astronomical knowledge. Some savants have held that there are other planets quite as great as those known to man. The number of spheres is also in doubt, for some authorities say there are nine spheres and some ten. There are even problems about the movement of the heavens, since some astronomers think that the sphere of fixed stars moves from west to east. If one accepts some of these hypotheses, astrology is completely overthrown. The remainder of the book is a discussion of the signs of the zodiac. These signs, asserts Pico, are the basis of

note

astrology; if they can be shown to be absurd, astrology is absurd. He argues first that the properties of a planet cannot be changed when it enters a sign if the sign is stable. He says that it is difficult to follow astrologers who argue about signs fixed, mobile, and common. He points out that the qualities of a sign are really determined by the images attached to them; even an astrologer like Ibn Ezra admits this. Yet if the astrologers were logical, Aries would be hot and moist. In truth, he says flatly, there is no virtue in the signs. The figures are merely the fabulous creations of astrological madness. There are no animals in the sky. Like the number of the spheres, the number of the signs has varied; the Chaldeans combined Libra and Scorpio into one sign. He concludes by denouncing the astrologers for profaning the heavens, the portico of God's temple, with a menagerie of inane animals.

Book Nine, because of its repetitions, is probably the weakest section of the *Disputationes*. Pico considers again the difficulty of determining the moment for taking the horoscope. He criticizes Ptolemy's theory of *animodar* (the moon at birth and the planets at coitus), and summarizes the attacks made on this theory by the Arabs and astrologers of other nations. He says that it is difficult to determine the fates of cities because historians never agree on the date of founding. In the seventh chapter, he returns to the old theme of the disagreements of the astrologers; then he quotes various authorities to prove that it is almost impossible to follow the movements of the stars. He says that most astrolabes and quadrants have been found to be inaccurate. In the last four chapters of the book, he again rehearses the contradictory arguments of the astrologers on the motions of planets, the eighth sphere, and other matters of controversy.

In the tenth book, Pico argues that *locus* can give no virtue to a planet; if it did, the planet would affect all things under the house and not only its own natives. In the fourth through the ninth chapters, Pico attacks the mathematical, parabolical,

numerical, astrological, and dialectical proofs for the assignment of certain houses to brothers, parents, friends, death, and
enemies. He then amuses himself with the theory that various
houses govern various parts of the body. He asks how many
parts there are in the body? On what basis are the houses
assigned? Is the assignment based on number, on hot, cold,
dry, and moist? Why is Pisces given to the feet? In the
twelfth chapter, Pico takes up the qualities of the signs again
and repeats what he said earlier; then he shows the confusion
among astrologers who argue the nature of a planet from its
elements or color. He attacks the theory that some planets are
evil. Saturn is consonant with earth; is earth evil? Mars is
consonant with fire; is fire evil? He asks if black bile is not as
necessary as blood? Most physical afflictions arise from bad
customs, not from the planets. He now shows that the astrologers disagree among themselves about which stars are fortunate and which unfortunate. In the fifteenth and last chapter, he refutes the notion that the planets are dominant in
certain days and hours, and returns again to the question of
the beginning of the year.

   In the first ten books of the *Disputationes,* Pico criticizes
astrology as a science; in the last two books, he tries to prove
that it is not an art. He states that the defenders of astrology
say that if it cannot be shown to be a science, it can, at least, be
called an art and enjoy the prerogatives of an art. Is there
any reason for this statement? Suppose that certain effects
were observed under certain constellations; in order to check
the relationship between the effects and the stars, one would
have to wait a thousand years for the same sidereal pattern to
return. If two people had the same birth stars and the same
careers, it would be no proof that their lives had been governed
by the stars. Pico now considers the reputedly long observations of the Chaldeans, Egyptians, and Arabs, and says that
their data apply only to the point of observation and have no
universal value. He doubts that the Chaldeans really observed

the heavens for thousands of years. If one subscribes to the theory of the eternity of the world, one cannot believe this legend, because one knows how often civilization has been destroyed by floods and other general catastrophes. If one believes in the Christian chronology, this lengthy stretch of time is quite absurd. The observations of these early astrologers were crude and inexact, for the refinements of astrology are the results of recent theorists. As a consequence, one cannot prove astrology an art by asserting its long history.

Since astrology fails in all its attempts to rationalize its practices, it sometimes claims to be a revealed art. Pico asks if it was revealed to the Chaldeans, to the Egyptians, to the Arabs? Some say that it was revealed to Adam, who passed the knowledge on to his descendants. How is this proved? Why didn't other occult learning come down to us? How did the patriarchs, who knew no mathematics, practice this art? In truth, astrology arose among idolaters, who made a cult of the stars. The learning of the Chaldeans and Egyptians was extraordinarily limited; for though they had astronomers and geometricians, they had no philosophers. The idolatry of these peoples made them think that all things came from the stars; and as men became more vicious and frauds like hydromancy and geomancy arose, astrology naturally took a supreme place. Pico now shows that many astrological notions like the theory of triplicities derived from primitive religious beliefs. He then describes the spread of the astrological superstition, which, he says, was not unaccompanied by satanic machinations. He traces the growth of the practice in Western Europe until the time of Michael Scot and John of Spain. Returning to the matter of the first book, he again mentions the ancients who opposed astrology and tells of the various edicts hurled against it. He concludes the treatise by praising recent writers against astrology like William of Auvergne, Nicholas Oresme, Henry of Hess, John Caton, and "Brenlanlius Britannus," an astrologer unknown to modern scholars but listed by Gesner, the great Renaissance bibliographer.

The publication of this gargantuan attack on astrology provoked widespread comment. Pico's mentor, Savonarola, published an epitome of the work with the title *Opera singulare del doctissimo Padre F. Hieronymo Savonarola di Ferrara contra astrologia divinatrice in corroboratione de le refutatione astrologice del S. Conte Io: Pico de le Mirandola.*[72] The first attack of weight came from Lucio Bellanti, whose *De astrologica veritate, et in disputationes Joannis Pici adversus astrologos responsiones* appeared at Venice in 1502. Bellanti takes the attitude that Pico would not have published this polemic had he lived, and lays the whole blame for its composition on Savonarola, who was infamous and dead at the time Bellanti wrote. The attitude of Bellanti towards Pico is consistently indulgent, for he thinks of him as a brilliant youth beguiled by an old monster. His book is divided into two sections: the first section presents the case for astrology, and the second section refutes the arguments that Pico had advanced against the astrologers. Bellanti is ready to agree with Pico on the broad questions of free will, providence, and human dignity; but he disagrees on many technical points.[73]

[72] The friar's epitome is admittedly for popular consumption, and, consequently, omits most of Pico's technical arguments. Like a good teacher and preacher, Savonarola uses texts and *exempla,* for he realizes that things of the sort stay in the pedestrian mind. The epitome is divided into three sections. In the first section of five chapters, Savonarola shows that the Bible, the fathers, the theologians, the canonists, and the jurists are opposed to the practice of astrology. In the second section of eight chapters, he offers many quotations to show that the philosophers and their philosophies condemn astrology. In the third section of four chapters, he summarizes the quarrels and uncertainties of the astrologers. Most of the material is drawn from the *Disputationes,* but Savonarola seems to have added some references of his own culling. The book was first published in 1497; I have used the Venice edition of 1556.

[73] Bellanti first considers if prognostications are still possible (Ar-A3r). He relates how the science was transmitted (A3r-A5r), and considers it as a theoretical and practical subject. He denies that it is entirely theoretical, and says that the part of it which deals with altitudes and motions is the only hypothetical part. Other sciences are also partially theoretical (A5r-A5v). He now argues that it is a natural

Prior to the publication of the *De astrologica veritate,* an attack on Pico's polemic was meditated by his friend and great contemporary, Giovanni Pontano. When the news of the *Disputationes* reached him at Naples, Pontano took up his uncompleted *De rebus coelestibus* and added three books to it. In one of these books he inserted a statement about Pico. This nobleman and genius, he said, was now persecuting astrology as he had once persecuted religion. He then told of Pico's heretical theses and the condemnation of the theses by Pope Innocent. Pontano knew Pico's weak spot, and there was a

science and as exact as mathematics (A5v-B1v). The sun's action proves that the elements are subject to the celestial bodies (B2v-B3v). Mixed bodies like stones and metals are influenced by the stars, since they have powers that could not come from the elements (B3v-B4v). Plants and herbs are likewise submissive (B4v-B5r). Since an influence is observable in these things, there must also be an influence on more sensitive things (B5r-B6v). There is likewise an influence over will and reason; for if the sensitive parts are influenced, the will must be influenced. Man cannot shun the forces of the complexions (B6v-C1v). He turns to the question of the universality or particularity of the sky, and says that particular effects arise from accidents or the diversity of matter (C1v-C2v). He insists that the effects of the sky can be thwarted if they are known in advance, so that the will can alter the inclinations (C3v-C4v). The light alone does not produce the influence, for the position of the star alters its light (C4v-C5v). He now asks if the stars are the causes of evil? They are not the whole cause of evil because they are essentially good; however, they may incline the matter, and should there be a weakness in the matter, evil might result (C6v). He now develops the theory that there are different qualitative powers in the stars. One can see with the naked eye that parts of the heavens are more luminous than other parts (D4v-D5v). The explanation of this idea is followed by a conventional discussion of the spheres (D6v-F1v). The fixed stars, he asserts, are stronger when they are closer to a potent planet (F1v-F2v). A number of subsequent pages deal with the virtues of planets in the normal fashion (F2v-M2v). The astrologer, he declares, can be deceived in numerous ways (M2v-M3v). He shows by arguments based on agricultural practice that it is important for one to decide on an auspicious moment for an action (M4v-M5r). With such knowledge, one may modify one's difficulties and at times eliminate them entirely (M5r-M5v). The formal refutation of Pico's arguments begins on Q1v. Since Savonarola had been put to death, Bellanti lays the blame for the *Disputationes* on him and says that the friar persuaded Pico to do the book in order to seduce the vulgar (Q2r). He points out that Pico's friend Ficino was a great disciple of astrology and used it in his *De Vita.* He says, contrary to Pico's remarks, that though Poliziano was uninstructed in the subject, he finally employed astrologers to teach him (Q3r). In the second section, Bellanti takes up points from the *Disputationes* like the uncertainty of the astrologers and tries to refute them by pointing out that the druggists are not very certain about their science. He says that the ignorant astrologer, like the ignorant doctor, will make errors, but that the learned astrologer will be successful (Q5r-Q6v).

barb in his remarks. Before the *De rebus* could be published, Pontano learned of Pico's death and expunged this statement from the printed text; it remained, however, in the manuscript, where Soldati later discovered it.[74] In 1501, Pontano published his *De fortuna,* and in that book he paused to recollect Pico's attack on astrology. "Giovanni Pico, a man of great nobility, genius, and learning, who recently tried to demolish the whole sidereal discipline, shall not frighten us," says Pontano.[75] But Pontano did more than mutter about Pico's *Disputationes;* he wrote vigorously and realistically in defense of astrology.

The career of Pontano is closer to the conventional life course of the Renaissance man than that of Ficino or Pico della Mirandola. Like Alberti, Guicciardini, or Ariosto, he was able to unite a life filled with political action to a life of letters and scholarship. He was the foremost Latin poet of his age and the author of numerous charming essays and dialogues in the fields of rhetoric, politics, ethics, and physics.[76] In his own era, he was accused of paganism, and some later writers have thought him superstitious; but he has been cleared in part of the first charge by Toffanin,[77] and a sympathetic inspection of his astrological writings, from which the second accusation arises, will do much to abrogate that imputation.

Like Ficino, Pontano undoubtedly acquired his taste for astrology early in life. His first teacher was Gregorius Tifernas, a master of the Greek tongue but, nonetheless, an adept in astrology. When Pontano came first to Naples, he met Lorenzo Bonincontri, who was, next to Pontano, the greatest astrological poet of the Italian Quattrocento. The friendship between Pontano and Bonincontri was very close, and the two men

[74] B. Soldati, *La Poesia Astrologica nel Quattrocento* (Firenze, 1906), p. 230.

[75] *Opera omnia* (Venetiis, 1518-19), I, 300r; see Soldati, *op. cit.,* p. 230.

[76] See E. Percopo, *Vita di Giovanni Pontano*, ed. M. Manfredi (Napoli, 1938), and A. Altamura, *Giovanni Pontano* (Napoli, 1938), for biographical details.

[77] *Giovanni Pontano fra l'uomo e la natura* (Bologna, 1938).

spent a great amount of time together studying their cherished science. They were later joined in their studies by another astrologer of repute, Tolomeo Gallina, and the influence of these early associates marked the thought of Pontano for the rest of his life.[78]

The earliest astrological compositions of Pontano are the translation of and commentary on the pseudo-Ptolemaic *Centiloquio* and the early books of the *De rebus coelestibus*. Soldati has offered sufficient proof to show that the translation and commentary was a first work and arose from Pontano's association with Bonincontri. The *De rebus coelestibus* was begun about the same time as the translation of the *Centiloquio,* but it was not completed until the news of the *Disputationes* moved Pontano to add three books and bring it to a close.[79]

note

As one turns over the pages of the *De rebus coelestibus* one is struck by the fact that one is reading a handbook of social psychology as well as a textbook of astrology. The characters of men and their social conduct are mentioned almost as often as the influence of the stars. The predilection of Pontano for psychology goes back to his basic theory. Drawing upon Aristotle as his authority, Pontano accepted the notion that the skies were a perfect substance and the elements corruptible substances. Extending this idea, he took the view that the perfect, incorruptible skies had a shaping power over the corruptible sublunary matter. Man, who is the product of the sublunar substance, is, as a consequence, influenced in both his body and his temperament by the stars. The physical temper of man influences in turn his moral temperament and so begets certain inclinations that may be called *character.*[80]

---

[78] Soldati points out (pp. 233-234) two references in which Pontano, like Ficino, sees the influence of the stars in his own career. In the *De rebus* (*op. cit.,* III, 131r-v), Pontano observes that no hereditary talents pushed him to study and poetry; the inclination to these arts must consequently be referred to the stars and the powers emanating from them. The second reference is found in the *Urania* (*Opera,* Venetiis, 1505, sig. D2v).   [79] *Op. cit.,* p. 238.

[80] This thesis is carefully delineated in the prologue to the *De rebus coelestibus* (*op. cit.,* III, 95r-96v).

Both Soldati[81] and Gothein[82] have noticed that Pontano passes over the spiritual element, the divine soul, which the scholastic had breathed into the Aristotelian system. It is this startling silence that turns Pontano's astrological system into a milestone in the history of social psychology.

Pontano's theory that the matter of man is inclined by stellar influences establishes the necessity of a horoscope. If one knows in advance what one's inclinations are, one can shape one's character according to these dispositions if they are good, and check those weaknesses that are unsocial. This thesis is developed in the twelfth book of the *De rebus,* which Pontano wrote after learning of Pico's *Disputationes* and dedicated to Paolo Cortese. In this book Pontano defends astrology vigorously by showing that the sciences of which Pico approved are filled with errors, and by asserting that astrology is the most certain science. One also perceives the position of Pontano. Unlike the vulgar astrologer, unlike even himself when he wrote his commentary on Ptolemy, he does not believe that the influence of the stars is a necessitating force. He does believe, however, that inasmuch as man is corporeal, the stars have the power to incline his matter, to make of him a definite character, unless his rearing or his moral environment offers a definite opposition to sidereal influences.[83] For further aspects of Pontano's astrological ideas, we turn to two of his ethical treatises, the *De prudentia* and the *De fortuna.*

In the fourth book of the *De prudentia,* Pontano defines three types of prudence, and says that there are numerous virtues like perspicacity, caution, versatility, haste and delay,

---

[81] *Op. cit.,* p. 239.

[82] *Die Culturentwicklung Süd-Italiens in Einzel-Darstellungen* (Breslau, 1886), p. 446.

[83] *Op. cit.,* III, 275r-280r. In this book, Pontano takes up Pico's arguments on the disagreements of astrologers; this, says Pontano, does not vitiate the truth of the science, for other scientists disagree. Truth hides itself and must be sought; astrology is conjectural and has no claim to infallibility. There are, of course, charlatans in astrology who claim accuracy; however, the true astrologer recognizes the limits of the science and knows that the stellar rays are altered by many things.

simulation and dissimulation, and diligence that arc ancillary to prudence. First among these attendant virtues is *consideration,* which derives its name from *syderum contemplatione.* It is, says Pontano, a transference of heavenly observations to things below. Before one engages in any action, one should consider it with grave care, one should leave nothing unknown or unconsulted; in other words, one follows in the contemplation of one's actions the same sort of process that a cautious astrologer pursues in the study of the stars.[84] As Percopo observes, Pontano thought of a virtuous man as one who knew how to ascertain a reasonable proportion between the disposition that the stars had given him and the means of modifying this disposition.[85]

The problem of fortune is touched on in various places in Pontano's writings, but his central theory, which is found in the *De fortuna,* is not only closely related to his doctrine of virtue but to his astrological bias. The nature of fortune and the remedies for fortune were two of the major questions of the Renaissance, and the humanistic treatises on these problems are many. Poggio, for instance, advises one not to seek after the external goods of fortune, but to cultivate a quiet and tranquil mind.[86] Coluccio Salutati, who denied the power of the stars[87] and believed like Pico in free will,[88] identifies fortune with providence[89] and believes in a sort of predestination.[90] Alberti, whose *Intercoenales* contains two interesting allegories of fortune,[91] also urges the life of contemplation as an anodyne for the blows of fortune.[92] Enea Sylvio Piccolomini says in a letter to Johannes Hinderbach that a tranquil mind can endure the jests of fortune;[93] but in his *Somnium de for-*

[84] *Ibid.,* I, 198r-v.   [85] *Op. cit.,* p. 278.
[86] *Oratoris et philosophi opera* (Basel, 1538), pp. 86-87.
[87] *Epistolario de C. Salutati,* ed. Novati (Roman, 1891-1911), I, 282.
[88] *Ibid.,* II, 147.
[89] *Ibid.,* I, 256.   [90] *Ibid.,* II, 115-117.
[91] *Opera inedita,* ed. Mancini (Florentiae, 1890), p. 132.
[92] *Opuscoli morali* (Venetia, 1568), pp. 270, 273, 274.
[93] *Opera quae extant omnia* (Basel, 1571), p. 791.

tuna, he has the poet Vegius urge men to follow fortune and points out that men are miserable only when they fly from the fickle goddess.[94] Pico, one recalls, mentioned this matter in the *Disputationes.* Nothing happens without a legitimate cause; if a man digs for a well, he remarks, quoting the Aristotelian illustration, and finds a treasure, this is not a gift of fortune but of God, who undoubtedly sent an angel to tell the digger where to dig.[95] Ficino likewise discussed fortune in a letter to Bembo. He finds a certain irrationality in the cosmic process, which causes the evil to prosper and the good to be cast down. This irrational factor must be fortune, the uncaused cause. Providence, he thinks, can overcome fortune and so can wisdom. Unlike Machiavelli and some of the other later political realists, Ficino denies that the wise man can take advantage of fortune. Wisdom and fortune, he declares, do not make a team, for wisdom can neither be the partner nor the servant of fortune.[96]

There is little doubt that most Renaissance men were convinced of the actuality of a power that they called fortune; in fact, one might describe the Renaissance spirit in terms of *fama, fortuna,* and *humanitas.* In the *De fortuna,* Pontano takes up this irrational factor in human affairs, and treats it in a way that is novel but at the same time in accord with his usual clear-sightedness and interest in society. Fortune is not a god, nature, intellect, or reason; it may be, he says in a passage in which he disposes of free will, the servant of God, who carries out his dictates. The true Christian is satisfied that the decisions of God are just; he does not ask for reasons. He also remembers, says Pontano sarcastically, that God has no time for petty details; He is a delegator of duties. Some of these duties are assigned to fortune.[97] The powers of fortune are limited to external affairs,[98] for it has no power over the body or mind[99] and no force over the reason, although the

[94] *Ibid.,* p. 614.
[96] *Op. cit.,* I, 748.
[98] *Ibid.,* I, 267v.
[95] *Op. cit.,* IV, 3.
[97] *Op. cit.,* I, 266r.
[99] *Ibid.,* I, 269r-v.

reason is sometimes useful in perfecting fortune.[100] The goods that fortune brings are not to be attributed to virtue; in fact, the fortunate man has no need for the Aristotelian mean in which the virtuous man must necessarily perform for all his days.[101] Like reason, prudence is also of use in enhancing the gifts of fortune.[102] Pontano takes a rational attitude towards fortune; and unlike Poggio, Alberti, and Ficino, he does not think that the goods of fortune—wealth, power, friends, and honors—are unnecessary to mortal happiness. It is better to be rich and honorable, declares Pontano, than to sit in a kitchen and wash dishes.[103]

The arch stone of Pontano's theory is his notion of the fortunate. Nature, he states, begets certain men who are the children of fortune and others who are not. The fortunate man, unlike the virtuous man, does not need to follow a code of conduct; he has only to follow his natural impulses, and he will be carried to the highest goals.[104] Pontano admits that he does not know why this is so; reason can no more explain it than it can explain why one man wins at dice and another man loses.[105] The fortunate are like prophets, sybils, and poets; they are agitated by a divine power.[106] Reason and study have nothing to do with their successful careers; in fact, the fortunate often lose their occult power when they try to reason or begin to study.[107] There are definite signs by which one may recognize the fortunate. They seize the occasion briskly; they attack and master fortune without thought or caution; they spurn counsel; and they close their ears to admonition.[108] Fortune, says Pontano, is variable and hence one must assault her boldly;[109] she is like a ship and requires a strong steersman.[110]

[100] *Ibid.*, I, 276r.
[101] *Ibid.*, I, 282r-v.
[103] *Ibid.*, I, 275v.
[105] *Ibid.*, I, 289r.
[107] *Ibid.*, I, 291v.
[109] *Ibid.*, I, 292v.

[102] *Ibid.*, I, 285r.
[104] *Ibid.*, I, 287r-v.
[106] *Ibid.*, I, 280v-281v.
[108] *Ibid.*, I, 292r.
[110] *Ibid.*, I, 289v-290r.

To this unusual theory of Pontano, Egidio da Viterbo, an Augustinian friar, objected strongly because the doctrine of providence had found no place in the book. Pontano, like many of his contemporaries, had an honest reverence for the friar's opinion, and so he added a third book to the *De fortuna,* in which he attempted to reconcile the doctrine of providence with his theory of fortune. This for Pontano was an easy task; he simply sought an answer in the stars. God, he says, created the stars and gave them power over everything below save the wills of men; therefore, fate is a sort of partner of men's wills in the governing of earthly business.[111] In a lengthy section which he calls "That good fortune is foretold by the stars," Pontano offers illustrations from the careers of Marcus Hordeonius and Tertullus to show that fortune is governed by the stars.[112] The last part of the book returns to his favorite astrological arguments, and he identifies fortune rather definitely with the stars. He repeats the caveat that one must consider the parents, kinsmen, and the region in which the person is born.[113] He relates again the powers of the planets,[114] and re-emphasizes the importance of knowing the natural inclinations of the native so that one may support or eradicate them.[115] The fortune that is caused by the stars, he calls a cause per se because it works in a natural way.[116] He makes a little bow to providence, saying that, of course, God rules everything through the geniuses or angelic intelligences, but he does not put this conclusion in capital letters.[117] In the end, he preens himself on his regularity; he has shown that fortune, since it is caused by a natural cause, is a cause; and he has granted (in a very quiet fashion) free will to men.[118]

The learned friar Egidio was also the begetter of Pontano's dialogue on free will and immortality that bears his name and complements its author's astrological treatises. An important

[111] *Ibid.,* I, 301v.
[112] *Ibid.,* I, 304r-306v.
[113] *Ibid.,* I, 306v.
[114] *Ibid.,* I, 306v-308v.
[115] *Ibid.,* I, 308v-309r.
[116] *Ibid.,* I, 309r.
[117] *Ibid.,* I, 309v.
[118] *Ibid.,* I, 309v.

section of the *Aegidius dialogus* is devoted to a discussion
on astrology between Poderico and Pardo, and Robert Greene,
the English novelist and playwright, was so pleased by this
little dialogue that he reproduced it in his *Planetomachia*.
Poderico is represented as a man who detests physicians and
astrologers, so the dialogue is essentially an oration by Pardo
in defense of the school of astrology to which Pontano belonged.

Pardo states the underlying principle at once. The stars
are active and prime causes, whereas inferior things are passive
and secondary causes. Our wills are free to command, and
sometimes the will is made stronger by the influence of a
favorable star. He postulates the influence of the sun and moon
on the humors, and relates the nature of the elements and the
doctrine of generation and corruption to the stars. He admits
that the region and the altitude in which one lives alter this
stellar influence, and explains by this the inconstancy of planetary forces.[119] Astrology is, consequently, conjectural, and by
prognostication is meant only that the predicted event usually
occurs. He turns the argument of Pico on the errors of mariners and farmers to advantage by saying that if they fail in
their simple prognostics, the astrologer should be allowed some
errors in his more complicated calculations.[120] He rehearses
the numerous physical difficulties that spoil the calculations of
the astrologers, and says that astrologers should beware of
particularized prognostications. In this latter remark, he seems
to parry Pico's doctrine of universal effects by agreeing with
it.[121] After this prelude, Pardo turns to consider the wills of
men.

If the will allows itself to be dominated by the senses, nothing is more weak and unstable; if it bridles the senses, nothing
is more strong. Cato, when loaded with honors and offices,
sold the horse that he had ridden through many campaigns.

[119] *Ibid.*, II, 168r.
[120] *Ibid.*, II, 168v.   [121] *Ibid.*, II, 168v-169r.

Why did Cato do this parsimonious deed? Was it because of his stars or his will? The stars may have inclined Cato to parsimony, but the sale of the horse was an act of volition.[122] Discussing the character of Nero, Pardo inquires if his iniquitous career was the result of the constellations or the matter of which he was formed? Was it not that his volition carried away by his ambition got the better of his reason? He follows this with a psychological explanation of the nature of choice. The will by its nature and election is free. If it is governed by reason, it keeps its liberty; if it becomes a slave to sense, it loses this liberty. It evinces its free nature when it struggles with the senses. As the stars have an influence only on the corporal man, they have no power over his will; consequently, astrologers who predict the future without taking the will into account are very foolish.[123] The stars can oppose the will only when the will requires the aid of corporal and external things; but when the action derives from the will, it is vain to speak of the action and force of the stars.[124]

When one adds Pontano's affirmation of astrology to Ficino's moderate or vacillating attitude and Pico della Mirandola's negative view, one has a complete idea of the manner in which Renaissance men looked at this science. In the light of present-day knowledge, we are inclined to make the award for rationality to Pico della Mirandola; but when we transfer ourselves into the milieu of fifteenth-century Florence, we are tempted to recall the prize. Pico's knowledge of astrology is broad but bookish; and in his polemic he fails to realize the ultimate purpose of astrological converts like Pontano. Pico's attempt to explain untoward occurrences by means of the angelic choir is to modern taste as superstitious a notion as the wildest theories of Bonatti. On the other hand, Pontano seems more clear-eyed; he saw that there were many strange fractures of the cosmic monotony, many discords in the harmonies of the spheres. Like a good scientist, he sought an explanation

[122] *Ibid.*, II, 169r-v.   [123] *Ibid.*, II, 170r-v.   [124] *Ibid.*, II, 171r.

for these extranatural events; like a good psychologist, he tried to understand why some men seemed always to succeed whereas others were dogged with failure. To explain these phenomena, he offered his theory of the stars and his theory of fortune, but he never insisted on them. His theories are always tentative; he continually cautions his reader and castigates those astrologers whose pretensions to infallibility place them foremost in the ranks of charlatans. Were we to judge these men on the basis of intellectual flexibility and seriousness of purpose, we should have to place Pontano, the master astrologue, in the highest place.

CHAPTER II

SOME CONTINENTAL ATTITUDES

THE UNCERTAINTIES and misfortunes of sixteenth-century life produced in men of that age a feverish desire to know something of the future. This desire, of course, is not peculiar to any century, for prescience is one of man's more elemental yearnings. In the sixteenth century, however, this yearning seems to have been stronger than it had been in the Middle Ages, and to have arisen, in part, from a growing skepticism about the verity of Christian doctrine. Man no longer endured the misfortunes of this life because they were a sort of gymnastic preparation for the pleasures of the celestial Eden. The humanistic creed had placed an emphasis on the joys of this world, and humanistic learning had shaken the certainty of a number of Christian beliefs. A fearful rumor was spread, and men wondered if this life might not be all that man had to enjoy. A desire to know of days-to-be became the anodyne to man's fears. But there were other reasons that made the divining arts, and especially astrology, attractive to Renaissance men. The new classical learning had brought Ptolemy, Manilius, and Firmicus Maternus to the attention of all educated men. Cicero, that almost beatified master of meandering prose and other men's ideas, marshaled the ancients against the prognostic arts in his *De divinatione,* but, as Luca Gaurico observed, Cicero condemned only the Chaldean form of astrology and was so learned in divination that he considered it to be given of God.[1] The attitude of Cicero towards astrology became a matter of constant quarrel between the defenders and enemies of astrology, but other demigods of classical letters like Vergil,

[1] "Oratio de laudibus astrologiae," in Joannis Sacro Bosco, *Spherae tractatus* (Venetia, 1531), sig. A2v.

Ovid, and Pliny seemed to be firmly on the side of the proponents of sidereal emanations. Then, too, there was the newly esteemed Plato, whose *Timaeus* has been suggested as an excellent basis for astrology; Plato was made a conscript in the army of astrology although the rationalists protested that they were unable to discover in the *Dialogues* any evidence that he subscribed to the tenets of the art.

A third stimulus to the study and practice of astrology came from the riches of research in classical mythology. Since the letters of antiquity were riddling without such studies, works like those of Palaephatus, Phornutus, Hyginus, and Fulgentius were resurrected from monastic sepulchers, and scholars like Boccaccio, Pylades, Conti, Gyraldi, and Cartari labored to produce new manuals. The relations between classical mythology and astrology are obvious. The planets were named for gods; the heavens were crowded with constellations whose origins mythology alone could explain; the days of the week and other time-counting devices bore the titles of deity; and by mythology, one was able to expound in an allegorical fashion the harmony between the moon and the sun or the sun and the earth. To the letters and mythology of Greece and Rome, one could also join the letters and mythology of the Hebrews.

For a long time, the Catholic Church had turned its face against astrology, although its princes were not averse to feeing astrologers. The Bible, unfortunately, was ambiguous on the problem. In the case of the witch of Endor, it was most certain and had presented the sixteenth-century witch-hunt with a glittering gonfalon; but astrology was a different matter, for one had only to turn to Genesis to read that the stars had been set in the heavens *ut sint in signa cum tempestatibus, tum diebus et annis.* One could also learn from the Scriptures that the stars fought against Sisera, that Joshua checked some of the major planets in their orbits, and that the birth of Christ was heralded by a *nova* of great magnitude. These allusions were known to all who could read, and there were other references that were adduced by the defenders of astrology and explained away by its opponents.

There were, moreover, other sciences that underscored the importance of astrology. Alchemy, which had set many an oven glowing in Christendom, was closely bound to the art of astrology. The relation between the stars and the essential metals was a gift of Hellenism and was based on color similarity. There were proper times to conduct experiments in the transmutation of metals, and as everyone knows, these moments were indicated by the positions of the planets. Medicine, as we have noticed in the discussion of Ficino's astrological attitudes, depended on the emanations of the planets for part of its philosophy and its mechanics. Various areas of the body had their governing planets and signs, whose position and relationship must be consulted before a cure could be attempted; the position of the patient's and the physician's natal stars had also to be considered. The practitioners of this school, which was allied to that of Paracelsus, although it claimed Galen as its founder, were confident that they could not only treat but prognosticate the course of any illness by a close study of celestial mechanics.[2] Natural science also looked to the stars. The influence of the moon on the seas and their inhabitants was carefully charted; it was held that pearls grew great with the burgeoning satellite and that the selenite reflected the lunar phases. The influence of the heavens on herbs and plants was so well known that the relation between these things was used as a motif in the gown that Queen Elizabeth wears in the Devonshire portrait. The farmer and the cattle raiser had

---

[2] Short accounts of astrological medicine appear in most histories of medicine. C. Camden, "Elizabethan Astrological Medicine," *Annals of Medical History*, N. S., II (1930), 217-226; Hugo Magnus, *Der Aberglauben in der Medizin, Abhandlungen zur Geschichte der Medizin*, IV (Breslau, 1903), 88-105; and C. A. Mercier, *Astrology in Medicine* (London, 1914), are important references. The best bibliographical study is by Karl Sudhoff and was published in 1902 as the second volume in the Breslau series with the title, *Iatromathematiker vornehmlich im 15. und 16. Jahrhundert*; see the Appendix for a summary of these works with some new additions.

also inherited a great mass of astrological lore that they took
into account whenever they sowed, planted, bred, or castrated.
Finally, the science of astronomy had progressed rapidly and
the discoveries of Copernicus and Kepler had turned the faces
of men towards the skies. The new findings of astronomy
brought with them new instruments, more precise instruments—astrolabes, quadrants, optic glasses, and star tables—
with which, the astrologer said, he was able to correct the
errors of his predecessors. Time, which both the astronomer
and the astrologer had to compute with care, was now measured with greater exactness by watches and clocks that were
unknown to the men of the previous century.[3] But in addition
to all these stimulating factors, there was the actuality of the
professional astrologer.

Long-bearded and long-robed, the astrologer moved
through the courts of nobles and ecclesiastics; and when he
dwelt in the courts, his humbler colleagues were not absent
from the city mews. Defrance says that thirty thousand sor-
cerers, alchemists, diviners, and astrologers lived on the credulity of sixteenth-century Paris.[4] One is inclined to question
this statement, for Albert Pigghe (Pighius), writing in 1518,
complains that hardly any students at the university were
interested in astrology,[5] but the very title of his book, *Adversus
prognosticatorum vulgus qui annuas predictiones edunt et se
astrologos mentiuntur astrologiae defensio,* may bear witness
to Defrance's conjecture. The alley charlatan is difficult to
trace save for those great rogues like Jean Thibault or Simon
Forman; the astrologer in the entourage of the great noble or

[3] The new timepieces moved some of the best Latin poets of the age to compose
laudatory verses. Nicodemus Frischlin's *Carmen de astronomico horologio Argentoratensi* (Argentorati, 1575) contains a long hexameter poem on the clock, with a
descriptive prose preface. The volume also contains a poem on the same subject by
Guilielmus Xylanderus.

[4] Eugène Defrance, *Catherine de Medicis, ses astrologues et ses magiciens-envou-
teurs* (Paris, 1911), p. 15. Since this chapter was written, Thorndike's fifth and sixth
volumes have appeared; Chapters XIII, XIV, and XV in Volume V add much sup-
plementary matter to this account.

[5] *Op. cit.* (Paris, 1518), pp. 1-4, contains a general account of conditions.

priest comes more readily to hand. In Italy, the court astrologer was an established officer at the beginning of the fourteenth century,[6] and from Italy he found his way to the court
of France.

Louise de Savoie, the mother of Francis I, was a great
believer in prognosis, and hired Henry Cornelius Agrippa as
her physician because he was also an adept astrologer. Agrippa
eventually lost this post and attributed his dismissal to the fact
that the queen was a more superstitious astrologer than the
astrologer himself.[7] The career of Luca Gaurico also provides
an illustration of the importance of the astrologer in the council
of kings. Gaurico was born in 1476 and had a long and distinguished career as an astrologer. He predicted the fall of
Giovanni Bentivoglio, tyrant of Bologna, and was punished
for his prediction although it eventually was fulfilled. He
predicted that Alessandro Farnese would become pope; and
when Farnese was Paul III, he summoned Gaurico to Rome,
knighted him, and eventually made him Bishop of Giffoni.
Gaurico is said to have predicted to Pope Paul III the exact
day of his death and the disease of which he would die; he
also informed Hamilton, Bishop of St. Andrews, that he
would end on the gibbet. In 1493, Gaurico announced that
Giovanni de' Medici would be pope within twenty years, and
in 1513, he was Leo X. Gaurico also announced that Giulio
de' Medici would have many political difficulties and beget a
great progeny, and Giulio, as Clement VII, quarreled with
Henry VIII and fathered twenty-nine bastards. After a rather
glorious Italian career, Gaurico was called to the court of
France and became an adviser to the gullible Catherine. The
young queen had him draw up a horoscope of her husband
and Gaurico seems definitely to have missed, for he predicted
that the king would live to be an old man; however, after

[6] J. Burckhardt, *Die Kultur der Renaissance in Italien* (Leipzig, 1928), pp.
481-492.

[7] L.-F. A. Maury, *op. cit.*, pp. 216-217, for Agrippa's career see Auguste Prost,
Corneille Agrippa: sa vie et ses œuvres (2 vols.; Paris, 1881-82).

Henry's fatal mishap in 1559, it was pointed out that Gaurico
had foreseen the accident in a prognostication of 1552.[8] The
queen apparently believed that Henry's death was predicted,
for she put herself completely in the hands of astrologers and
was guided by the advice of seers like Regnier, Nostradamus,
Cosimo Ruggieri, Oger Ferrier, and Simeoni.[9] Catherine, however, was not the only French ruler who trusted the astrologers;
Henry IV summoned the astrologer Larivière at the moment
of Louis XIII's birth; and on the wedding night of Louis XIV
and Anne of Austria, the astrologer Morin, hidden in the
apartment, drew up the horoscope of the future dauphin.[10]
Nobles were not the only trusters in astrology; humanists like
Cardan, Henri Estienne, and Campanella believed in the art.[11]
Even Kepler, one of the fathers of modern astronomy, was not
averse to issuing prognostics, although his apologists insist that
he did this in order to secure funds for his more legitimate
investigations.[12]

So astrology triumphed in the courts and the back lanes,
in the laboratory of the alchemist, the astronomer, and the
physician, and in the study of the scholar, humanist, and publicist. The reasons for this triumph are manifold, and it is
impossible to determine which reason is the most important.
In spite of the popularity of the art, men were not blind to its
nature. Astrology was not confused with the science of astronomy. Divining by the stars had been attacked too long
and had been the subject of too many ecclesiastical edicts for
men not to know that it was prohibited. As one looks over

[8] E. Defrance, op. cit., pp. 216-217; E. Percopo, Luca Gaurico, ultimo degli astrologi; notizie biografiche e bibliografiche, Atti della reale accademia di archeologia,
lettere e belle arti (Napoli, 1896), XVII, ii, 39.
[9] E. Defrance, op. cit., p. 97.   [10] L.-F. A. Maury, op. cit., p. 217.
[11] Erasmus likes to make jesting remarks that would suggest that he believed in
astrology (Epistola, 1832), but his true attitude is probably found in the Antibar-
barus (Opera Omnia, X, 1695), where he supports free will, and Epistola 1005, where
he writes that he will seek "what makes us happy" in the earth, not in the stars.
[12] H. A. Straus and S. Straus-Kloebe, Die Astrologie des Johannes Kepler: Eine
Auswahl aus seinen Schriften (München u. Berlin, 1926), p. 8; Franz Boll and Carl
Bezold, Sternglaube und Sterndeutung (Leipzig, 1931), p. 42.

the treatises of astronomy and physics published during the
sixteenth century, one discovers that a sharp distinction is
made between the art of astrology and the science of astronomy.
Most writers say that astronomy is the study of the orbits of
the planets and the *situs* of the fixed stars,[13] whereas astrology
is an art that attempts to determine the future from the stars.[14]
One lexicographer, at least, brands astrology as superstitious,[15]
but some men who were partial to the art sought to enhance
its repute by making various philosophical distinctions. Gartze
says that astronomy is the sister of mathematics and astrology
the child of physics,[16] and Jacob Milich (Milichius) states that
astrology is that part of physics which ascertains the influence
of starlight on the elements and consequently on mixed
bodies.[17] Marstaller defines astrology as a science that is approved by the agreement of the learned and by everyday
experience,[18] and Peucer finds that astrology is a science in
its methodology and an art in its antiquity.[19] The famous
Henry, Count of Rantzau, says cautiously that it is a begetter
of truth when the observations are careful and the instruments
accurate.[20] Finally, one may quote the definition of John Dee,
the learned and much maligned astrologer of Queen Elizabeth: "...for, Astrologie is an Art Mathematicall, which
demonstrateth reasonably the operations and effects of the

[13] Gregor Reisch, *Margarita Filosofica,* tr. G. P. Galluci (Venetia, 1599), p. 339;
Nicolaus Raymarus, *Fundamentum astronomicum: id est nova doctrina sinum et
triangulorum* (Argentori, 1588), p. 1; Joachim Ringelbergius, *Institutiones astronomicae ternis libris contentae* (Basileae, 1528), p. 2; R. Göckel, *Urania cum geminis
filiabus hoc est astronomia et astrologia* (Francofurti, 1615), p. 11.

[14] J. Ringelbergius, *loc. cit.,* R. Göckel, *loc. cit.;* Jacobus Carion, cited in G. Marstaller, *Artis divinatricis quam astrologiam seu iudiciariam vocant, encomia et patrocinia* (Pariis, 1549), p. 14. The dictionaries of the day with the exception of Calepine,
who confuses the two definitions, follow these forms.

[15] B. de Chasseneaux, *Catalogus gloriae mundi* (Lugduni, 1546), p. 210v.

[16] Joannes Gartze, *Astrologiae methodus* (Basileae, 1576), sig. A3r-A3v.

[17] G. Marstaller, *op. cit.,* p. 13.   [18] *Ibid.*

[19] C. Peucer, *Commentarius de praecipuis divinationum generibus* (Servestae, 1541),
p. 389r.

[20] H. von Rantzau, "Ad lectorem," *Tractatus astrologicus de genethliacorum thematum iudiciis pro singulis nati accidentibus* (Francofurti, 1602), p. 7; see J. Taisnier, *Astrologiae iudiciariae ysagogica* (Coloniae, 1559), sig. A3-A3v.

naturall beams of light and secret influence of the Stars and Planets in every element and elementall body at all times in any Horizon assigned."[21] There was truly no confusion of terms in the Renaissance; the astronomer might practice astrology, but he knew when he crossed the line that limited the domains of the two areas.

During the sixteenth century, there were many attacks on astrology and an equal number of treatises in defense of the art. There is, of course, little in any of these writings that is new. The arguments of Pico della Mirandola and other earlier opponents of astrology are repeated *ad nauseam;* the illustrations and the wording are sometimes new, but the basic arguments are ever the same. A like monotony governs the defenses, but there were at least three methods of supporting astrology. The first method was that used by Bellanti, Schonheintz, and Pirovano; a foe of astrology is singled out and his arguments are subjected to point-by-point refutation. The second method is to present a general essay in favor of astrology and to follow it with an astrological manual. The author of this type of book supposedly assumed that his general preface would convince the reader, who would then wish to learn the science. The third method, and by far the most ingenious one, is to offer a series of historical horoscopes to show that the facts of history bear out the predictions of the stars. None of these methods is original, and they are mentioned in order to provide a backdrop against which the English controversialists may be exhibited.

A history of sixteenth-century continental attitudes on astrology might very well begin with the writings of Luca Gaurico, whose career as a successful astrologer has already been delineated.[22] Gaurico was the author of many prognosti-

---

[21] Euclid, *Elements of Geometry,* ed. T. Rudd (London, 1661), sig. G3.

[22] The names of many astrologers can be learned from G. Hellmann, "Versuch einer Geschichte der Wettervorhersage im XVI. Jahrhundert," *Abhandlungen d. preussischen Akademie d. Wissenschaften* (Berlin, 1924), and from the entry "Almanack and Prognostication" in any of the great library catalogues. In this chapter I

cations and calendars; in 1539 he published a *De eclipsi solis miraculosa in Passione Domini celebrata,* in which he attempted to establish the date of the Crucifixion and of other events in the life of Christ. Prior to the publication of the *De eclipsi,* Gaurico printed his *Oratio de inventoribus et astrologiae laudibus habita in Ferrariensi academia,* a sort of listing of astrological immortals which concludes with the praise of astrological amulets. Gaurico's most famous book was his *Tractatus astrologiae iudiciariae de nativitatibus virorum et mulierum,* which appeared first in Italian in 1539 and was issued in Latin many times after 1540. It is mainly a collection of aphorisms arranged under convenient headings and it is illustrated by six books of horoscopes. The first book contains the horoscopes of towns and cities; the second book those of popes and cardinals; the third book those of kings and princes. The fourth book, which has the horoscopes of men illustrious in the arts and sciences, is most interesting to the modern student. In this book we learn that the careers and fates of Pico della Mirandola, Petrarch, Poliziano, Luther, Melanchthon, and Michelangelo were shaped by the stars. The fifth book of the *Tractatus* contains the horoscopes of those who died violently, and the last book those of monsters and deformed. Each horoscope has an historical appendix which proves that the astrologer's predictions were fulfilled. Gaurico did not stop with this work; he compiled a *Super diebus decretoriis axiomata,* which belongs to the history of astrological medicine, and other works of a more technical nature, before his death in 1560.

A more popular type of work than those of Gaurico was the *Introductiones apotelesmaticae elegantes* of Jean de Hayn (ab Indagine), a work that discussed chiromancy and physiognomy as well as astrology. The book was printed at least a dozen times before the close of the seventeenth century and

---

have tried to discuss only those essays that seemed symptomatic; I have not intended to write a complete history.

seems to have introduced the general public of this period to
the notion that the facial and physical conformities of men
depended on their natal stars. The astrological sections of
this book came at the end, but there is a preface dated June 1,
1522, in which de Hayn attacks the scholastics for attacking
astrology. In the latter sections of the book, he makes a curious
distinction between "artificial" and "natural" astrology, which
he never defines exactly. It seems that an artificial astrologer
considers all of the planets, whereas a natural astrologer considers only the sun and moon. De Hayn makes the usual bow
to free will, but discusses in detail the influence of the stars on
the humors and complexions. He seems, however, to be careful about arguing that future events can be predicted by the
stars.

A defender of astrology against the opponents of astrology
and the vulgar astrologers was Pedro Cirvelo, whose *Apotelesmata astrologiae Christianae* was printed at Alcala in 1521.
The first part of this work is devoted to the method of making
weather predictions and all other legitimate predictions—but
not those in which so many vulgar astrologers deceived their
clients. The second part of this book contains a *Centiloquium,*
and the third part an attack on Pico. Pico's incompetence, of
which one hears a good deal later, is stressed, and Cirvelo, like
Bellanti, offers instances of the count's technical errors. A
supporter of astrology with an attitude similar to that of Cirvelo was Albert Pigghe (Pighius), who was also a theologian
and who was involved in the controversy over the watery
conjunction of 1524 which was to terrify half the astrologers
of Europe. In 1518 Pigghe published his *Adversus prognosticatorum vulgus qui annuas predictiones edunt et se astrologos
mentiuntur astrologiae defensio,* in which he leveled his pen
at the charlatans in his profession.

A most bitter attack on astrology was written at this time
by Henry Cornelius Agrippa, who has been mentioned as the
physician of the Queen of France. Famous enough for his

divinations to be mentioned by Marlowe in *Faustus,* Agrippa composed in 1530 an amusing book called *De incertitudine et vanitate omnium scientiarum et artium,* in which he castigated astronomy, astrology, and all forms of learning save the highest type of theology. The next year Agrippa printed his *De occulta philosophia,* in which he affirmed all the occult sciences that he attacked in the *De incertitudine;* so one cannot congratulate him on his consistency and must consider his attack on astrology as formal rather than sincere. Agrippa begins his satire of astrologers by portraying the arrogance of the star-gazers, who go about as if they were descended from the heavens. Astrology is, he says, a sort of nationalistic science because the Chaldeans, Moors, Arabs, Jews, Greeks, and Latins differ in their theories. The same confusion, however, occurs among the adepts, who argue whether there are eight, nine, or ten spheres and who debate the velocity of celestial motions. In spite of this wrangling, they try to convince the credulous that their science was founded by God.

In cynical fashion, Agrippa tells of his former pursuit of learning in astrology and astronomy. He says that he learned the sciences from his parents and wasted a great deal of time in them. He came finally to the conclusion that they had no foundations outside the imaginations of men and he tried to forget them; but the importunities of the great, who often use genius to bad ends, and his own domestic needs kept him bending over his books and peering at the stars. Astrology, he admits, may be of value in interpreting the fables of the poets, who have peopled the heavens with their monsters and who get along better with astrologers than with other men; but it has no other value.

In the main, the astrologers make him merry. They derive the effects and influences of the stars from the most remote ages, from before the time of Prometheus and Noah. They pretend that the hidden natures and powers of stones, metals, plants, and animals depend on the powers of the stars, and fail to notice that God created plants, herbs, and trees before the heavens and stars. Agrippa names the philosophers who were opposed or indifferent to astrology, and observes that even Ptolemy admitted that it was impossible to make accurate predictions because of conflicting factors like education, diet, locality, and freedom of will. He talks about the disagreements of astrologers, who depend on chance like children on books of fortune. After all, the main desire of astrologers is to suck a little money out of their clients. Agrippa says that the more cautious astrologers utter their predictions in ambiguous terms so that they cannot be pinned down. There are so many stars in so many positions that the ordinary astrologer usually makes a guess, and often his simple client is led by this guess to fulfill by his own efforts the star-merchant's predictions. Generally, sneers Agrippa, the astrologues are rather clever in showing how they predicted some past event and equally cautious about events in the future.

Agrippa regrets that astrologers are so well received by princes from whom they draw such excellent salaries, for no man is so injurious to the commonwealth as the astrologer. They are the enemies of Christ and all Christians. If anything depends on the stars, he says, let us trust in them and the God who made them and forget this astrological foolishness. If, however, there is no power in the stars, why bother with the astrologer? They are truly Doctors of Lies, who get more credit, because of human stupidity, for one half-truth than blame for a hundred known falsehoods. While they search the heavens, they do not know what is going on in their own houses. Agrippa mentions a number of astrological inconsistencies, but he is chiefly angered by the remarks and investigations of astrologers on religious events. These shocking people credit the stars with the birth of Christ, with Moses' laws, with miracles, and with other holy matters. For this reason, Agrippa, basing his attitude on Pico della Mirandola and the *patrologiae,* consigns the astrologers to the hell that holds the Manichees and other heretics.[23]

One of the most formidable assaults on astrology at this period was the *Adversus falsos quorundam astrologorum augurationes* of Cornelius Scepper (Scepperius), the secretary of King Christian of Denmark and the envoy of Denmark to numerous governments. This book, which appeared first in 1523, was aimed at the (premonstrative writings/ of Johann Virdung von Hassfurt, Pietro Tommai, and Philologus, whose predictions on the conjunction of 1524 are said to be astrologically illogical. Scepper opens his treatise by listing himself with Pico and Nifo as one of three champions who had dared attack astrology.[24] He is especially annoyed by the insistence of the astrologers on the universal importance of their theories. Scepper, who employs a dream motif, describes the astrologers surrounded by their apparatus and mumbling their cant and lying hypotheses. They overextend themselves, he says, when they take shelter in the argument that their art incites men to religion and the love of God, for the true protectors of Christianity are doctrine, piety, and good examples.

So that no one will mistake his attitude towards the astrologers, he places them among the heretics and describes them bivouacked in a diabolical encampment surrounded by banners on which they have painted the signs of the zodiac. The astrologers, Scepper states, try to appear pious, but this is a pose, for at heart they are the most wicked and pernicious of men. He now attacks them on their own ground, for he is

---

[23] *Op. cit.* (Francofurti et Lipsiae, 1693), pp. 123-148. To Agrippa's attitude we may add Reisch's remarks on why astrologers fail. They try to include too much. They make predictions based on the fixed stars, which are not only innumerable, but astrologically unknown, quantities. They also wish to be known as masters as soon as they have learned the rudiments. Reisch, whose work is highly medieval in character but whose methods influenced later encyclopedists like Di Fonti, Recorde, Malespina, and Maiolus, in his larger section on astrology repeats most of the standard arguments that we have noticed before and shall notice again (*op. cit.,* pp. 429-447).

[24] *Op. cit.* (Coloniae Agrippinae, 1547), p. 5.

well read in authorities and slows his book with his continual
citing of titles. He demonstrates by astrological reasoning that
Noah's flood did not occur in a watery sign, that Ogygius'
flood, Deucalion's flood, and the great Italian flood of 1487
cannot be explained by astrology. He proves that the revolutions of Saturn have nothing to do with great catastrophes,
and that the various fearful conjunctions and triplicities have
no certain effects on the earth.[25] He gives reasons to prove
that eclipses are not the causes of local or general inundations,[26]
and goes so far in his hate of astrological hypotheses that, like
Pico, he denies the influence of the moon on the tides.[27] Scepper finds that the age is essentially impious and ungodly.
Because of this lack of religion, men go to the astrologer, for
the irreligious live in fear of God's impending wrath.[28] The
latter part of the treatise is devoted to the usual discussion of
astrological inconsistencies; one astrologer, he declares, will
stand by Albumasar, another will cling to Ptolemy, and a third
will differ from both the others. Altogether, Scepper's book
is in the tradition; his major charge against the astrologers is
that of heresy, a charge that was centuries old. His chief merit
is that, in confuting their theories, he met the astrologers on a
field of their own choosing.

As we have noticed before and will observe again, the possession of a theological degree or theological interests was no
bar in the sixteenth century to the practice of astrology. The
famous heretic Michael Servetus took sides for the defense of
astrology when, in 1538, he published his *Apologetica disceptatio pro astrologia* at Paris. The occasion of this pamphlet was
an attack made on Servetus by the dean of the medical faculty
at Paris when he discovered that the wandering scholar was
discussing astrology in his lectures on geography and astronomy. Servetus' apology takes the form of an announcement of
his own successful predictions and an attack on physicians for

[25] *Ibid.*, pp. 2v-18.   [26] *Ibid.*, pp. 29-30v.
[27] *Ibid.*, pp. 40-46v.   [28] *Ibid.*, p. 19.

their skepticism. Galen taught the importance of astrology, and most plagues are caused by the stars.[29] The dean of the medical faculty did all that he could to prevent the publication of the *Apologetica;* he even went to the inquisition. Finally, Parlement decreed on March 18, 1538/39, that all copies of the book were to be recalled and burned.

The attacks of Pico and Scepper brought many defenders[30] to the banners of the diabolical encampment. In 1549 appeared the *Artis divinatricis quam astrologiam seu iudiciariam vocant, encomia et patrocinia* of Gervase Marstaller (Marstallerus), which included the defense of Melanchthon and Heller. Marstaller plants his defense on several foundations. On the basis of experience he postulates—all sciences postulate—the celestial influences and the ability of skilled men to use these influences in predictions.[31] He divides astrology into two sections, the natural and conjectural. By natural astrology, he writes, one predicts future plagues and pestilences, for by the rays of the stars the air is first moderated, then the blood, and, finally, the body. By conjectural astrology one predicts future events *contingenter, et non necessario,* because inferior causes do not always agree with celestial ones. He clarifies this position by saying that Mars in a threatening aspect does not mean an immediate war but merely an inclination among men to war.[32] In some respects, Marstaller's position is not unlike Pontano's in that he does not accept the influence of the stars as an agent of necessity.

A number of sections in the *Encomia* are devoted to a consideration of the relation of the stars to human depravity. This problem was very popular with astrologers, and some of them held that the fall of Adam was produced by an unfortunate

[29] *Op. cit.,* ed. H. Tollin (Berlin, 1880). The circumstances of the publication and banning of the book are related by Tollin in his preface.

[30] For minor defenses see B. de Chasseneaux, *op. cit.,* p. 210v, and J. Calderia, *Concordantiae poetarum philosophorum et theologorum liber* (Venetia, 1547), p. 151v.

[31] *Op. cit.* (Pariis, 1549), p. 13.   [32] *Ibid.,* pp. 16-17.

conjunction.[33] Marstaller regrets that the stars have an influence on sublunar things, for, though the influence is constant, the effects are different. "We are led by reason and piety to seek good and resist evil and are fitted by a superior temperament to resist the infection of the stars." Unfortunately, all men are not so provided, for some men are evil in disposition because of the influence of Satan, and the noxious forces of some of the planets impel them to ill deeds.[34]

For the sake of embellishing his book with some Aristotelian touches, Marstaller expounds the four causes in astrological terms. The efficient cause, he says, is the motion of the celestial bodies, the *loci* of the stars, and the light and peculiar powers of the stars. The material cause, in the objective sense, is simply the search made by the astrologers after the final cause. The formal cause is the foreseeing or the observing of the events which either precede or follow within a reasonable time from the forces which reside in the stars and are shed on the world and the discovering by what aspects of the stars these events are caused. The final cause is the desire of predicting future events from the influences of the stars or the ascertaining, by the same means, of the causes of past events.[35] This series of definitions is obviously open to attack, and Marstaller fares better in the latter pages of his defense, where he lists and illustrates the ten triumphs of astrology.

The art of astrology, he declares, explains the dissimilarities not only in various regions of the world but also in the customs

---

[33] A long discussion of this question appears in Valentine Nabode, *Enarratio elementorum astrologiae* (Coloniae, 1560). Nabode, who was also the author of an *Astronomicarum institutionum* and a *Primarum de coelo et terra institutionum*, asks how the stars, which are the good creatures of a good Creator, can incline men to evil? He answers by saying that the same wine produces different effects in different men. Are these various effects caused by the virtue of the wine or the nature of the drinkers? We were given good natures in the beginning, but we have despoiled ourselves. "Sic siderum naturalem actionem in intaminata et sincera nostrorum corporum animorumque materia proculdubio omnes effectus bonos producturam, malos impetus nonnumquam et pravas inclinationes, morbos, brevitatem vitae, et tales pestes infligere, nullam ab aliam causam, nisi propter sordes et impuritatem nostrae naturae, cogitare et credere decet" (pp. 1v-3r).

[34] *Ibid.*, pp. 19-20.   [35] *Ibid.*, pp. 25-26.

of those regions; it determines the differences among men in stature and mind; it shows what fates await individual nations; it foretells meteorological conditions almost to the minute; and it predicts whether harvest will be good, average, or poor. In addition to these things, it announces the danger of war, famine, drought, flood, pestilential air which may ruin crops and destroy animals, uprisings, changes in government, and the deaths of noblemen. In every case, says Marstaller, the astrologer can indicate the exact place of the threatened event. Astrology further informs farmers and physicians of the best moments for the practice of their professions.[36] Besides all this, it enables one to formulate calendars and accounts of future years with the minutest accuracy. Finally, the art of the astrologer permits the discovery of one's temperament as well as one's momentary dispositions, alterations, and inclinations. Knowing this, one is not only able to guard one's health, but to rule both one's manners and one's life in a happy and useful fashion.[37] The remainder of Marstaller's book is given over to an expansion of these points and to a full account of the benefits bestowed by astrology on all other professions.[38]

Perhaps the most important defender of astrology in the mid-century was the eminent reformer Melanchthon, who like many of his fellows was deeply interested in the occult arts. As a young man Melanchthon dedicated one of his orations to Johann Stoeffler, whose astrological prediction precipitated the panic of 1524; and in his preface to his edition of Sacrobosco's *Sphaera* in 1531, Melanchthon defended astrology against its calumniators. All through his life Melanchthon clung to his belief in astrology, a fact that is established by his numerous prefaces to works of this type and by the astro-

[36] In Erasmus Rheinholt's *Ptolemaei mathematicae constructionis liber* (Basileae, 1549), the author lists medicine, economics, mining, architecture, theology, geography, and history as aided arts (sig. A2v-A3v).

[37] *Ibid.*, pp. 32-33.

[38] *Ibid.*, pp. 34-38; see Nabode, *op. cit.*, pp. 4-4v.

logical references in his epistles and other writings.[39] A good example of Melanchthon's attitude may be found in his preface to the *De iudiciis nativitatum,* which his friend Johann Schöner published in 1545. Like many of the defenders of astrology, Melanchthon divides the art into two departments: one department concerns itself with motion, the other with divining.[40] Light, says Melanchthon, provides the first qualities, and the secondary qualities arise from the action of these in the body. This has been proved by years of experience, during which it has been discovered that droughts and heavy rainfalls resulted from eclipses and certain conjunctions. The stars temper the body of man although much of his nature is derived *a materia seu a semine;* an individual born during a conjunction of the moon and sun will, he writes, probably be a lunatic.[41]

To the governing of life, says Melanchthon, the science of astrology is most useful. "What is true discipline except the diligent ruling of life, but this is impossible if the distant causes are unknown. This divining art is manifestly necessary to the conduct of life, for it shows what one's natural inclinations are and allows one to exercise one's good qualities and bridle one's vicious instincts."[42] He compares astrology to medicine and observes that they both search for the causes of things; the difference between the two sciences is that medicine seeks material causes and astrology celestial causes. Astrology, Melanchthon insists, cannot be called superstitious because men are taught by it to magnify the works of God. He supports this statement by likening the labors of the astrologer to those of the herbalist, who studies the occult virtues of plants.[43] He does not claim that astrology is an exact science, but he feels that it is a probable science.

[39] K. Hartfelder, "Der Aberglaube Philipp Melanchthons," *Historisches Taschenbuch* (Leipzig, 1889), pp. 233-269.

[40] G. Marstaller, *op. cit.,* p. 47.   [41] *Ibid.,* pp. 50-51.

[42] *Ibid.,* p. 53.   [43] *Ibid.,* p. 55.

I must confess that there is small proof of the influence of the
stars. But if something can be drawn from them, which can rightly
and prudently be adapted to the conduct of life, they can be considered of great effect. Yet we are frequently deceived in this, more
frequently than in other arts. I confess this indeed and I must also
admit that it is no art. What is more familiar to man than to err
and ramble in his thoughts? Nevertheless there are some truths
in it, which some men more skillfully and others less adroitly ac-
commodate to matters under their consideration; but when one is
pondering future things, it is both important and useful to possess
even the smallest foresight.[44]

This attitude, which was inherited from Pontano, places Melanchthon among the moderate and more rational exponents of
astrology.

Joachim Heller, a friend of Melanchthon and professor of
mathematics at Nürnberg, was also a defender of astrology.
He was the editor, in 1546, of *Albohali Arabis astrologi anti-
quissimi ac clarissimi de iudiciis nativitatum liber unus;* and
in 1548, he wrote a preface to the *Epitome totius astrologiae*
of the twelfth-century compiler, John of Seville. In this preface
Heller divides the opponents of astrology into two parties—
the epicureans and the impious. In the sixteenth century, these
titles smacked of the halter and the stake, and Heller was,
without question, returning the compliments of those who
called astrologers atheists and heretics. It was assumed by
Heller that the stars were the means by which God governed
the world and expressed the concepts of his divine reason. To
oppose the astrologer was, consequently, rank impiety.[45] After
this opening volley, Heller considers the charges of vanity and
sacrilege that the enemies of astrology had always hurled at
the science. His defense against the first indictment is authoritative; he cites philosophers and fathers in support of the
validity of astrology; he draws upon the works of naturalists
to prove the existence of celestial influence; and he repeats

[44] *Ibid.,* p. 57.   [45] *Ibid.,* pp. 90-117.

a number of historical events which, he says, were effected by the stars.[46] The charge of impiety is met in the same way. The timeworn passage from Genesis is made the spearhead of the argument, and other Biblical passages are brought up to support it.

Another associate of Melanchthon was Jacob Milich (Milichius), a professor at Wittenberg and a physician, whose *Oratio de dignitate astrologiae* was delivered sometime between 1524 and 1533 when it was printed. This is a conventional defense. Astrology is not perfect, but what sciences are? Milich points out the advantages of astrology to the other arts and suggests that a knowledge of one's complexion is especially useful. He uses the old argument that if one knows the future, one can avoid it. A true die-hard, Milich observes that though the conjunction of 1524 did not produce a flood, there was very wet weather for the subsequent two years. Many other members of Melanchthon's group like David Kochhafe (Chytraeus), Achilles Gasser, and Joachim Camerarius were practicing astrologers; but perhaps the most interesting document in the history of divination was written sometime before 1553 by Melanchthon's son-in-law, Caspar Peucer, who had a reputation as a historian and who succeeded Milich as Rector of Wittenberg.

Peucer's *Commentarius de praecipuis divinationum generibus* was printed first at Wittenberg in 1553, but its popularity was such that it was reprinted at least six times and even translated into French. The work begins with a general discussion of divining; then Peucer turns to a discussion of oracles, theomancy, magic, and incantations. Following this are lengthy sections on divination by entrails, augury, lots, divination by

---

[46] *Ibid.*, pp. 117-122. His doctrine that God created the stars with definite powers is found on pp. 88-89. The same matter is taken up in Taisnier's *Astrologiae iudiciariae ysagogica* (Cologne, 1559), where one reads that astrology is a special gift from God and enables man to distinguish himself from animals (sig. A4v-A5). He also elaborates on the Genesis quotation and recommends astrology because it leads men from darkness to light (sig. A3-A3v).

dreams, medical prognosis, meteorology, physiognomy, chiromancy, divining by insects, animals, plants, and minerals, astrology, and prodigies. It is, in truth, a very complete book.

In the earlier sections of the book, Peucer speaks of the constant suffering of man and of man's eternal yearning to make his life happier and his future more secure. Man, he says, finds it difficult to associate cause and effect, and is haunted by the fear of God's vengeance; hence, he has a just reason to learn by any means possible what joys and sorrows await him in the future. Investigations of this sort, if they are natural in method, cannot be called superstitious.[47]

As a suggestion of what the reader may expect, Peucer discusses, in an early section on the various forms of divination, some of the proofs for the truth of astrology. He says that God intended us to look at the stars and to observe the sympathy between them and natural objects; it was for this reason that God provided men with eyes. The study of the stars is more difficult than other forms of natural observation, but in time man will master it. The knowledge of these sympathies, Peucer states, was transmitted by God to the first parents and they passed it on to their descendants, who have perfected the technique. This original lore has been supplemented by what later men have learned of other relationships in the sublunar world. From the stars, we can determine the causes of various effects, but we must always remember that the will of man is free, even when it is incited or hindered by various causes. If, however, there is some cause that does not emanate from the volition of man, foreknowledge will enable man to alter it by diligence, caution, or an appeal to God. The difficulties that beset men, says Peucer, arise because men are ignorant of the future and are unable either to govern their own conduct or cry to God for aid.[48]

[47] *Op. cit.* (Servestae, 1591), p. iv.
[48] *Ibid.,* pp. 68v-69v. The origin of astrology was a question variously debated; Pico's attitude on its antiquity has been noticed in the first chapter, but his arguments seem to have had little or no influence on the sixteenth-century astrologers.

When we turn to Peucer's special chapter on astrology, we find many of these arguments repeated. He founds the philosophy of astrology on the Aristotelian doctrine of motion, but admits that astrology has been abused in past ages when men degenerated and the science of physics decayed with them. The Prince of Hell, the author of superstition, has also tainted the art of Adam with his insidious suggestions. Peucer discusses the known effects of planets, the doctrine of critical days, and the influence of the stars on humors and complexions. He believes that the customs of nations are subject to their governing star and illustrates this with an example of the baleful influence of Saturn on Nürnberg. Peucer's theory is that since action is dominated by the will, the evil coming from the stars can be removed, altered, or checked by meditation and discipline.

Peucer defends astrology against those who attack it with passages from the Bible, by showing that these opponents abuse the Scriptures. He takes up the arguments drawn from the diverse careers of twins and from those born under different stars who share the same fate; a moment's error in reckoning the horoscope will, he insists, make this apparent difference. He attacks the notion—that he attributes to the Chaldees— of celestial necessity, and devotes the remainder of his essay to establishing his thesis of the star-governed matter and the free

Many astrologers agreed with Peucer in deriving the art from Adam, but astronomers also turned to that origin. Adrianus Metius writes in the preface of his *Doctrinae sphaericae libri V* (Frankfort, 1602): "Nec dubium est primum generis humani parentem suam posteritatem de motibus coelestibus, de ordine et situ stellarum, de anni et dierum spaciis docuisse as suis studiose monstrasse certa divinitatis vestigia ac testimonia de Deo in ordine motuum coelestium, posituque corporum mundi et forma" (p. 4). Others, like Bartholomeus Vespucius in his *Sphaerae tractatus* (Venetia, 1531), followed Lucian and named the Aethiopians as the fathers of the science of stars (sig. A8r). A most original attitude is found in the *De elementis et eorum mixtionibus libri quinque*, which Gasparo Contareni published at Paris in 1548. Though fate and chance, says Contareni, really arise through privation, the later Peripatetics have omitted this entirely and have sought the source of these uncaused causes in celestial necessity. "Inde nata est astrologia haec diviniatrix, caeteraque huiusmodi inanes artes" (pp. 10-11).

will.[49] Without doubt, Peucer was more convinced of the
essential truth of astrology than was his father-in-law, Melanchthon, for he accepts all the notions of the professional
astrologer save that of fatal necessity. Peucer's belief in free
will makes him a moderate, but one discovers that there were
degrees of moderation.

Writing about the same time as Peucer, Erasmus Rheinholt
(Rheinholdus), the student of Milichius and the teacher of
Johannes Gartze, comments on the various aspects of astrology.
When we remember that Rheinholt was among the first to
perceive the elliptic orbits and that he was the author of numerous technical works on astronomy, we realize that a belief in
astrology was not confined in the sixteenth century to the
ignorant and credulous. In the preface to his *Primus liber
tabularum directionum discentibus prima elementa astronomiae necessarius et utilissimus,* Rheinholt mentions the influence of the stars on political conditions. He modifies his
position by saying that God has various ways of punishing the
wicked and protecting the just, and that the stars are not the
sole causes of alterations which depend, in the end, on the
will of God. He does not, however, hesitate to attribute the
uprisings in Saxony to a conjunction of Saturn and Mars in
Capricorn during February, 1548.[50] Rheinholt's awareness of
the disfavor into which astrology had fallen is indicated in an
epistle that he prefixed to an edition of Georg Purbach's *Theoricae novae planetarum.* In this preface, he narrates the discovery of the relationship between planetary movement and
cause, and recounts the definite laws concerning these relationships that had once been usefully established. Astrology, he
writes, was once the philosophy of kings and princes, but now
the art is neglected by nobles and scorned by universities. Its
safeguarding depends on a very small number of philosophers.
The art should be cherished and endowed, but where can

---

[49] *Ibid.,* pp. 389r-421v.
[50] *Op. cit.* (Tübingen, 1554), sig. A2v-A3v.

patrons be found? "Was there ever an age so unfriendly to philosophy as this, in which the study of our art is impeded by domestic dissensions and foreign wars? Our arts love truth and modesty and to these virtues they attract the minds of men, but in times of civil discord, they are without honor."[51]

Among the most cogent writers of the Renaissance is the many-sided Alessandro Piccolomini. In the course of his continual search for knowledge, Piccolomini investigated all the divisions of learning indicated by Aristotle and wrote a large number of highly important books. The best known of his works are the *Della institution morale,* which colored the ethics of the *Faerie Queene,* and the *Filosofia naturale;* for his longest excursus on astrology, it is necessary to turn to a lesser known work, *La prima parte dele theoriche o'vero speculationi dei pianeti,* which was published at Venice in 1558. Piccolomini's remarks are reasonably conventional, but he straddles the question of the reality of stellar influences in an interesting fashion.

As a good Christian, he opens his digression by assuring the reader that though the skies may incline one to evil, one can conquer all these influences by the powers of reason and will. He assures the reader that geography, navigation, and agriculture have been advanced by the efforts of the astrologer, but with these remarks he concludes his commendation of astrology and turns to the attack. Superstitious or judicial astrology is vain and fallacious. It is impossible to imagine the noble planets of the heavens having anything to do with this world of mud and offal. The incorruptible does not traffic with the corruptible. Piccolomini observes how horrible life would be if the tenets of judicial astrology were true and we could foresee all that was in the future. It is also absurd to make preparation for predicted events that never occur. There is a God-given form of prediction that permits us to know the future from sure causes; we can count on high prices after a

[51] *Op. cit.* (Pariis, 1553), sig. A2r-A3r.

long war, or we can assume that a patient will die after a long and wasting fever. The evil method of prediction considers neither cause nor effect.[52] He closes by admitting that there probably is some sort of stellar influence, but urges man to oppose it with his free will.[53]

Though astrologers liked to call Calvin one of their supporters, it is only by a twisting of the evidence that the acid reformer could be placed in their company. As Savonarola fought astrology in the fifteenth century, so the protestant Calvin combated it in the sixteenth century and rallied many theologians to his standard.[54] Calvin was particularly opposed to those arts by which man tries to learn what God does not wish him to know. Human curiosity caused Adam's fall; and man, he regrets, has never given up his desire to be a god. Hand in hand with this yearning to know that which is forbidden goes the means by which man seeks to learn. Sober knowledge, says Calvin, is the best; one should strive to know only that which it is permissible to know.[55] Calvin's formal attack on astrology, the *Contre l'astrologie,* was translated into English in 1563 as *An Admonicion against astrology iudiciall* and published at London. It is patterned on the conventional polemic against astrology.

Calvin regrets that in his time astrology has the patronage of the wise as well as of the foolish. He says that it is a useful science for explaining the motions of planets and the mechanics of eclipses, and he admits that there is justice in the astrological

---

[52] *Op. cit.* (Venice, 1558), sig. A3r-B3v.

[53] *Ibid.,* sig. B4v. Portio Piccolomini, who wrote *Parte terza della filosofia naturale* (Venetia, 1585), says that the stars cannot influence the matter of men or their spirits; only the qualities of the body are affected (pp. 16r-16v). See G. Rosaccio, *Teatro del cielo e delle terra* (Fiorenze, 1594), p. 53, for the same view.

[54] For other theological views see Calvin, *Commentaries on the First Book of Moses called Genesis,* ed. J. King (Edinburgh, 1847), p. 84; Joannes Brent, *Opera* (Tubingae, 1576), p. 13; Gervase Babington, *Certaine Plaine, briefe, and Comfortable Notes, upon every chapter of Genesis* (London, 1596), p. 14; Andrew Willet, *Hexapla in Genesin* (London, 1608), pp. 11-12; David Pareus, *In Genesin* (Francofurti, 1608), cols. 217-221.

[55] *Opera* (Brunswigae, 1863-1900), XL, 554.

theories of the influence of the moon on bloodletting. The full claims of the astrologers are, of course, absurd. He attacks astrology on some of its weak points. The hour of conception is really more important than the hour of birth, but the astrologers, he states incorrectly, never consider it. If two mothers, he asks, have children at the same moment, will the stars or the complexions of the parents determine the temperament of the children? He insists that a person's temperament is determined by the seed of the parents, the mechanics of conception, and the grace of God. He objects vigorously to Pontano's notion that God uses the stars to help in the government of mankind. He asks if all the men killed in the same battle were born under the same conjunction,[56] and says that if men were really ruled by their stars, no deliberative body would ever agree.[57] At the conclusion of this section, he admits that the stars may have some influence on the earth, that there is a certain agreement between the nature of the heavens and such natural phenomena as rain, whirlwinds, drought, and pestilence. The relationship is, however, not as great as the astrologers would have it to be.[58]

The second section of Calvin's book is consecrated to a discussion of the Biblical attitude towards astrology. In a long introductory section, Calvin lists the various Biblical events in which the stars had no share. He italicizes Isaiah's scorn of the Chaldeans and Egyptians, who could not foresee their own fates, and mentions Daniel's God-given success against the ignorance of the astrologers. True to his own genius, he says that those who consult the stars do not look into their own consciences or trust in God.[59] He is disturbed by the pious attitude and the theological arguments of the astrologers.

Wherefore it is an impudent slander wherewith they slander us, in that they go about to make men believe that we do destroy

---

[56] *Op. cit.*, sig. A5v-B5r.　　　[57] *Ibid.*, sig. B8r.
[58] *Ibid.*, sig. C1r-C1v.　　　[59] *Ibid.*, sig. C2r-C7r.

the order which God hath established in takyng awaye from the
starres the propertie that they have to signifie things aforehand:
yea that we condemne a very excellent and profitable science. All
this cloke is taken away in one word: when we put a difference
betwixte the naturall Astrologie and this bastardly Astrologye which
the Magicians have fayned. I know that to knowe the course of the
starres, their vertue, and that which is of this sort is not onely very
profitable to men: but also doth styrre them up to magnifie the
name of God in his wonderfull wisedom which he sheweth there.[60]

Calvin refutes the interpretations of the Biblical passages adduced by the astrologers in their own behalf. Joseph's star was
divine and surpassed that of the Egyptians; Moses may have
known the tenets of astrology, but he was guided by the word
of God; the sign that will foretell the coming of Christ will
be more extraordinary than the astrologer's conjunction.[61]

In the same era that Calvin drew up his confutation of
astrologers, Cyprian Leowitz (Leovitius), a member of an
aristocratic Bohemian family, came to the defense of astrology.
Leowitz was well known in England, where his calendars and
prognostications were reprinted in translation. He believed
that the world would be destroyed in 1584, and was the author
of numerous predictions that never were realized. In his old
age, he was visited by Tycho Brahe, who had admired his
works and referred to them in his own books. In 1554, Leowitz
published a book that was intended to prove the veracity of
astrological predictions, for he pointed out that there had been
a warning conjunction for every disaster mentioned in history.
Since there were several fatal conjunctions in every year and
sublunary catastrophes were equally frequent, Leowitz had
no difficulty in establishing his case.

Leowitz assures the reader that a conjunction in Sagittarius
in A.D. 73 resulted in the fall of Jerusalem, that a conjunction
in Capricorn in 312 brought Constantine to the Roman scep-

[60] *Ibid.*, sig. D1r-D1v.   [61] *Ibid.*, sig. D3r-D4v.

ter.[62] Charlemagne's rise, he says, was at the beginning of a fiery triplicity with a conjunction in the end of Cancer and the first of Leo; his death was marked by the comet of 814.[63] Contrary to the statements of the historians, Leowitz attributes the rise of Richard III to an eclipse of the sun in Gemini.[64] The years 1514-1515, when there was an eclipse of the sun in Pisces, filled the annals of the astrologers with direful happenings. The Duke of Wittenberg attacked the Swabians; George of Saxony invaded Frisia; Wilhelm and Ludwig of Bavaria battled over their father's crown; Franz von Sickingen fought a decisive skirmish; the Duke of Milan was captured; the King of Hungary died; Luther proclaimed the Reformation; and Huss made his famous confession.[65] Leowitz's accounts of the influence of the stars on early Tudor history are equally diverting. The comet of 1529 brought a plague of sweating sickness in England,[66] and a comet of 1533 produced not only the Anabaptists but Henry VIII's break with Rome.[67] An eclipse of the sun in Virgo in 1542 effected the war between England and Scotland,[68] and an eclipse of the sun in Aquarius joined with three eclipses of the moon sent Henry's army to Boulogne.[69] The death of Mary and also that of Charles V was caused, says Leowitz, by the comet of 1558.[70]

To modern men, Leowitz's book is patently ridiculous, but a most intelligent and cautious defense of astrology was composed at about the same time by Jerome Wolf (Wolfius).

[62] *De coniuntionibus magnis insignioribus superiorum planetarum, solis defectionibus, et cometis, in quarta monarchia, cum eorundem effectuum historica expositione* (Langingae ad Danubium, 1554), sig. B3r.

[63] *Ibid.*, sig. B4r. The ever-present fear of comets during the age is discussed by a variety of writers. Bishop Frederike Grau (Nausea) says that all comets are not formed as Aristotle says, but are the creations of God to warn us against His just vengeance (*Of all Blasing Starrs in Generall, as well Supernaturall as Naturall*, tr. A. Fleming, London, 1577, sig. B2v). See also Scipion du Pleix, *La physique ou science des choses naturelles* (Lyons, 1620), p. 278.

[64] *Ibid.*, sig. E4v.

[65] *Ibid.*, sig. F4v-G1r.

[66] *Ibid.*, sig. G3v.

[67] *Ibid.*, sig. G4v.

[68] *Ibid.*, sig. H3r-H3v.

[69] *Ibid.*, sig. H3v-H4r.

[70] *Ibid.*, sig. K1r-K1v.

Wolf was born in 1516 of an aristocratic line, but his youth was filled with many misfortunes. In time he became one of the greatest of Greek scholars and translated sixteen Greek authors into Latin besides seeing many editions of classical writers through the press. His little-known *Admonitio de astrologiae usu* was printed as a preface to Leowitz's *Brevis et perspicua ratio iudicandi genituras, ex physicis causis et vera experientia extructa* and published at London in 1588. Wolf represents the astrologers who descended from Pontano and who were opposed to the extravagant claims of many of their less cautious colleagues.

Wolf opens his essay by stating that he will not answer all the charges brought against astrology; too many of them are just and arise from the fact that there are many mediocre astrologers, who, rather than admit an error, will deny the truth. After this announcement, he mentions all the arguments that can justly be hurled against astrology. He admits the impossibility of determining the exact minute of conception or birth in taking a horoscope, and says that false predictions about twins probably result from this difficulty. All prognostications of shipwrecks, the fall of cities, pestilences, the slaughter of armies, and earthquakes are open to error because it is difficult to set up a correct figure when there are so many thousand stars to be observed. The same difficulty prevails when one attempts to establish the horoscopes of the numerous people who are born at the same time, but who become kings and shepherds, philosophers and tyrants, hunchbacks and noblemen. The reason for most astrological errors rests with the astrologer who attempts to split hairs. A cynic has said, writes Wolf, that it is not the stars but the astrologer who errs; however, it is not the true astrologer who makes mistakes but the false one, who for the sake of gain arrogates the title of astrologer to himself although he is either ignorant of the art or at best only half-taught.

After this general exordium, Wolf uses the question and

answer method to advance the claims of the honest astrologer. He divides the bulk of his defense into sections on the seasons and the changes of the atmosphere, on the alterations in politics and religion, on the making of astrological amulets, and on the study of individual fortunes. The last section is separated into three divisions: the genethliacal art, elections, and matters that cannot be learned from the stars.

Wolf now tests the certainty of astrology by the syllogistic method. One assumes, he remarks, that either the observation of the stars is folly (and no one is so insane as to assert that), or that a diligent study of the stars combined with great personal prudence can make for a probable judgment of the future. As there is a science of astronomy, so there is one of astrology. When the efficient cause is ascertained, who would doubt or question the result? This, Wolf declares, is especially true when one considers that the power of the stars is demonstrated daily to be ameliorating in its effects upon the health and temperament of mortals. At best, this is very feeble logic, but one must remember that Wolf took his text from his opponents.

· Asked by his interrogator to expound the utility of astrology, Wolf keeps his answers on a moderate level and does not praise the art as the handmaiden of physicians, sailors, and farmers. His answer may be inspired by Ficino, for he replies that if one's mind is not corrupted by bestial delights, astrology will enable one to ascend to God. The questioner asks how this may be accomplished, and Wolf replies that having learned how much greater than the earth are the moon and sun and being aware that God made the whole universe, we can perceive in a limited way the greatness and power of God. This conception should fill us with reverence, admiration, wisdom, and love.

This discussion leads the questioner to ask if it is not presumptuous to attempt to foresee a future that belongs to God? Wolf is ready with the answer. It is true that God has the past, present, and future immediately before him, but man may arrive at a knowledge of the future by digressions. Of course, what man can learn of the future is to the knowledge possessed by God what the peasant's mite is to the treasure house of a king. It is a speck of dust in the cosmos. As God gave men eyes to behold the present and a memory for the retention of the past, so he has given him reason with which he may discern the future. God, says Wolf, would not have men live as beasts who know only the moment, and God indicates that he wishes men to know the future by warnings that he has sent them in visions and dreams. God, he declares, has written in the heavens; and if we could read perfectly, we would be wise men. Does anyone, asks Wolf, accuse the farmer of impiety because he foretells the nature of his harvest or the physician of irreligion because he prognosticates the course of a disease from the pulse, urine, and physical condition of the patient? Is the political expert called blasphemous because he predicts the future fate of a nation from present circumstances?

The course of the essay turns now to practical matters, and Wolf hedgingly answers the question whether or not astrology prepares us for all future events. By the invocation of God and diligent preparations, many impending evils, he asserts, can be mitigated or avoided; this fact has been known for ages, thanks to the investigations of pious men. Wolf attaches great importance to the horoscope, for by it we may learn for what professions we are fitted, what good we shall enjoy, and what evils we should avoid. It also informs men in what actions they will have good fortune, and in what they will fail. It is the duty of a father, Wolf notes, to take the horoscope of a son before he thrusts him into a profession. In like manner, an individual may learn from the stars to what diseases he is subject, and, as a consequence, he may avoid them by natural means.[71]

Wolf's preface closes with an analysis of why astrologers

[71] *Op. cit.,* sig. B2r-C2v.

err. One should always remember that the astrologer is not a divine oracle, but simply a learned and erudite man, who can be deceived like other men. "Who will not bump his head among so many shadows; who will not stray among the windings of such a twisted labyrinth?"[72] One of the reasons that astrologers misjudge events is that they are unable to agree on some of the essentials of the science; they disagree about the method of setting up the horoscope and about the significance of certain stars. These quarrels result in error, but there is no discipline without its controversies. The decrees of the stars are also altered by circumstances of location, education, law, custom, parentage, religion, and other factors. Besides these sources of error, there is such a variety of actions, practices, and accidents that it is almost impossible to predict for an individual; yet individual predictions are required of the astrologer by clients who refuse to accept general conclusions. Sometimes the error arises from misunderstandings; the client, like the supplicant at Delphi, garbles the astrologer's remarks. The major source of error is, however, the unskilled and ignorant astrologer, who plumes himself on his amateurish skill and so brings the whole art of astrology into disgrace.[73]

Perhaps the most readable essay in the history of Renaissance astrological polemics is Pontus de Tyard's *Mantice ou discours de la verite de divination par astrologie*. The book is a discussion in the Ciceronian fashion between Curieux, who attacks astrology, and Mantice, who defends it. The author obviously inclines to the side of Mantice, but it is to his credit that he does not make Curieux a man of straw.

Curieux opens the debate by saying that if astrology were able to perform all that it promised, it would be the first of sciences.[74] He relates the ancient estimates of the art and notices that neither Plato nor Aristotle favored it. He recalls that Eudoxus, Plato's pupil, attacked it. He points out the

[72] *Ibid.*, sig. C4r.
[73] *Ibid.*, sig. D1r.   [74] *Op. cit.* (Lion, 1558), pp. 4-5.

mathematical errors in the works of Firmicus Maternus, and says that the Arabians—Haly, Alamansor, and Albumasor—were barbarians. He thinks that Ptolemy's theories of planetary influences and the sex of stars are absurd, and lectures modern astrologues like Bonatti and Cardan for attributing the miracles of Jesus to the stars. The ancients, he asserts, honored true scientists, but they satirized astrologers in the fables of Icarus and Bellerophon.

Curieux now offers his own theory, which is essentially that presented by Pico in the *Disputationes*. The stars furnish light and heat, which produce variety in nature. There is no place in the world, he declares, that we consider incapable of sustaining life; no island is so barren and deserted, no place under either pole so dead that we think of it as void of living things. We assume, however, that the sun, moon, Saturn, Jupiter, and all the other celestial bodies, which we say are composed of more generous matter than our own earth, are utterly devoid of inhabitants and exist for only our utility and pleasure. It is easier, says Curieux, to believe in a plurality of worlds than to believe that these planets were created just for our benefit. He laughs at the logic of the astrologers; they would say that the coming of the sparrows is the cause of spring and not a sign of spring. If the stars are the causes of all sublunar happenings, why is virtue praised and vice condemned; why bother to be good or great if everything depends on one's natal planets?

Curieux now offers some arguments that have a trace of Gallic wit. If the birth stars mean so much, why don't women delay the births of their children to secure more favorable stars? He narrates with unconcealed mirth the story of the astrologer Bonatti, who was asked what would happen if two opposing generals joined battle in an hour favorable to both, and replied that the stronger army would win.[75] He makes sport of the astrologer's claims to antiquity; and observes that

[75] *Ibid.*, pp. 8-30.

though the same conjunctions have appeared several times, neither the old religions nor the old empires have revived.[76] The folly of the astrologers and their arguments take his attention. If one points out that the planets can have an influence on matter but not on passion, the astrologer replies that it is not the planets but their stations that have the influence.[77] The remainder of the discussion is devoted to conventional matters about the disagreements of astrologers, their impiety, and the arguments of Bardesanes the Syrian against them.[78] Curieux concludes his arguments with an apostrophe to reason.

Mantice now begins his arguments for the other side. If an art or science should be abandoned because it is difficult, he says, astrology should be abandoned. But if a science should be embraced because it is certain, necessary, and embellished with subtle and pleasant contemplations, then one should embrace astrology. He relates the long history of the art and places a great deal of emphasis on the ancients, who lived for hundreds of years and were able to determine the influence of the stars by repeated observations in the course of their own lives. He admits, however, that a great deal has been lost in the normal decay of things. He considers the influence of the stars on plant growth, precious stones, and the humors, and deduces from this their influence on the temperaments of men.[79] He sees no reason why one should accept the influence of plants, gems, and animal parts on men and doubt the force of great and beautiful things like planets.

To Mantice the horoscoping of Biblical figures and the astrological analysis of Scriptural events does not seem impious. When Jesus descended to the earth, he placed himself under the influence of the stars.[80] He thinks that the critics of astrology should be more charitable and not condemn the whole profession for the blunders of a few of its members. He re-

[76] Ibid., pp. 32-33.
[77] Ibid., p. 35.
[79] Ibid., pp. 55-71.
[78] Ibid., pp. 36-53.
[80] Ibid., pp. 78-81.

peats the traditional panegyric on the usefulness of astrology
to the other professions and ascribes the quarrels of the astrologers to the decay into which all of the arts and sciences have
fallen.[81] He concludes by saying that, unlike Curieux, he will
not deny that the stars have power; but before he can accept
the science with a cheerful heart, its inconsistencies must be
removed and it must be restored to its pristine eminence.[82]

One of the most famous of scientific thinkers of the mid-
century was Cardan, whom we have already seen condemned
by Curieux for his astrological practices. No Renaissance man
was possessed of learning vaster than Cardan's, and few men
were more certain of the truth of astrology. In the *De libris
propriis,* Cardan provides the reader with a profession of
faith,[83] and astrological allusions are scattered through the
other works.[84] But the interest of Cardan in astrology was not
casual. He annotated Ptolemy with the affectionate care of the
converted scholar, and he wrote a defense of astrology which
he called the *Libelli quinque* and which was frequently mentioned in this century with both favor and disfavor. The
greater part of this book is devoted to the horoscopes of a
hundred famous men. Cardan prints the figures and prognostications for humanists like Petrarch, Trapezuntius, Filelfo,
Erasmus, Alciati, Pico, and Bembo; for rulers like Nero, Lodo-
vico Sforza, and Henry VIII; for artists like Dürer; and for
reformers like Luther. Each horoscope shows that for these
men the stars predicted correctly. Cardan got the idea for the
book from Gaurico and it is, of course, a splendid example of
post factum reasoning.

In his preface to the book, Cardan speaks in astrology's
defense. In the beginning, he states, no one attributed any
powers to the stars. Later power was granted to the sun, but
it was soon apparent that this was not a correct surmise since

---

[81] *Ibid.,* pp. 85-86.   [82] *Ibid.,* p. 97.

[83] *Opera omnia* (Lugduni, 1663), I, 144.

[84] *Ibid.,* V, 523, 527, 724; X, 102, 460.

it did not account for phenomena like the changes of the seasons, the growth of trees, plants, and gems, the floods of the Nile, and the tides of the sea. The hypothesis was then altered to permit the moon to add her influence and later the powers of the stars were admitted. Cardan differs from other astrologers in that he writes with extreme confidence. He never apologizes for a science that he considers true. He says that he has never heard of an astrological prediction that failed to materialize.[85]

The late 1560's produced another attack on astrology by Thomas Liebler (Erastus), a professor of medicine at Heidelberg, the author of numerous medical and theological works, and a constant opponent of astrology and Paracelsian theoric. In his preface to the "pious and Christian reader," Liebler explains that he had come upon Savonarola's attack on astrology and had been so pleased with it that he had translated it into "nostra lingua." As soon as it was published, Christopher Stathmion strode into the arena against it and forced him to defend it.[86]

The early pages of Liebler's short pamphlet are simply an omnium-gatherum of philosophical and theological diatribes against astrology. His own attitude, which is eventually stated, suggests that he belonged like Bodin, Delrio, and others to the society of Renaissance devil-hunters. The art of astrology, he says, does not derive from true causes and is obviously the work of Satan. Since the ethnics thought that demons were gods, they respected astrology; but "we, who have been instructed by Heaven, know that they are not gods, but the sworn enemies of God and men."[87] Liebler denies that the

---

[85] *Op. cit.* (Norimbergae, 1547), pp. 1r-2v.

[86] *Defensio libelli Hieronymi Savonarolae de astrologia divinatrice, adversus Christophorum Stathmionem* (Heidelberg, 1569), pp. iiir-iiiv. I have not been able to see Stathmion's book, but I judge from Liebler's defense that it is a point-by-point attack not unlike the second half of Bellanti's work.

[87] *Ibid.*, p. 12. The emphasis on diabolism gets firmer as the century passes. In Alsted's *Philosophia digne restituta; libros quatuor* (Heborniae-Nassoviorum, 1612), astrology is said to be the art of cacodaemons (pp. 279-280).

stars are God's means of warning men, and attempts to deprive the astrologers of their special position by saying that the
ancients numbered them among the common diviners. In a
very tenuous section, he proves by means of Aristotle's theories
of sense perception and causation that the future cannot be
learned from signs. Having established a proof that is satis-
factory to him, he bursts into a rhetorical praise of God.[88]

Liebler offers four arguments against astrology which he
feels will confine the science to the hell from whence it came.
The astrologers admit that the stars are not necessary causes;
they say that they incline but do not compel. If they realized
that a necessary cause cannot produce a contingent effect, they
would give up divining. This argument indicates that Liebler
was pointing his guns at the moderate school of astrology,
that he would not tolerate those forms of astrology that many
of the other critics of the art were willing to permit. He
berates the astrologers for disregarding species, genres, and
individuals; they never predict that the summer will be hot
and the winter cold, but offer exact data about rains, winds,
and harvests. They make the same sort of error when they
cast horoscopes. If their predictions were about the nature of
the species, they would have some hope of being accurate;
but they insist on predicting for the individual. In the main,
their method of prognostication is too limited. The farmer,
sailor, physician, and political expert predict according to a
multitude of signs like the quacking of ducks, the gabbling
of geese, the redness of the sky, the moistness of walls, and
the condition of pools and streams; the astrologers use only
the planets. They also predict inanely. When they announce
the date of a future war, they do not use historical information
about the beginning of other wars, but base their whole prediction on the fact that Mars is in a certain sign or that the sun
or moon will be eclipsed.[89]

Although he published other books, the sixteenth-century

[88] *Ibid.*, pp. 16-43.   [89] *Ibid.*, pp. 59-62.

reputation of Johann Gartze (Garcaeus), a Brandenburg preacher, rested on his *Astrologae methodus*. Like many other of these works, it is a practical manual of the astrologer's art, but in the preface and conclusion, Gartze rises to the defense of astrology. He divides the uses of astrology into four categories, and like his old mathematics master, Peucer, relates the history of the art and its degeneration through the activities of Satan. He is unusual in that he believes that the influence of the stars comes from their motion, and he agrees with Wolf that astrology teaches one to be pious, sound of body and mind, and fortunate. Like Wolf, Gartze also admits that astrology cannot foresee everything; but when life is so generally wretched, he says, it is good to be informed of impending difficulties. He insists that astrology is not condemned by the Bible when it is based on physics and not on infernal contracts.[90] Most of these notions are repeated in the conclusion, where Gartze also introduces a proof of astrology drawn from the theory of qualities.[91]

A few years after the publication of Gartze's *Methodus,* the *Catalogus imperatorum, regum ac principum qui astrologicam artem amarunt, ornarunt et exercuerunt* was written by Henry, Count of Rantzau (Ranzovius). Rantzau was the first gentleman of Germany, for he was possessed of vast wealth, wide experience, and great learning. He wrote books on medicine and compiled a number of calendars; his works on military history were justly esteemed because he had distinguished himself as a soldier under Charles V. In his introduction to his historical defense of astrology, Rantzau covers himself with the cloak of piety. By means of stellar signs, he writes, we are able to seek God's aid in our behalf; since God is above fate and the stars, he can overcome any malign influence that

---

[90] *Op. cit.* (Basileae, 1576), sig. A3v-A5v. The pious note is frequently struck in Iofrancus Offusius' *De divina astrorum facultate, in larvatam astrologiam* (Paris, 1570). Offusius' defense is quite conventional, but he consigns the foes of astrology to the ranks of atheists "who scorn to study the order of nature and by this deny the Creator."   [91] *Ibid.,* p. 391.

threatens us.[92] The main body of the work is a series of historical anecdotes about famous men who practiced or favored astrology. Among the adepts are Adam, Abraham, David, Job, Democritus, Caesar, Charlemagne, and Mahomet.

In 1580, Francesco Giuntini (Iunctinus), one of the most sincere of astrologers, published at Cologne a book of method and debate which he called *De divinatione, quae fit per astra, diversum ac discrepans duorum catholicorum sacrae theologiae doctorum iudicium scilicet Francisci Iunctinus Florentini, ac Ioannis Lensaei Belliolani Professoris Louaniensis.* The book was to represent both sides of the question, but it is hardly as judicious as De Tyard's *Mantice.* Since the preface to the book is extracted from Pico's opponent, Bellanti, we can see that the work begins with a definite bias.

Giuntini's section of the book is devoted to answering an opponent, who had attacked him on twenty-two points. Most of the points deal with appeals to the authority of the Bible or the fathers, and Giuntini refutes them by citing a similar quotation in favor of astrology or by twisting the reference. He disposes of Isaiah 44:25 by saying that it is a prohibition of "superstitious divination." He announces that his position is between that of Democritus, Heraclitus, Empedocles, Aristides, Sentirius, Frenetius, and Possidonius, who said that the stars controlled everything, and the phyrronists, who contended that they had no power at all.[93]

Giuntini's defense is personal, but Lensaeus' attack is general and follows the formal method that a hundred years had approved. He says that astrology tries to slip in among the arts in a disguise, and to prove that it has no place in such select company, Lensaeus turns to authority. If astrology were not hostile to Christianity, it might be permitted; but it abducts men from virtue, confirms them in erring ways, and seduces them from truth by ascribing all evil to the stars. Through the first three chapters of the polemic, Lensaeus defends free

[92] *Op. cit.* (Antverpiae, 1580), pp. 10-11.   [93] *Op. cit.,* pp. 1-3.

will and the power of God. In the fourth chapter, he proves by authority that the stars have no influence on the temperaments of men and insists on the importance of heredity. In the eighth chapter, he seems to unbend. We can decide, he declares, that we wish to honor God, become priests or soldiers, give our efforts to honest deeds, or pass our lives in ease and ignorance; the stars can determine, on the other hand, that we will be intelligent or stupid, in good or bad health. He brings up the stereotyped argument about the careers of twins and repeats Pico on the relation between the names of the signs and their influences. The eleventh and twelfth chapters are devoted to a reinterpretation of Scriptural passages that seem to support astrology, and the thirteenth and fourteenth chapters to proving that astrology belongs to the chorus of the witch of Endor. In the closing chapter, Lensaeus exhorts the reader to stay away from the astrologer, who is the deceiver of deceivers.

The pillar of strength in the anti-astrology movement of the 1580's was the celebrated physician and mathematician, Sixtus van Hemminga (ab Hemminga). Van Hemminga was no amateur in the art of astrology who relied on old arguments or contented himself with the compilation of a mass of authoritative quotations; he selected the astrologer's own weapons and defeated them at their own contest. The major part of the *Astrologia, ratione et experientia refutata* is devoted, like the works of Gaurico and Cardan, to the horoscopes of famous men. Van Hemminga shows that in no case did the lives of these people keep the promises of their natal stars. Some of the famous people whom he considers are Charles V, Mary of England, Ludwig of Bavaria, and Duke John of Saxony; but the horoscope that van Hemminga draws up for himself is the most interesting, for it permits him to reveal his native wit—a characteristic not indicated by his stars.[94]

[94] *Op. cit.* (Antverpiae, 1583), pp. 225-237.

In the preface to this book, van Hemminga speaks, like other opponents of astrology, of the evil curiosity of man. All the divining arts, he asserts, attempt to push their way into God's secrets; but astrology, a famous and even respected art, is the most successful of all in trapping the minds of men. Its results, however, are utterly fruitless, for it keeps men in ignorance and precipitates them into the abyss of misery and despair.[95] He urges the astrologers to prove that the stars have influence before they make predictions from them,[96] and objects to the generality of their prognostications.[97] Their cocksureness annoys him. If one shows them a figure, they begin to predict without inquiring whether the subject of the figure is alive, whether it is a man or a woman, whether it is sane or a lunatic, whether it is well or ill, or whether it is a prince or a pauper. In a world that is in flux, it is sheer imbecility, says van Hemminga, to try to foresee anything.[98] He considers the dire predictions that are made when a comet appears, and inquires whether the effect of comets is local or general, immediate or constant.[99] His main argument is essentially his collection of false horoscopes, and his conclusion is that the stars have a general influence, but no one knows what it is.[100]

Three years after van Hemminga's acerous attack, the German poet Nicodemus Frischlin published his *De astronomicae artis, cum doctrina coelesti, et naturali philosophia.*[101] In the course of this book, Frischlin has frequent occasion to mention astrology and astrologers, but mindful of friends like Schöner, Milichius, Peucer, and Winzemius, he urges his reader to remember that he is not animated by his hate of individual men but by a pious desire to examine the truth for the glory of God.[102] Certain astrologers, he says, are guilty of both impiety

[95] *Ibid.*, p. A2v.　　　[96] *Ibid.*, p. 45.
[97] *Ibid.*, p. 60.　　　[98] *Ibid.*, pp. 7-8.
[99] *Ibid.*, p. 13.　　　[100] *Ibid.*, p. 18.
[101] The astrological activities of another early sixteenth-century German man of letters have been recently made available in Moriz Sondheim's *Thomas Murner als Astrolog* (Strassburg, 1938).
[102] *Op. cit.* (Francofurti, 1586), pp. 2r-2v.

and audacity towards heaven. They say, for instance, that the stars provoked Adam's fall, and one of them, Cardan, has had the effrontery to cast the horoscope of Christ. Even theologians (he may be thinking of Gartze) are besotted by the art.[103] God, declares Frischlin, made the world in harmony; he arranged that nothing, with the exception of day and night, could change of itself or be altered by a superior body. He made man and gave him memory for the past and understanding for the present, but he reserved the knowledge of the future for himself, for in him all things are present. Why should God teach Adam to read the stars, asks Frischlin, when he had made Adam in his own image and shed the light of his wisdom, justice, and holiness on him?[104]

In the beginning, writes Frischlin, God did not wish the elements either to alter or interact; he did not wish the air to be hot, then cold, and then moist. All things were to keep their own vital force and remain ever the same. We learn from Moses that there was no rain until man sinned; before that event, the earth was moistened with a gentle dew. The seeds of growth were in the earth and the elements, not in the celestial bodies, and men admired the stars for their motive force, not for their powers of generation. Frischlin now describes the decay of the original universe, a notion that haunted the century. He admits that there is a problem in the astrologer's assertion that the stars acted on man only after Adam's fall. He tries to argue his way round this question. If the stars originally had the power to act on man, reasons Frischlin, it was no punishment to be under their influences after the fall. If God had endowed the stars with this force prior to the fall and man had not sinned, God would have acted in vain. If he gave the stars this power after the fall, he acted contrary to the Biblical account, for he cursed the heavens then as well as the earth. We must then assume, says Frischlin, that the

---

[103] *Ibid.*, p. 4v.   [104] *Ibid.*, pp. 3-4.

decline from the golden age was not caused by the stars but by God's curse on the earth.

Frischlin also takes up the disputed Genesis passage and presents some ideas that had not occurred to the theologians. The stars, he writes, were made as signs of God's bounty, and there is a celestial parable in their motion and change which reminds man of the realm in which there is neither alteration nor shadow. The stars are the work of God's fingers and the registrars of time, but they should not be studied for themselves because this is to transfer to the created, admiration that belongs to the Creator.[105] Frischlin now describes the nature of the sky, its infinity, the force of the sun in generation, and other matters of Aristotelian provenience. From time to time, he returns to the astrologers, whom he considers the greatest of deceivers.[106] In his conclusion, he opposes to the doctrines of the astrologues his own common sense. Cut your hair and nails, he advises the reader, when they are long enough; do not put on a new cloak until it is completely sewn; buy when you have money; sell what is yours and what is unwanted; celebrate a wedding when it is convenient; and have a vein opened when the surgeon advises it.[107]

Jacques Fontaine, a Provençal physician, joined with Frischlin and van Hemminga in the crusade against judicial astrology. In 1581, Fontaine published at Paris his *Discours de la puissance du ciel sur les corps inferieurs et principalement de l'influence contre les astrologues iudiciares;* and in 1622, he issued his *De astrologia medica liber* at Lyons. Fontaine, like most of the opponents of judicial astrology, does not deny the influence of the planets; he simply does not approve of some of the astrologers' tenets. He points out, for example, that one of the arguments used to prove the influence of the stars is that certain animals seem to be produced without insemination. The astrologers find the reason for this generation in the stars, but Fontaine thinks that the influence of the stars in such

---

[105] *Ibid.,* pp. 5-9.   [106] *Ibid.,* p. 142.   [107] *Ibid.,* pp. 464-465.

cases is only partial. The influence of the planets is a real thing to Fontaine, and he likens it to the force of the magnet; like a good astrologer, he also believes that the stars, through their influence on matter, can incline the mind and determine the complexion.

The forty years that elapsed between the publication of this first book and the printing of the book on astrological medicine did not change Fontaine's attitude. In the second book, he admits that the stars may influence the air, but he insists that if the physician can determine the nature of the air, he need not worry about the constellations. He continually urges his practitioner to observe matters that are close at hand. He says that an individual's character is not settled by his horoscope, and, like some of his fellows, believes that successful predictions are the work of magic or Satan.

During the closing years of the sixteenth century, a formal polemic against all forms of magic and certain types of divination was written by Benito Pereyra (Pererius), a member of the Society of Jesus and the author of two widely read books, the *De communibus omnium rerum naturalium principiis et affectionibus* and the *Theatrum rerum creaturarum*. The *De magia, de observatione somniorum, et de divinatione astrologica* was published in 1593 and supplied the pattern for Jesuit treatises of this type written during the seventeenth century.

Pereyra opens his section against astrology by quoting the Bible, the fathers, and the council edicts against the art. He rehearses the astrologers' impieties and is shocked by Albumasor's theory that one should pray in a favorable hour. He summarizes the astronomical ineptness of the astrologers and says that their notions have been upset by the recent *nova* in the sphere of fixed stars. This remark is interesting because the opponents of astrology seldom made use of the new astronomy. Pereyra now proposes to confute astrology with eight arguments: the stars are not particular causes; the as-

trologer cannot explain the diverse careers of twins; the case
of those that share the same fate but not the same stars is a
blow to astrological theory; the customs of a land have more
to do with the lives of men than their stars; free will confutes
astrology; the art has no sure foundation and is horrent with
errors; learned men have never approved of astrology; and
none of the essential hypotheses of astrology is sound. The
astrologers say that the stars have the qualities of the elements,
but since they have light, they cannot be moist or cold. The
course of life cannot be foretold by the stars, because it is a
product of the gestation period, the nature of the parents, and
the education of the child. He is also amused by the astrologers,
who will take the horoscope of a city, but not that of a plant or
animal. He quotes Pico against the astrologers' claim to antiquity, and insists that the stars are neither causes nor signs.
He concludes his attack by explaining some possible reasons
for the occasional success of astrologers. Perhaps, he says, they
have a pact with Satan; or for some hidden reason, God tells
them the answer. Often, however, their stupid clients inad-
vertently fulfill the prediction which the astrologer made on
the basis of his common sense instead of his astrological knowledge.[108]

A learned defense of the moderate school of astrology was
attempted by Tycho Brahe's pupil, Kort Axelsön (Conradus
Aslacus), in the latter part of his eclectic *Physica et ethica
Mosaica, ut antiquissima, ita vere Christiana.* He inaugurates
his defense with the following six postulates: the stars influence the seasonal changes; the sun and moon affect animal
and vegetable life; the results of the ascension and declension
of the Pleiades, Orion, and Arcturus are well known; the
influences of eclipses are certain; the conjunction of planets
brings known aerial disturbances; and alterations in the lower
world are often caused by conjunctions. He points out that
the influence of a planet cannot be constant because it is some-

[108] *Op. cit.* (Coloniae Agrippinae, 1598), pp. 156-235.

times hindered by clouds and other earthly exhalations, by fixed stars that revolve oppositely, and by the will of God.

Axelsön does not believe that the stars dominate man completely; he acknowledges the force of free will. One knows, however, the influence of the sun and the moon on the humors, but no planet inclines man to evil—the powers of Hell alone do that. Axelsön examines the Scriptural passages adduced against the astrologers and blunts their edges with sophistry. Jeremiah said that the stars are not to be feared; if they are not to be feared, their influence must be real, for Christ told us not to fear Satan. Genesis states that the stars are signs; if they are signs, they must be signs of something.[109] Axelsön is ready to grant that the stars do not foretell everything; they do not foretell events that arise from God's will, events that come from man's free will, and happenings that are fortuitous.[110] These qualifications permit Axelsön to strike a blow for the moderate school of astrology and he strikes with great spirit.

The followers of Pico and Frischlin, who relegate astrology to Orcus, writes Axelsön, are just as heinous as the presumptuous Arabs, who make all things depend on the stars. He speaks of the five important arguments advanced by the foes of astrology and says that he will refute them. It is said that the philosophy of the astrologers is untrue because it is not based on exact hypotheses. Axelsön states that there are two kinds of proof: *a priori* proof on which physics is based, and *a posteriori* proof on which astrology is established. Experience has shown that an influence emanates from sidereal motion and the accidents of this motion. It is also said that astrology violates the definition of a science by dealing with particulars. No science, Axelsön insists, is without particularity; like other sciences, astrology has some elements that are particular and probable, others that are universal and true. The

---

[109] *Op. cit.* (Hanoviae, 1613), pp. 233-241.
[110] *Ibid.*, p. 24.

opponents of astrology say further that the predictions of the astrologers are usually untrue. The errors of astrology, Axelsön replies, are the errors of the astrologer; like all general sciences, astrology is fallible when applied to particulars. The enemies of astrology also say that if the art were as ancient as the astrologers claim, Adam would have predicted his own fall. Adam's fall, however, came from his own free will and not from the stars. Finally, the foes of astrology argue that if the stars are the good creatures of a good Creator, they cannot predict such evil things as bad weather, famine, war, and pestilence. To this Axelsön retorts that though the good creatures of God have good effects, they sometimes become the instruments of Divine wrath and inflict a merited punishment on men.[111]

In Axelsön, one detects the friends of astrology shifting their ground to meet the assaults of their enemies. The theory of stellar influences has altered since the beginning of the sixteenth century, and the astrologers of the seventeenth century are ready to admit free will as an important factor in mortal actions. The foes of astrology are less flexible; they abide by the old arguments, which they reiterate constantly. Occasionally one comes upon a writer like Frischlin, who has something new to say, but the voice of the rationalist is seldom original in tone. Among the more intelligent and adroit opponents of astrology in the early part of the seventeenth century is Andreas Libau (Libavius), a great student of medicine and chemistry and the author of four extremely lucid works on alchemy. His polemic against astrology is printed in his *De universitate et rerum conditarum originibus,* a work on Christian physics.

Libau laughs at those who assign human passions to the stars and who publish calendars with crosses denoting the fatal days. God is able, says he, to scatter rewards and benefits without the aid of the sky. How can the skies threaten when they were made for kindness? He admits that the earth and

[111] *Ibid.,* pp. 242-245.

sky have probably been weakened by man's continual sinning, but has not God the power to change all evil to good? God may have created cause and effect, but he is not controlled by them and his providence governs all alterations; even the stars cannot change their places of their own accord, and they are quite incapable of love or hate.[112] Libau was charmed by the *reductio ad absurdum,* and so he invites the scientist to learn about plants, animals, and minerals from the stars that tell the astrologer so much about men. One could learn the properties of gold from the sun, or those of iron from Mars, if the astrologers' theories were true.[113]

Libau also points out what the astrologers must do before they have a perfect science. Each astrologer must be thoroughly instructed in human and divine wisdom; he must have continual practice in observation, a minute knowledge of the past and present, and a perfect comprehension of history. The findings of the Babylonians, Egyptians, and Chaldeans will have to be adjusted to modern circumstances. The astrologer must also be able to show what effect a stellar disturbance over India will have on his own city. Finally, the astrologers will have to reconcile the disagreements between members of their own confraternity like Röslin and Crabbe. In order for all of this to happen, says Libau, the stars will have to work harder than ever before.[114]

A completely unrevised defense of astrology appeared in Rudolph Göckel's (Goclenius) *Acroteleution astrologicum,* which was printed at Marburg in 1618. Göckel was made professor of physics at Marburg in 1589 and professor of mathematics and logic in 1603. He devoted a half century of tireless effort to learning and published in a wide variety of fields. He is the author of an *Academia seu philosophica panegyris,* an *Observationes linguae latinae,* a *Conciliator philosophicus,* a *Physica,* a *Politica,* a *Physiologia,* an *Idea philosophiae pla-*

---

[112] *Op. cit.* (Francofurti, 1610), p. 404.
[113] *Ibid.*, p. 410.   [114] *Ibid.*, p. 450.

tonicae, and many other books. We mention these works of Göckel to indicate again that the proponents of astrology in the Renaissance were by no means ignorant men; only too often they were more erudite and more skillful investigators of nature than many of their opponents.

Köke

Like Axelsön, Göckel feels that those who reject astrology are men of limited intellectual horizons, and he regrets that he must enroll Pico, "vir doctissimus," among these men. He plans not to refute their arguments, but to expound the doctrines of astrology. He follows his predecessors in a discussion of planetary influences and in authoritative arguments; he then girds himself to attack the heretics of the art. The real sinners, says Göckel, are those astrologers who say that all things depend from the stars, who make the planets the weapons of fate. These astrologers have been rightly damned by all learned men, for they are men who have no faith in God. He speaks of himself as one "who travels the middle and safest way, for he is really a physicist, who takes careful observations and learns by experiment." He tells the reader that his motto is "ex effectis contextis."

He defends astrology from the charge of error, by relating the mistakes in other sciences, and inquiring if they are vitiated by these blunders.[115] He concludes this section by attacking astrological heresies like the notion that the stars are the homes of the blest and Albumasor's "hour of prayer." He insists, however, that the stars are important in the governing of health and in the many accidents of mortal existence.[116] In support of the latter claim, Göckel prints pages of illustrations to prove that the predictions of the astrologers are often correct. Ladislaw's mother was told by an astrologer that her son would have a short and glorious life; he became king at the age of twenty and was slain at the Battle of Varna.[117] The brief life of Pico della Mirandola[118] and the death of Charles of

[115] *Op. cit.,* pp. 8-27. For his panegyric of astrology see his *Discursus apologeticus pro astromantia* (Marpurgi, 1611), p. 11.
[116] *Ibid.,* pp. 29-31.   [117] *Ibid.,* p. 32.   [118] *Ibid.,* p. 43.

Burgundy[119] were foretold. The stars, says Göckel, are type slugs in the heavenly printing office; they are also the legates sent by God.[120]

In the closing pages of his book, Göckel, in spite of his moderate and scientific attitude, takes up the ubiquitous question of free will and goes back to the era of Pontano. The stars, he writes, have no influence on the will, but man is divided into two kingdoms, the material and the spiritual, the body and the soul. The stars affect only the material parts of man, but the material man has a certain influence over the spiritual man. If the body is well inclined, Göckel declares, the soul will be well inclined; if the body is inclined to evil, the soul will bend to sin.[121] With this statement, Göckel, one of the most learned of Renaissance Germans, reverts to a position that the more enlightened astrologer tried to avoid.

Before the close of the Jacobean age, a polemic against astrology, which is comparable in many ways to Pico della Mirandola's *Disputationes,* was published on the continent. This work was by Alessandro degli Angeli (de Angelis), a Jesuit father, and bore the title *In astrologos coniectores libri quinque.* Published at Lyons in 1620, this book derived its form from the *De magia* of Pereyra and much of its matter from Pico della Mirandola. Fra Alessandro had, however, four times as many pages as Pereyra had, and so he was able to extend his arguments at length. He seems also to have taken a hint from the *Il serraglio degli stupori del mondo,* which Tommaso Garzoni published at Venice in 1613 and which contained a series of arguments against astrology. Each of Garzoni's arguments is supported by several pages of quotations from important writers who back his opinions.[122] Fra Alessandro's method of attack is to follow the outline of Pereyra but to expand the argument with a wealth of examples and quotations. The polemic is well organized in five books which

---

[119] *Ibid.,* p. 46. [120] *Ibid.,* p. 60. [121] *Ibid.,* pp. 66-67.
[122] *Op. cit.,* pp. 407-472; in Garzoni's *La piazza universale* (Venetia, 1601), pp. 369-391 are devoted to astrologers and astronomers.

bear the following headings: "De coeli actione in haec inferiora generatim," "De conceptu et foetu," "De natali et partu," "Quo astrologia astrologicis conclusionibus exagitatur," and "Qui et exotericus."

In his first book, Fra Alessandro makes many admissions. He grants the influence of the stars on the sea, on plants and animals, on the changes of season, on invalids, and on men living in widely separated localities. These effects, he says, are the result of light and heat, but not of planetary motion, which does not extend as far as the earth. He says that the sky can have no influence on particulars, and hence has no influence on either the intellectual or the procreatory processes. Sympathies and antipathies can develop more easily from the elements than from the stars. He criticizes the theory of Fernelius that plagues come from the stars. Has not one seen the air foul, asks Fra Alessandro, when the skies are salubrious; is it not more reasonable to think of these diseases as produced by putrid bodies than by a putrid sky?

In the second book, he notes that if the stars influence anything, it must be the body; but he exhorts his readers to consult the physician and the philosopher instead of the astrologer. He argues that the astrologer can observe nothing during a pregnancy when so much depends on the food, sleep, activities, and mental condition of the mother. He laughs at the astrological notion that the stars of the parents mingle to produce the character of the child and offers a physiological explanation of why children look like their parents. In the third book, he begins, as usual, by insisting that the will of man is free. It is a rule of nature, he states, for the noble to dominate the ignoble; hence the stars cannot dominate the mind. Man was created to fix his mind on God; hence the mind cannot be dominated by the stars. The mind also controls the matter of the body, so it cannot be governed by the matter of heaven.

After this digression on the will, Fra Alessandro turns to the theme of the book. The astrologer cannot know the mo-

ment of conception or the moment of birth with any accuracy;
he also depends, when he establishes a horoscope, on too few
stars. He centers the remainder of the book on such regulators
of character as food, exercise, wives and children, and conscience. In the fourth book, he talks of the lack of scientific
technique among the astrologers, but he is chiefly alarmed by
their trickery. He says that Cardan, who is one of his special
targets, predicted in his horoscope of Edward VI that the king
would die in the third month of his fifty-fifth year; but when
he issued his book of horoscopes—the *Libelli quinque*—he
falsified Edward's and made it seem that he had predicted
his death in his sixteenth year. Fra Alessandro relates in a
detailed fashion the errors and inconsistencies of the astrologers
and borrows many of the arguments used by Pico della Mirandola. He draws upon Pereyra for his explanation of the astrologers' occasional successes, and concludes his chapter by listing
the numerous times when the predictions of the astrologers
failed to materialize.

The last book of the *In astrologos* is little more than a compendium of authorities. Some of the chapters are simply
sections from the works of Augustine or Ambrose. In the
latter pages of the book, Fra Alessandro relates the unhappy
fates of men who put their trust in astrology and concludes
his polemic with a homily addressed to Cardan, who was by
then beyond the reach of all homilies.

> What say you, Cardan? What have you gained from so many
> years of study in the astrological arts? After expounding your hun-
> dred horoscopes, after noting the births of so many famous kings
> and emperors, after editing the seven books of aphorisms and writ-
> ing so many comments on Ptolemy, have you not become an adept?
> Why did you not tear the axe from your son's hand? Why did you
> not take heed lest he marry an unchaste woman? You, who exam-
> ine all the hidden places of nature, why did you not foresee the
> shame of your son's marriage? One of two things must be admitted;
> either you were ignorant of your son's unhappy fortune and are

unable to determine future events from a horoscope, or you were aware long before of your miserable son's death, but could not offer any aid to him whom the stars had devoted to the sword. Rightly we scorn a fruitless art of this sort; if it is of no use to itself, to whom is it profitable? First take counsel for your own affairs; then you may anticipate, by your great foresight, the misfortunes of others. We cannot believe that those whom we find unwitting of their own impending fates are seers.[123]

With this analysis of Fra Alessandro's polemic, the history of the continental debate on the validity of astrology is concluded. The arguments on both sides of the question are obviously very conventional; it is unusual to find either novelty of thought or originality of approach. The enemies of astrology drew for the most part on the vast treasures of the Middle Ages or thumbed through the encyclopedic treatise of Pico della Mirandola. Most of them seem to be utterly unaware of the new astronomical findings; no one of them thinks to ask how the stars can shed down their influences in a universe in which there are no ups and downs. A few of them mention the comets observed during the latter part of the century in areas above the sphere of the moon, but no one of them realizes that this discovery was the supreme argument against the system of Ptolemy and the cosmology of Aristotle.

The defenders of astrology are a more pliable breed. They, too, have a penchant for ancient argument and delight in ringing the traditional changes; but, with certain exceptions, they are ready to shift a flank to meet a lateral attack. Few of the later defenders insist that the stars dominate all terrestrial inhabitants; most of them admit the freedom of the will and limit the influence of the stars to the creatures of the elements. There is also a definite tendency for the moderate astrologers and the liberal anti-astrologers to draw together, for an astrologer who admits the freedom of the will is not unlike his

[123] *Op. cit.*, pp. 349-350.

opponent who focuses his attack around a defense of free choice. Only a name kept these two groups apart.

In conclusion, we wish to point out again that the defenders of astrology were not ignorant and superstitious men. Some of the greatest scientific minds of the age believed in the art of the stars. As we look over these books, we notice to our amazement what intelligent writers most of the astrologers are; on the other hand, we are only too often confronted with an anti-astrologer who is both ignorant and dull. There are various reasons for this. To be a ranking member of the astrologer's profession in the sixteenth century required a mastery of astronomy and mathematics, sciences in which the stupid never excel. To be an opponent of astrology, one needed only enough Latin to read Pico and abridge his arguments. The underlying reason for the war against astrology had also a share in shaping the character of the defender. The Renaissance debate about the verities of the astrologer's creed has only a small place in the history of rationalism, but it merits a generous chapter in the history of religion. The force that impelled Pico to write his *Disputationes* was the force that inspired most of the writers of the sixteenth century; and when the brotherhood of Christian believers marshals its dogma for an offensive, it takes both courage and intelligence to move against it.

CHAPTER III

ATTACK AND DEFENSE IN RENAISSANCE ENGLAND

THE CONTROVERSY over the basic tenets of astrology which had sent some of the most learned polemicists of the continent to their writing stools was not without repercussions in Renaissance England. A study of the state papers and official transactions of Tudor and Stuart rulers reveals the hovering and sometimes sinister presence of these cicerones of the celestial avenues in the residences of nobles. The Spanish astrologer, Jehan, had a role in the plot against Henry VII which Sir John Kendal, Prior of the Order of St. John of Jerusalem, fabricated to his own misfortune;[1] and Henry, the object of the plot, was himself not averse to heeding the predictions of priests who had repute as prognosticators.[2] Astrologers who were not retained by the registrants of Battle Abbey found employment elsewhere, for ambassadors like the Provost of Cassel were known to consult with them about the proper courses of diplomatic action.[3] Unless, however, one accepts the mythological Mother Shipton as an historic personage, one is forced to conclude that most of the practitioners of practical astrology during the early period of Tudor rule were of foreign extraction. The true-born English astrologer comes into his own with the reign of Henry VIII.

Henry was, we know, a devotee of astronomy, and, as Roper relates, often had Sir Thomas More "up into the leads,

---

[1] A. F. Pollard, *The Reign of Henry VII from Contemporary Sources* (London, 1914), I, 116-122. For surveys see C. Camden, "Astrology in Shakespeare's Day," *Isis,* XIX (1933), 26-73; E. B. Knobel, "Astronomy and Astrology," *Shakespeare's England* (Oxford, 1916), I, 444-461.

[2] A. F. Pollard, *op. cit.,* I, 205; II, 231.

[3] *Ibid.,* I, 306.

8

there to consider with him the diversities, courses, motions, and operations of the stars and planets."[4] These discussions were undoubtedly on the white side of the science, for in his *Utopia,* More writes that though the priests of the island were skilled in astronomy, they never dreamed of divination by planets.[5] John Chamber, however, informs us that Henry's physicians used the planetary positions in diagnostics and that the king did not hesitate to use the precepts of astrology on other occasions.[6] In 1541, an act was established which made the practice of sorcery a felony, and Bosanquet thinks that this act included the manipulations of the astrologers and accounted for the apologetic preface to Andrew Boorde's prognostication for 1545.[7] The tenure of the act of 1541 was not long, for it was repealed early in the reign of Edward VI, and after its rescission we discover the native astrologer not only compiling and publishing prognostications but also taking an important place in the life of the court and the city.[8]

In England, as on the continent, piety and learning were, by no means, bulwarks against the temptations of astrology. Reginald Scot writes in his *Discoverie of Witchcraft* that "though there be many of them learned and godlie, yet lurke there in corners of the same profession, a great number of counterfets and couseners."[9] When one considers the English astrologers, one is forced to discriminate between the sincere and scientific investigators of planetary influence and the mountebank and charlatan who throve on the credulity of all classes of society. Among the learned men who interested themselves in this art was Thomas Allen, a mathematician,

[4] *The Life of Sir Thomas More* (London, 1925), p. 7.
[5] *L'Utopie. Texte latin,* ed. Delcourt (Paris, 1936), p. 139; this attitude is consonant with the Utopian's scorn of all forms of divination; cf. p. 191.
[6] *A Treatise against Iudicial Astrologie* (London, 1601), p. 29.
[7] *English Printed Almanacks and Prognostications. A Bibliographical History to the year 1600* (London, 1917), p. 5.
[8] For an important study see Sanford V. Larkey, "Astrology and Politics in the First Years of Elizabeth's Reign," *Bulletin of the Institute of the History of Medicine,* III (1935), 171-186.   [9] *Op. cit.* (London, 1584), p. 171.

philosopher, and antiquary, who owned the friendship of distinguished thinkers like Harriot, Taporley, Warner, Bodley,
Camden, Selden, and Spelman. Allen was a favored intimate
of Leicester's circle, and, as Fuller writes, he "succeeded to
the skill and scandal of Friar Bacon."[10] Another learned prognosticator was Anthony Ascham, who was probably a brother
of Roger Ascham. Since Anthony Ascham was a graduate
of Cambridge and held the living of Burneston, Yorkshire, one
may suspect that he had some learning and at least a dash of
piety. Allen left only manuscript works on astrology, but
Ascham was the author of an herbal, a treatise on astronomy,
and the iatromathematical *Treatise of Astronomie, declaring
what Herbs and all Kinde of Medicines are appropriate, and
also under the influence of the Planets, Signs & Constellations.*
A further member of this group was Leonard Digges, the
father of the famous astronomer Thomas Digges,[11] whose
defense of astrology and astronomy forms the introduction to
his famous *A Prognostication of right good effect.* Though
widely read in astronomy, Digges calls upon the authority of
Melanchthon, Bonatti, and Cardan and follows the medieval
classification of sciences which resulted in the confusion of
astrology and astronomy.[12] In addition to these learned devotees of astrology there were others like Sir Thomas Smith[13]
and Peter Baro,[14] the French-born Cambridge professor of
Hebrew.

English physicians, men who could hardly be called unlearned though the taint of Sextus Empiricus might besmirch
their piety, shared the interest of their continental colleagues
in astrology, and many of them undoubtedly diagnosed and
treated diseases according to the prescriptions of the stars.[15]

[10] *The History of the Worthies of England* (London, 1811), II, 310.
[11] See Francis Johnson, *Astronomical Thought in Renaissance England* (Baltimore, 1937), pp. 161-210.
[12] *Op. cit.,* Old Ashmolean Reprints III (Oxford, 1926), pp. xiii-xiv.
[13] G. Harvey, *Smithus; vel Musarum Lachrymae* (London, 1578), sig. F3v-F4v.
[14] R. Harvey, *An Astrological Discourse* (London, 1583), p. 5.
[15] C. Camden, "Elizabethan Astrological Medicine," *Annals of Medical History,*

One of these physicians was Doctor Henry Low, who practiced
at Salisbury "near to the Close gate" and who for many years
published an annual prediction. Thomas Twyne, who had
studied at Cambridge under John Caius and who lived at
Lewes, was another physician who was skilled in astrology.
Twyne was a close friend of John Dee and the author and translator of many books. A medical associate of Low at Salisbury was Doctor John Securis, who had been educated at
Paris and Oxford and who, in addition to his frequent pro-
posals for the reformation of the medical profession, was the
author of numerous astrological prognostications. The medical man who was guided by the precepts of the astrologer was
not, however, restricted to provincial England, for two of the
most famous of London doctors, William Cuningham and
Richard Forster, were renowned for their skill in astrology.
Cuningham was educated at Heidelberg under Liebler, whose
reputation for astrological learning was world-wide. Returning to England, Cuningham began to practice at Norwich—
where a moderate astrologer, Thomas Browne, was to work
later—but leaving this residence, he moved to London, where
he became a fashionable physician and wrote on astronomy,
cosmology, and medicine. Richard Forster, like Cuningham,
was the author of prognostics and eventually became the Presi-
dent of the College of Physicians. He did not feel that he was
acting in a manner unbecoming to either his place or his profession when he defended astrology in the preface to his *Ephemerides* for 1575 and called the art the handmaid of medicine.

So far we have presented the portraits of only the learned
and scientifically minded investigators of the *ars astrologica*,
but there is, of course, an obverse to the medallion. In spite
of Miss Fell-Smith's attempt to rehabilitate his reputation and
to prove that he was the simple dupe of ignorant but shrewder
men, John Dee, the astrologer of Queen Elizabeth, must still

N.S., II (1930), 217-226. Professor Camden provides notices of Recorde, Boorde,
and Vicary, and for that reason I do not mention them.

be regarded with some doubt. Learned, unquestionably pious, and an experimenter of immense callidity, Dee was, nonetheless, ready to be feed by the great for labors that were distinctly of a swindling nature, and until a judicious account of him appears, he must be considered as more sincere but not too far above the lower order of prognosticators. Younger than Dee, and definitely below him in character and learning, was Simon Forman, whose life seems almost the invention of an intemperate romancer. Forman, a virtually uneducated Englishman, succeeded, in spite of numerous imprisonments and the hostility of the whole medical profession, in acquiring a lucrative practice among the great and in securing honorary degrees from the universities. This astrological quack, whose love for the theater has provided Shakespearean scholars with invaluable information about *Macbeth, The Tempest,* and *Cymbeline,* was not only a marvelous rogue but the closest approximation to Don Juan that the Elizabethans knew. In the same category with Forman was John Lambe, who was regularly arrested for his malpractices but who succeeded in securing the patronage of the notorious Duke of Buckingham. Lambe's evil influence on the Duke was made the theme of ballads, and he eventually died of injuries received in a street brawl. Late in the seventeenth century, he became the subject of a popular chapbook and so passed into the literature of roguery.

There is in the careers of men like Dee, Forman, and Lambe enough glitter to compensate for their manifold craftinesses and gargantuan deceits. Far below them in both wit and foul dealing was a great mass of petty rascals, predaceous offscourings who patrolled the by-lanes and holed in the alleys.[16] The names by which they were known—Edward Alavantrevor, David Upan, John Uprobert—have all the characteristics of an alias, and one suspects that they were no better than they sound or than the English opponents of astrology say that

[16] For some annotations on this see *The Lives of those Eminent Antiquaries Elias Ashmole, Esquire, and Mr. William Lilly, written by themselves* (London, 1774), pp. 17-23, 29-45.

Summary

they were. What one perceives, however, is that the art of astrology was extraordinarily popular in Renaissance England; the high and the low, the rich and the poor, the learned and the ignorant, the pious and the impious shared a common belief in the influence of the stars. There were, of course, gradations in the fixity of this faith, but the scholar of the twentieth century must not lose sight of the fact that in the sixteenth century disbelief in the essential hypotheses of the astrologer was the exception rather than the rule. In the subsequent pages, the polemics in the formal debate about the verity of the art will be outlined, and one should observe that though the English attacks on astrology are seldom original, their authors, like their continental compeers, were men of courage and even intellectual audacity whose opinions, supported by canon law but not by ecclesiastical performance, were diametrically opposed to the common view.

The first Englishman of the Tudor era to write a formal attack on astrology was William Fulke. After graduating from Cambridge, Fulke came to London to study law at Clifford's Inn, but finding the pandects little to his taste, he returned to his university and pursued advanced studies in mathematics, languages, and theology. His life was a long controversy, for he early attached himself to the Puritan cause and published at least one pamphlet a year in defense of his religious attitude. His opposition to astrology is at first difficult to understand, for he was the compiler of prognostics licensed for the years 1561 and 1563, and he is listed among astrological adepts by Richard Harvey;[17] this seeming incongruity of attitude and performance is, however, removed by noticing that Fulke, like many of the opponents of astrology, was against only the judicial phases of the science.

Although Fulke's opinions on the superstitious and irrational claims of the astrologers can be clearly indicated by a survey of his polemic against astrology, it might be illumi-

[17] *Op. cit.*, p. iii; see E. Bosanquet, *op. cit.*, pp. 194-195.

nating to notice that like Montaigne he turned his face against all types of superstition and was especially irritated by those folk legends that annoyed Bacon and produced Browne's *Pseudodoxia Epidemica.* In 1563 he published a neo-Aristotelian work called *A Most Pleasant Prospect into the Garden of Naturall Contemplation,* and in this work he tried to erase by means of the doctrines of Aristotle such popular superstitions as the flaming Satan that was said to have flown over the Thames and to have been stocked at Stratford.[18] Although he is ready to accept such phenomena as the immunity of the eagle and the bay tree to lightning[19] and the magic properties of certain springs and wells,[20] he is equally ready to deny even Aristotle when his own experience points toward a negative conclusion. He writes, for instance, that the occult powers of gems are due more to the "superstition & credulitie of him that useth them, then of the vertue of the stones."[21] He takes up the ancient question of comets, whose malignant nature had been certified by some of the more rational minds of his day,[22] and though he admits that they may corrupt the air and bring physical misfortune to the delicately reared members of the upper classes, he adds:

Yet these predictions have a shewe of reason, though it bee nothing necessarie: but it is a world to see, how the Astrologians dote in such devices. They are not ashamed, to an earthly substance, to ascribe an heavenly influence, and in order of iudgement to use them as very starres. Surely, by as good reason as to the celestiall starre, they attribute divine influences and effectes. But this their folly hath beene sufficiently detected by divers godly and learned men, and this place requireth no long discourse thereof.[23]

This challenge to all superstitions and this attitude of careful skepticism prevail throughout Fulke's *Antiprognosticon contra inutiles astrologorum predictiones Nostrodami, Cun-*

---

[18] *Op. cit.* (London, 1602), pp. 10v-11r.
[19] *Ibid.*, p. 31r.   [20] *Ibid.*, p. 59v.   [21] *Ibid.*, p. 71r.
[22] C. Camden, "Elizabethan Almanacs and Prognostications," *The Library*, XII (1931), 201-205.   [23] *Op. cit.*, p. 16v.

ninghami, Loui, Hilli, Vaghami, et reliquorum omnium, which was published at London in 1560 and turned into English in the same year by the famous translator and compiler William Painter. The translation, besides containing some verses and a letter of Painter, has an additional essay by Fulke which is titled: *A shorte Treatise in Englyshe, as well for the utter subversion of that fained arte, as also for the better understanding of the common people, unto whom the fyrst labour seemeth not sufficient.* The *Antiprognosticon* is aimed at all the superstitious disciples of astrology, but the attack is definitely pointed by the mention of names in the title. In the translation, only the name of Nostradamus is mentioned on the title page, but in one of the prefatory verses, Painter holds up Doctor Cuningham and Vaughn as special targets.

Fulke introduces his attack on astrology with a general discussion of the divining arts. It were a small matter, he says, if astrology were limited to the forecasting of weather, but "they must fyl the whole world at their pleasure with warre, sycknesse, and rebellion."[24] He scorns the astrologers' thesis that they understand the government, both physical and mental, of men in particular; and though his purpose in writing the *Antiprognosticon* is essentially didactic, he also subscribes to the medieval notion of the limitability of the knowable which Saint Bonaventura had emphasized and against which Marlowe's Faustus struggled in vain. "Those thynges that are aboue vs, perteyne nothyng vnto vs: and those thynges which are aboue our reache, ar not to be sought for, with muche curiositie."[25] As an indication that the older confusion between astronomy and astrology still existed, one may notice that Fulke praised astronomy and exhorted his readers not to condemn it because it had been misused by the astrologers.

After reminding the reader of the number of times that

[24] *Antiprognosticon that is to saye, an Inuectiue agaynst the vayne and vnprofitable predictions of the Astrologians* (London, 1560), sig. A3r-A3v.
[25] *Ibid.,* sig. A5r.

astrologers have been wrong, Fulke turns, as did almost all of his continental precursors, to an examination of the essential postulates of astrology and declares that they are both uncertain and inconstant. He complains that the economic balance is often upset by untrue predictions of the astrologers about crops and markets, and he explodes a broadside against the fears produced in the previous year by the prophesies of Nostradamus. To his remarks about the notorious French seer, he adds others concerning the English prophets Hill, Low, Vaughn, Ascham, and Cuningham, and shows that like the ancient premonstraters, they always predict in an ambiguous fashion which allows them to escape the consequences of an unfulfilled prophesy.

Fulke explains how demonstrable and indubitable the bases of a true science are and indicates how contrary to this are the grounds of astrology. He is moved to mirth by the astrologers who plead the distance between man and the stars as the cause of error and uncertainty. Astronomers, says Fulke, whose science is firmly established, do not complain of this distance. He takes up the natures and special influences attributed to the planets by the astrologers and shows that it is far easier to prove that the planets have powers contrary to those posited by the astrologers than it is to prove the actuality of the assigned powers. He applies the same method of criticism to other tenets of the astrologer to indicate that none of the basic hypotheses of the art depends on exact demonstration. Astrologers can only avoid his arguments by boasting of "somme reuelations to bee geuen unto the inuenters of theyr arte."[26]

If, however, the astrologer insists on revelation, Fulke is prepared for him. Honest revelations are conveyed by angels; dishonest revelations have their origin in Hell. He attacks the ancient arguments from Genesis with equally ancient arguments. He admits to a ready belief in a stellar influence of some sort on the matter of men, but he denies that anyone can either

[26] *Ibid.*, sig. B5r.

ascertain or predict the nature of this influence. Some years
before, says Fulke, Cuningham announced a sudden and total
destruction of the lands of Egypt, Babylon, Constantinople,
and the cities of Italy; a citizen of these realms who trusted the
prophesies of Cuningham before those of Jeremiah might well
be afraid.

O blockeheade, that must haue thy Natiuitie caste, howe dooest
thou determyne to leade thy lyfe, lyke a bruite beaste, that thou
wylle suffer all thynges to woorke vpon thee. Wherefore serueth
thy reason which thou dost not vse? nay rather which thou dooste
abuse in suche vanities. Knowynge thy fortune (yu saist) by thy na-
tiuity thou wilte endeuour thy selfe to seeke for good thynges, and
auoyde euyll thynges. Why wouldest thou not haue doon so, although thou haddest neuer asked counsell of the sothsaier.[27]

Against the astrologers and their clients, Fulke hurls the
testimony of the patriarchs and early philosophers; he repeats
the arguments—that we have encountered before—about the
 naming of the planets and the transferring of the qualities of
the name to the star. At the conclusion of this first section,
Fulke considers an epistle in defense of astrology that Doctor
Cuningham had prefixed to one of his prognostications. Cuningham had said that all the calumniators of astrology repeated
the same two arguments: that astrology was an enemy to physics and that the astrologer cannot foretell by the stars. By an
appeal to Hippocrates, Cuningham had attempted to confute
the first objection, but Fulke was too good a classical scholar
not to trace him to his source. Fulke discovered that Cuningham had read a misleading Latin gloss, but had apparently
not read—perhaps he could not read—the Greek of Hippocrates. Reading the Hippocratean text, Fulke learned that the
great ancient was by no means a disciple of the astrologers.
The second argument of the anti-astrologers had been refuted
by Cuningham with the old brief drawn from the customs of
mariners and physicians. Fulke is unable to see that this is an

[27] *Ibid.*, sig. C2r-v.

argument, for the observations of physicians and mariners are based on sure foundations whereas those of the astrologer have nothing certain in them. Fulke concludes the first section with a witticism at the expense of Cuningham, who was unable to relate more than two truthful predictions, both of which occurred in a far country and in a remote age. One cannot be corrected, says Fulke, if one limits one's proofs to events that happened long ago; but over a period of two thousand years, two or twenty successful prognostications do little to establish the verity of astrology.

The second section of the *Antiprognosticon,* which appears only in the Painter translation, is addressed to the common order of mankind and is, as a consequence, extremely elementary. Fulke first discusses carefully and patiently the impossibility that man could ascertain the virtues of the planets. Fulke now argues that the stars do not cause wars; they arise from the evil workings of the minds of kings. He shows that weather is the product of natural causes and reasons that sickness is likewise dependent on the natural order of things. He reproves the astrologer physician, who should know "that the causes of sycknes and helth hang nothynge vppon mouyng of the celestiall bodies."[28] Fulke now attacks the doctrine of nativities by asking if at a certain moment all children born are kings or if at another moment everybody is a thief. He concludes this second part of the treatise with a common-sense discussion of good and bad days that recalls the remarks of Frischlin. Sow and plant in good weather, go on journeys when you must, buy and sell on market days, and get married on any day in the year.

Fulke's *Antiprognosticon* contains no arguments that cannot be read in some continental polemic; nevertheless, it is one of the most important documents in the war against astrology. In the first place, it introduced the English to the time-honored arguments against the art, and Painter's immediate translation

[28] *Ibid.,* sig. D7v.

placed the book at the service of the vast middle class, who, without doubt, contributed vastly to the support of the astrologer. In the second place, Fulke's espousal of the cause against astrology linked that movement in a fashion with Puritanism and in this way secured another touching place with Calvinism. Finally, in Fulke's work we have a premonstration of the English scientific movement of the seventeenth century, for in eschewing superstition and preconceived notions and in urging the employment of reason and common sense as the touchstones of truth, Fulke was adding a few stones to the foundation of Bacon's College of the Six Days Works.

A year after the publication of Fulke's book, Francis Coxe printed his *Short Treatise declaringe the Detestable Wickednesse of Magicall Sciences.* Coxe was a professional astrologer after the fashion of Forman and Lambe; he was summoned before the Privy Council in 1561 on the charge of sorcery, and after examination and punishment, he was forced to confess publicly at the Pillory in Cheapside. His book is essentially the recanting pamphlet of a felon under the screw and contains nothing more worthy of mention than a recommendation of Fulke's book to those who wish to go more deeply into the arguments against astrology.[29]

After these treatises of the 1560's, a calm of twenty years duration prevailed before another tempest of controversy about the merits of astrology caught the attention of the Elizabethans. A nobleman, two scholars, and a famous clergyman took part in this new controversy, which had reverberations in the world of polite letters. The nobleman was Henry Howard, the Earl of Northampton, whose penchant for playing with fire secured him a place in the annals of England. In the early 1580's he was tried for heresy, and after his acquittal he retired to St. Albans, where he wrote his *A Defensative against the poyson of supposed prophecies.* In this work Howard attacked all forms of divination and especially rebuked the type of predic-

[29] *Op. cit.,* sig. A6v.

tion that encouraged conspirators or stirred up civil dissension. In this respect Howard is, perhaps, following the example of Fulke, whose work, as Larkey suggests, was partially inspired by the quasi-political nature of the prognostication of Nostradamus. A generous portion of the *Defensative* is given to a polemic against astrology, but Howard does little more in this section than borrow—without acknowledgment—his arguments from Pico and other continental controversialists.

In a preface to Sir Francis Walsingham, Howard tells us that since the green days of his youth he has read avidly and stored up arguments against false prophecies and that he now proposes to attack all predictions, all forms of divination that do not come under the "law of Moses."[30] Following the continental convention, he attributes the desire of men to know the future to their unguarded and uncontrolled curiosity and to their distrust of God. In the third chapter, Howard writes at length of the vain and rash credulity of men.

We need not rifle in the Monuments of former times, so long as the present age wherein wee live, may furnish us with store of most strange examples. For though we have beene yearely mated, and abused with blinde Almanacks, in such a sort, as whosoever buyes the same as directories eyther of the weather or of the world; may be truly said, to bee made a foole for good lucke sake upon the first of Ianuary.[31]

Howard's formal confutation of the principles of astrology begins with the tenth chapter and continues to nearly the end of his book. Astrology, he writes, was spawned by Satan and unlike all other sciences has no foundation in sense data. The same authorities that Pico had used are summoned to prove that the ancients had no respect for the art. Howard doubts the antiquity of astrology and argues that it was Ptolemy, not the Chaldeans—those inordinate liars—who invented its methods. Like Pico, he insists that the heavens are a universal cause

[30] *Op. cit.* (London, 1620), p. 4r. The first edition was printed in 1583.
[31] *Ibid.*, p. 11r.

and can influence the seed of man no more than a setting hen
can influence the plover eggs that have been placed in her nest.
This universal influence, Howard states, is derived from the
motion and heat of the stars, and as the planets share the same
light, he cannot understand how they may have different effects. He denies the validity of the more modern theory that
the influence of the planets is benign, but that this benignity
is thwarted by the accidents of matter. He admits, however,
that he would rather believe this notion than accept the hypothesis that the stars imparted a second nature to their natives.
All things under the moon, he writes, are under the universal
influence of the heavens, but nothing is changed or altered by
the planets. This chapter is then little more than an English
summary of the third book of the *Adversus astrologiam*.

In his next chapter, Howard treats of the astrological houses
and achieves little that is not conventional; however, like most
of the English polemicists, he is skillful at the introduction of
concrete illustrations, and so, unlike most of the continental
writers, he is able to get down on all fours with his ordinary
reader. He argues, for example, that the heavenly bodies are
not subject to mutability and illustrates the point by inquiring
if one becomes a mercer by passing under a mercer's sign or a
goldsmith by entering a goldsmith's shop. In the twelfth chapter, Howard continues his discussion of the signs and borrows
from Pico a great deal of material about the astrologers' disagreements over the value of the signs. In the thirteenth chapter, Pico again provides the matter necessary to ridicule the
aspects and sex of signs. The following chapter contains many
conventional arguments against the assignment of certain
planets to certain parts of the body. Howard also denies the
utility of astrological images and considers the problem of
providence and stellar malignity. The chapter concludes with
remarks about the foolishness of drawing up the horoscope of
cities, but this argument has already been met with in Pico.

Chapter XV contains Howard's discussion of the importance

of experience in astrological practice. Like the continentals, he observes that the length of years between certain conjunctions makes nugatory the testimony of experience. He thinks that the astrologers who say that a planet has a definite effect are absurdly mistaken when they say that this effect is decreased or increased by the near presence of another planet. One can learn something about the secret powers of herbs, he writes, but the influence of a planet is too momentary to be recorded; if the planet has an influence, it is probably more in the mind of the observer than in the planet. Howard points out that there is a human tendency to combine contiguous events; it sometimes thunders when swans are hatched and so the rustic connects the hatching of swans with the phenomenon of thunder. On the other hand, people do not seem to connect such contemporary events as the elocation of the haven at Sandwich and the building of Tenterden steeple. In the subsequent chapter, he handles the question of comets in a less usual way; if comets are really injurious to delicately nurtured noblemen, he asks, why are they not harmful to women? All in all, princes are probably more endangered by indigestion than by comets. From the discussion of comets, Howard passes to a consideration of the unnaturalness of astrology, which, like alchemy, seeks to alter the course of nature. He admits that certain natural objects seem to be influenced by the planets, but he cannot find that this influence is general. He is willing to admit that the planets may hold the elements within bounds, but he does not believe that they encourage the violence of the elements.

After some interrupting chapters on various forms of divining, Howard returns to astrology in the twentieth chapter and draws again upon Pico for a discussion of astrological impieties. In the traditional fashion, he summons the fathers to testify against the astrologers, and in the following chapter, he controverts the doctrines of astrology with Bible references. The twenty-second and twenty-third chapters provide the reader with illustrations of the lying predictions of the astrolo-

gers and with examples of the evils—especially the political
evils—that these predictions have caused.

It is obvious to anyone that Howard's book contains few
arguments that are not borrowed from continental sources; in
no sense is it as original a work as Fulke's *Antiprognosticon*.
The influence of the *Defensative* in England was undoubtedly
less than that of Fulke's book, for Howard's unsavory political
reputation and his well-known Catholic bias would militate
against his tractate. The value of the *Defensative* rests on the
simplicity of its style and on the fact that it introduced to the
English reader a great body of continental material. In a way,
the chapters on astrology in Howard's essay are little more than
digested translations of the better portions of Pico's *Adversus
astrologiam,* and so, after a fashion, this is the second appearance of a composition of Pico della Mirandola in English. Four
years after Howard's death, during the age of the great Jacobean witch-hunt, the *Defensative* was reprinted in folio, but
by that time it was an Elizabethan curiosity, for its matter had
been superseded by that of more authoritative works.

Shortly after the publication of Howard's polemic, a more
colloquial attack on astrology appeared. This new work bore
the title *Foure Great Lyers, striving who shall win the silver
whetstone* and was published at London in 1585. The author
of the work hid his identity under the modest initials "W. P.,"
and for many years bibliographers debated whom these letters
might represent. This mystery was solved by Professor Dick,
who noticed that the second section of this book—"A Resolution to the Countrey-man"—was reprinted in the 1613 edition
of the works of William Perkins. In his later years Perkins
was famed as the author of *The Reformed Catholic* and as a
teacher of theology at Cambridge, but there were dark stains
on his youth. Fuller uses Perkins as his example of "The Faithful Minister" in *The Holy State*[32] and expands this biography

[32] London, 1648, pp. 80-81.

in *Abel Redevivus;* in the second work we find the following remarks:

When first a Graduate, he was much addicted to the study of naturall Magicke, digging so deepe, in natures mine, to know the hidden causes and sacred quallities of things, that some conceive that he bordered on Hell it selfe in his curiosity. Beginning to be a practitioner in that *black Art,* the blacknesse did not affright him but name of Art lured him to admit himselfe as student thereof. However herein we afford no certaine beliefe, the rather because other mens ignorance might cast this aspersion upon him: Who knowes not that many things as pretty as strange may really be effected by a skilfull hand, lawfull and laudable meanes? which some out of a charitable errour will interpret a Miracle, and others out of uncharitable ignorance will nickname Sorcery. A very Load-stone in some Scholars hand, before a silly Townsmans eye is enough to make the former a Conjurer.[33]

Fuller does not say that Perkins was a necromancer; he apologizes, in fact, for the rumor of sorcery. The rumor, nevertheless, was vigorous enough to demand recording. If the popular belief about Perkins' youth was true, the English had a Henry Cornelius Agrippa. Such men were the most formidable of astrology's enemies.

The first twenty-one pages of *Foure Great Lyers* are a parallel presentation of the daily predictions of four professional astrologers.[34] The predictions always disagree. This graphic method of mocking the astrologers was, of course, not new. We recall van Hemminga's use of comparative nativities and Pico's remarks about his experiments with the prognostications of professional astrologers. In 1569, Nicholas Allen had published *The Astronomers game for three Whetstones, played by two Masters of Art and a Doctor,* a brief pamphlet in which the predictions of Buckmaster, Securis, and Doctor Low were compared, to the embarrassment of all astrologers. Without

---

[33] *Op. cit.* (London, 1651), p. 432.
[34] Perkins gives only the initials "B," "F," "T," and "D," but they probably stand for Buckminister, Frende (Forster), Twyne, Digges (Dade).

doubt, Perkins was consciously imitating Allen in the first pages of *Foure Great Lyers*—the similarity of titles suggests it—but he was also following the tradition of other rationalists who had lived before him. Laughter over the contradictory premonstrations of astrologers was frequently heard during the sixteenth century; even Adrian Turnebé, the learned teacher of Montaigne, amused himself in this fashion.

The early pages of *Foure Great Lyers* do not appear in the 1613 edition of Perkins' writings. As Dick justly conjectures,[35] the editors of this edition probably thought of them as much too ephemeral, too lacking in point at that late date, to reprint. As a consequence, only the second part, "A Resolution to the Countrey-man, prouying it vnlawfull for him to bye or vse our yearly Prognostication," was reissued. This section sounds very much like a satire; and ever since the publication of Bosanquet's bibliography, Perkins' work has been listed as an almanack satire. This, however, is not the case. "A Resolution" is a direct and forceful attack on astrologers and a caveat to those who support astrology by buying prognostications. It is a formal polemic and belongs in the same category with Fulke's *Antiprognosticon*.

Perkins accuses the purchasers of prognostications of immoderate care, distrust in God, and contempt for providence. One should never have a thought beyond the day, he says, for to worry about the future is to distrust God. Adopting the "stream of consciousness" method, he imagines the sort of conversation that a man of immoderate care might hold with himself.

I can neuer be quiet, nor take my sleepe, untill such time as I haue knowne the state of the yeare ensuing, that I may frame my busines accordingly: This next yeare there will be much rayne, it will rotte corne vpon the groŭd, it wil be spoyled, I will keepe my corne untill the next yeare following: I finde that corne wil be

[35] "The Authorship of Foure Great Lyers (1585)," *The Library*, XIX (1939), 311-314.

deare about halfe a yeare hence, I wil not sell my corne now, but keep it, that I may haue plenty of money for it, and sufficient beside, to maintaine my house: the sea and land is calme & quiet this yeare, the next yeare many shipwrackes & troubles in many countreys will fall, now I will fraught my ships that I then may be quiet.[36]

In this way Perkins chides the simple countryman for running to the astrologer and putting his faith in constellations without thinking of the providence that directs the stars. He is, Perkins writes with a certain philosophic modernity, like the man who owns an expensive clock, but who "neuer extolleth or thinketh on the wit and inuention of the clockemaker."[37]

The lecture to the astrologers is of great length. Perkins first takes up the inability of the astrologers to make truthful predictions. This failure in prognostication arises, he writes, from the misuse of the heavens, which were established for the glorification of God, the reproving of sinners, and the signalizing of seasons and times. Another reason for the fallibility of prognostications is that the astrologers run counter to the providence of God. In this connection, Perkins questions the theory promulgated by Pontano, who had said that the stars are the agents of providence. God, Perkins insists, does not effect his will by means of second causes.[38] A third reason for the errors of forecasters is their lack of experience. The physician knows that rhubarb is a purge because he has often administered it, but the continual alteration of the heavens vitiates any possibility of astrological certainty. Perkins' final argument is based on the thesis that the astrologer is ignorant of particular causes and errs in accepting contiguous events as cause and effect. To fix these abstract arguments in the minds of countrymen, Perkins uses Howard's figure of the setting hen and adds a new illustration drawn from the compounding of herbs.[39] To conclude this part of his case, Perkins lists the six impediments to successful prediction that one meets fre-

[36] *Op. cit.*, sig. B2v.
[37] *Ibid.*, sig. B4v.
[38] *Ibid.*, sig. C3v.
[39] *Ibid.*, sig. C8v.

quently in the continental polemics. Like most of the opponents of astrology, he admits that the stars have some influence, but he cannot perceive how this influence can be either measured or predicted.

Perkins' subsequent objections to astrology arise from the manifestness of the astrologers' falsehoods. He considers the untruths arising from the astrological anatomy, the power of signs, the doctrine of elections, the contradictions about the nature of the houses, the dignities of planets, the theory of combustion, and the moment of planetary impulse. For a continental, these astrological fallacies and inconsistencies would be the stereotyped matter of controversy; but for the ordinary Englishman who could not or did not read the continental polemics, it was undoubtedly novel material. In his remarks about the moment of planetary impulse, Perkins indicates that he believes that eclipses of the sun and moon have extraordinary terrestrial effects; he does not, however, think that these effects can be plotted before they occur.[40] His personal attitude is put in humble terms for his readers' benefit:

> For example, suppose, thou being a man toward marriage, in the *Almanacke* thou findest a good daye noted by the *Prognosticatour* to marry in: thou takest thy opportunitie: after a while, thou art wearie of thy life: the first daye of thy marryage was the last daye of thy ioye. What is the cause of this? All the Planettes which were signifiers of thy marriage in thy nativitie, were then euilly affected, and peraduenture also, at the first thou wast borne, they receaued some disgrace. So then thou maiest laye all blame, partly vpon thy selfe for beleeuing and partlie vpon the *Prognosticator,* who deceiued thee.[41]

In the closing pages of his essay, Perkins attacks the astrologers for their impieties and deceits. He lashes them for suggesting that the stars have the power to make men religious and condemns them for predicting immoral actions and crimes whereby dissolute people "ar stirred up to liue prophanely."[42]

[40] *Ibid.,* sig. F1r-F2v.   [41] *Ibid.,* sig. D5r-D5v.   [42] *Ibid.,* sig. F6r.

Perkins also alludes to the jargon used by the astrologer, which both impresses and benights the ignorant layman. He has equal sport with the ambiguity of all prognostications. Sometimes, he says, the astrologer phrases his prediction so that no matter what happens he will be right; at other times he goes in for general truths, predicting, for example, that there will be shipwrecks during the winter months or that old men will be in danger of dying. The second part of *Foure Great Lyers* is, then, more of a polemic than a satire, for it repeats in a simple fashion the views that previous writers had expressed more abstractly. The virtue of the tract lies in its absolute simplicity, and it is one of the few anti-astrological writings of the Renaissance to put its case in terms that could be grasped by the relatively unlearned.

In the course of his book, Perkins refers to a discourse written two years earlier about the conjunction of Jupiter and Saturn. This discourse, he writes, came from the pen of a learned man and was so terrifying that it had people settling their worldly affairs and scanning the heavens for signs of the impending catastrophe.[43] This remark might be an allusion to some work like Sheltoo a Geveren's *Of the end of this worlde and seconde commynge of Christe,* which was printed in 1578 and was the precursor of the dire prophecies for 1588. Perkins, however, is probably referring to Richard Harvey's *An Astrological Discourse upon the great and notable Coniunction of the two superiour Planets, Saturne & Iupiter which shall happen the 28. day of April, 1583,* a work that provoked the laughter of Thomas Nashe and effected a great controversy.

As Richard Harvey shared in the thirsty ambitions of his family, he dedicated his book to the Bishop of London and defended his astrological interests by pointing out to his prospective patron those pious contemporaries who were also devotees of the art. His brother Gabriel, he states, has called his attention to the Roman legislation against astrologers; but in the

[43] *Ibid.,* sig. B4r-B4v.

days of Rome, the art was very imperfect and the laws of the Romans cannot be cited against modern astrologers. Richard Harvey opens his formal prognostication with an address to Gabriel Harvey in which he states that his great brother had objected to the study of astrology as fruitless. He insists that astrology is not a vain study, as Gabriel, who has now "taken some reasonable paines therein," knows. The "slight" arguments of Pico and Agrippa, he declares, have been answered by Bellanti, Schöner, Melanchthon, Cardan, and Giuntini. A large number of Englishmen, he announces happily, have become adepts in the astrological philosophy.[44] Harvey then announces his predictions, which are all rather dire. He says that there will be violence, persecution of ecclesiastics, declensions among the nobles, barrenness and sterility in the earth.

> Eyther a marvelous feareful and horrible alteration of Empyres, Kyngdomes, Seigniories, and States, together with other wonderful, and very extraordinarie accidents, as, extreme hunger, and pestilence, desperate treasons and commotions, shall then fall out, to the miserable affliction, and oppression of huge multitudes: or else, that an utter, and finall overthrowe, and destruction of the whole world shall ensue.[45]

This tale of woe and destruction is supported with the famous prophetic verses for the year 1588 that the astronomer Regiomontanus was said to have discovered.

To this work of Richard Harvey, John Harvey added an appendix which he called *An Astrological Addition, or supplement to be annexed to the late Discourse upon the great Coniunction of Saturn and Iupiter.* In his dedicatory preface to Justice Meade, John Harvey says that he has composed this addition to satisfy Richard Harvey's learned friends, stop the mouths of his enemies, and enable pious Englishmen to prepare themselves for the coming catastrophe. He also hoped, he adds modestly, to gain practice in the dignified art of astrology.

---

[44] *Op. cit.* (London, 1583), pp. 3-4.
[45] *Ibid.*, pp. 44-45.

John Harvey does little more in his book than augment the number of authorities that Richard Harvey had cited in support of his thesis. At the end of his pamphlet, he mentions a number of other books that had been written about the conjunction. One of these works was "the French almanack," which John Harvey hesitates to criticize because of his imperfect knowledge of the French language; another work was Robert Tanner's *Probable coniectures from the course of tymes* and *A Prognosticall Iudgement*. The latter work, according to John Harvey, is little more than "a mingle mangle of stealths and patcheries" out of Leowitz, Rogers, and Richard Harvey; from the latter work, the unscrupulous Tanner "hath more then once, or twise culled out whole sides *verbatim,* without any mention of him."[46] The modern reader of these treatises is, of course, less surprised than John Harvey was that one astrologer should steal from another.

In the same year Henry Howard answered all of these works in a general way, but a special document—*A manifest and apparent confutation of an Astrological discourse, lately published to the discomfort (without cause) of the weake and simple sort*—was written by Thomas Heth and directed against Richard Harvey. Heth was no opponent of astrology, but, on the contrary, a very competent astrologer whose purpose in writing this book was to correct the mathematical errors of Richard Harvey. Heth's book is then one of those perfect illustrations of the astrologers' inability to agree; the opponents of astrology were undoubtedly pleased with it. According to Heth, Harvey and the other writers on the dire conjunction had erred in their calculations and had selected the wrong hour. He urges his readers not to lose faith in astrology—that excellent science—because two of its practitioners disagree. It would be well, he writes, if "the unskilfull Astronomer, which takes vppon him the Art without knowledge thereof" would be better advised before he publishes his calculations.[47] Heth gives

[46] *Op. cit.* (London, 1583), sig. E6v-E7v. [47] *Op. cit.* (London, 1583), sig. A3v.

every evidence of being "well seen" in astrology. Unlike John Harvey, he could read French, and he is familiar not only with the more important astrological authorities but also with the discoveries of the new astronomy. He describes, for example, the "simple Astrologian" as one who knows nothing of *"Copernicus his Hypotheses, Reinholts observations, or Peurbachius."*[48] Harvey had set the time of the fateful conjunction for noon of April 28, but Heth's calculations indicated that it would occur fifteen hours later. As a consequence of this alteration in time, the results of the conjunction would be benign rather than evil.

A Harvey, unfortunately, could not be silenced by either the quips of a Nashe or the careful mathematics of a member of his own sect, and so in 1588, John Harvey published another book, *A Discoursive Probleme concerning Prophesies, How far they are to be valued, or credited, according to the surest rules, and directions in Divinitie, Philosophie, Astrologie, and other learning.* John Harvey is now on the other side of the wicket, for he is attacking the sort of prediction that he had supported five years earlier. The prognostications of 1583 had all pointed to 1588 as a particularly fearful year, and there seems to have been a number of prophecies circulating that are no longer extant. John Harvey opens his essay by complaining that few of the current forecasters have any skill in any science;[49] he then turns to the various theories of the termination of the world and the legend of the Platonic grand year to show that there is a wide divergence in opinion among the authorities on these matters. He holds the prophecies of the Sybilla Tiburtina, of Ambrose Merlin, and of a variety of English charlatans up to ridicule,[50] and says that they were begotten like the tales of Robin Goodfellow, Bevis of Southampton, Amadis of Gaul, and Orlando Furioso to "busie the minds of the vulgar sort" and "to avert their conceits from the consideration of serious, and graver matters."[51] Harvey insists that he is not attacking

[48] *Ibid.*, sig. B7v.
[50] *Ibid.*, pp. 41-58.
[49] *Op. cit.* (London, 1588), p. 3.
[51] *Ibid.*, p. 68.

legitimate prophecy, but by legitimate prophecy he does not mean only Christian prophecy, for he mentions certain ethnic prognostications with careful deference. Astrology, he thinks, is still valuable, for when it is used with "modest discretion," it may foresee the consequences of "*Naturall or Morall* effects" by a contemplation of "the antecedent causes, or apparent signes, either *Naturall* or *morall*."[52]

Harvey now looks over the verses discovered by Regiomontanus which his brother Richard had discussed in his treatise of 1583. He doubts that the year 1588 will be as disastrous as these verses indicate or as many people think. He relates the great consternation occasioned by the conjunction of 1583 and the theories that learned men advanced about it; then he writes— as if his name were not Harvey: "I cannot sufficiently marvell what mooved so famous learned men in this facultie, to ascribe, or attribute so exceeding much unto that silly *Coniunction*."[53] The intellectual complexion of John Harvey had certainly altered in the five years since 1583, for he insists, in spite of three eclipses of the moon and the direful predictions of the astrologers, that the year 1588 will not be either especially unfortunate or unusual. It is curiously ironic that because of this change of heart, Harvey did not foretell the storms that would overwhelm the floating hosts of Spain.

After these heated treatises of the 1580's, formal defenses and attacks on astrology are wanting in England until the early years of the seventeenth century. At that time there was a recrudescence of polemics and a debate not unlike that which had raged on the continent after the publication of Pico's *Adversus astrologiam*. The reason for this new outburst cannot be ascertained. Perhaps the assumed decline in public morality which had produced the satirical papers of the late nineties had something to do with it; perhaps the failure of nerve which characterized the declining years of Elizabeth produced a sort of astrological "boom." After the coronation of James, who

[52] *Ibid.*, p. 77.   [53] *Ibid.*, p. 110.

was no friend to sorcery and divination, one needs no commentary, but prior to that time, one's explanation must be a
matter of conjecture.

The quarrel was reopened by John Chamber, who published
A Treatise against Iudicial Astrologie in 1601. Chamber, a
Canon of Windsor and an excellent Greek scholar, had lectured at Oxford on the Ptolemaic system, and to his attack on
astrology he appended his *Astronomiae encomium,* which he
had delivered at Oxford in 1574 and which indicates his wide
reading in astronomical authorities. Chamber's remarks about
astrology were answered in 1603 by Sir Christopher Heydon,
a member of Parliament. Heydon's *A Defence of Iudiciall
Astrologie, in Answer to a Treatise lately published by M. Iohn
Chamber* is a work of learning and sophistry; its central thesis,
moreover, seems to have annoyed Chamber, who meditated a
reply and eventually wrote out "A Confutation of Astrological
Daemonology in the Devil's School," a work which was never
printed. A defense of Chamber's book was written by George
Carleton, Bishop of Chichester, but this book was not printed
until twenty years after the original controversy had taken
place.

Chamber complains, in the first pages of his book, of the
unfairness of a system which punishes witches and allows an
astrologer to go free. He notices that most of the astrologers
of his time have become so ashamed of their profession that
they are compiling only reformed almanacks and no longer
meddle with the wind and the weather. He regrets, however,
that many of them still attribute everything to the stars, and
adds that if they are right, "then God may have an everlasting
playing day, and let the world wag."[54] In the second chapter,
he marshals the traditional Biblical references and quotations
from patristic writers against the astrologers and points out
that if demons, angels, and saints do not know the future, these
"wizards" cannot hope to encompass such knowledge. In the

[54] *Op. cit.* (London, 1601), pp. 3-4.

next chapter, Chamber introduces his technical argument. He says that the astrologers do not know the exact number of the stars, and he mentions the upsetting of their hypotheses by the *nova* of 1578. The expounding of technical flaws in the art of astrology is continued in the fourth chapter, and Chamber amuses himself with the picture of an astrologer standing on a hill and peering at the stars while he listens for the midwife to strike a bason and inform him of the birth of the child whose horoscope he wishes to cast. While the sound runs through the air, Chamber remarks, the heavens will have turned part of a degree and the astrologer will err in his calculations. The following chapter is devoted to the traditional arguments about the diverse fates of men born at the same time and under the same stars, and the subsequent chapter recites the difficulties attending those astrologers who make their astrological reckonings from the moment of conception. In the seventh chapter, Chamber sets problems for the astrologer. He asks him why he does not test his theories by drawing up the horoscope of a nest of eggs or a handful of seed corn. He wonders why the astrologer does not foretell events that will happen on the morrow. Sometimes, he admits, the prognosticator does forecast the weather correctly, but, as a rule, he does it so infrequently that it is obvious that it is a matter of luck.

It were infinite to lay their lies together: that one of 1588 may stand for many, and the rather because it hapned in our memory. It were well that all of that trade had those two figures .88. seared in their foreheads, that when they meet, they might laugh one at another, as did the *Aruspices* in olde time. Howsoever they might laugh, it was no laughing matter to the Catholike king, and his invincible Navie, who will be famous for that exploit till 88 come againe. The *Spaniards* belike thought, that this consummation of 88 would be by water, and therefore very politikely they began to prepare for it betime, longer a great deale then ever Noah did for the flood. And sure they might have done well, if they had bin provided of a pilot such as was *Hen. Nicholas in Chaucer*. But it fell out reasonable well with them, for they sped almost as well in their *Calloones,* as if they had bin in his tubs.[55]

From this reference to Chaucer, Chamber passes in his ninth chapter to a denial of the verity of predictions. One cannot foretell, says Chamber, necessary and casual events, events that are produced by the will, and events that depend on matters of sense, art, philosophy, and civil policy. Chamber, in the next chapter, develops his argument against the premonstration of necessary events. Even if these events could be foretold, he writes, they could be avoided. The eleventh chapter extends and augments the medieval argument about the fates of twins, and the twelfth and thirteenth chapters summarize in conventional fashion the attitudes of ancient kings and philosophers towards astrology. Chamber takes as the text of his fourteenth chapter the notion that only fools visit the astrologer. Flies and gnats get caught in the web, but the wise man, who knows that God alone perceives the future, plunges through the mesh like the beetle. In the fifteenth and sixteenth chapters, Chamber sets out to confute the widely held theory that Thales and Eudoxus Gnidus were astrologers. Thales, he insists, was not an astrologer but a man who employed his ample knowledge of natural science; and Eudoxus, though he was the first Greek to study astrology, scorned it. He now turns the tables on the astrologers, who had contended that astrology was the noblest of the divining arts, by asserting that there is a greater possibility of certainty in those forms of divining that required the touching and handling of the objects of divination.[56]

In the eighteenth chapter, Chamber borrows Pico's remarks about the contradictions and controversies of the astrologers, and plunders Pereyra for the reasons for the occasional success of prognosticators. Since he was fond of the racier parts of English literature, Chamber illustrates one of his latter points with an extract from the so-called "Jests of Skelton."[57] The

[55] *Ibid.,* p. 43.   [56] *Ibid.,* pp. 84-86.   [57] *Ibid.,* pp. 94-103.

twentieth chapter is especially interesting because it contains a general attack on superstitions, an attack that foreshadows Browne's *Pseudodoxia Epidemica*. Chamber questions the validity of palmistry and throws doubt on the common fear of the grand climacteric. He informs the reader that he has pulled the mandrake and that the root does not resemble the figure of a man. He is equally skeptical of the various superstitions about leap year. The last chapter of the book is a little homily, embroidered with all the colors of rhetoric and all the figures of pulpit oratory, which urges man to love God and hate astrology.

Sir Christopher Heydon, who wrote the reply to Chamber's work, was a man of a completely opposite character. Chamber is light and concise; Heydon is ponderous and prolix. Chamber is witty and enamored of literary and topical allusions; Heydon is downright pedestrian and tramps through his discussions on feet of lead. We are convinced, however, that Heydon knows his subject much better than Chamber does, for he has read widely enough in the literature of the astrological controversy to detect like a conscientious pedant all of Chamber's unacknowledged borrowings. Heydon, in spite of his immense reading, falls short of his purpose, and he fails for several reasons. Because he is such a thorough scholar, Heydon is a poor publicist; even the most hardened reader is graveled by his extended and overwhelming arguments. Like a professional controversialist, Heydon will always make his case even if the evidence is thin; he twists here, he glosses there, and, behold, he produces the proof of his hypothesis. His book contains the same number of chapters as Chamber's, for his method is to answer each of Chamber's chapters in one similarly numbered. He depends, unfortunately, on weight and not on deftness; and, as a result, his book is four times the length of Chamber's.

Before he begins his careful confutation of Chamber, Heydon gossips to the reader of his own experience with astrology.

He has long been a student of astrology and has discovered that it leads one to a complete admiration of the first cause. He had read Pico and the other "Astrologie-whippers" and he has observed that they all were at some time students of the art. This discovery has given him the clue to their disaffection. Astrology is the most difficult of all subjects to master, and these men, lacking both intelligence and patience, perceived that they could never learn the art. As a result of their chagrin, these opponents, before they were half through with the study, broke "out into a choler, and bitterly declaymed against it." Chamber, he says, must have followed the same course, for he knows nothing of astrology from experience and his book is simply a "rhapsody of other men's fragments and fancies." He regrets that Chamber was not more discriminating when he attacked all astrologers. He should have abused only the bad astrologers. He informs Chamber that he is like the man who rails against all Englishmen because there are a few bad Englishmen. After this prolegomenon, Heydon proceeds to refute Chamber chapter by chapter.

Heydon opens his rebuttal by taking up the charge of witchcraft that Chamber had flung against the astrologers and insists that the astrologian is no wizard, for he is never impious and never denies the doctrine of fatal necessity. He says that he is deeply offended by the opprobrious titles that Chamber conferred on astrologers; he is like those scoffing citizens who refer to reputable physicians as quacksalvers and mountebanks. Only the bad astrologers, he writes, deny the powers of providence; the good ones say that God governs by the stars. Heydon's personal attitude is that the stars foretell the constitution of the body, the natural inclinations, and nothing else. In the second chapter, Heydon looks over the authoritative quotations that Chamber used against the astrologers and informs the reader that they were all borrowed from Pico della Mirandola via Pereyra. All of them, he says, were shown long ago to be either favorable in purport or innocuous when rightly interpreted. With a great display of erudition Heydon attempts to circle all of Chamber's authorities and even argues that the demons do know the future. The stars, he thinks, influence the humors; there is no need to call God from Heaven to attend to these matters.

Heydon's refutation of Chamber's technical arguments begins in the third chapter. There are few stars in the heavens, he asserts, that are not on the star maps; the *nova* that Chamber said appeared in 1578, he correctly observes, appeared in 1572 and its appearance did not abolish any fundamental notions of astrology. In the following chapter, he laughs at Chamber's picture of the astrologer on the hill and the midwife sounding the bason. The astrologer does not have to stare at the skies to know where the stars are. He himself has been instructed in these matters by Edward Wright of London and owns a watch by which he can accurately set the moment of birth. If he lacked both this knowledge and this instrument, he could still use the "platick aspect" which permits a correct observation within eighteen days. With a certain justice he accuses Chamber of being either ignorant of astrological methods or untruthful in his relation of them. He admits in the fifth chapter that all that Chamber has to say about the fates of twins and the common fates of men born at diverse times are in accord with the best astrological theory. These differences are caused by the seed, and all good astrologers take the parents, the country, and the mores of the native into account. The universal influence of the heavens postulated by Pico is, says Heydon, pleasing to all good astrologers because they are able to show that this influence is particularized by matter. Heydon refutes the contents of Chamber's sixth chapter by arguing that Chamber is ignorant of the new methods and instruments of astrology by which the moment of conception can be ascertained with the highest degree of correctness.

In his seventh chapter, Chamber had inquired if one could take the horoscope of a nest of eggs or a handful of seed corn.

Heydon scorns this type of question and says that those who ask them are like the worshipers in the Temple of Minerva, who asked the oracle if they might bring their chamber pots into the sanctuary. Receiving an affirmative answer, they inquired of the weary oracle if the pots should be of earth or metal and received the reply, "Neither." Heydon answers Chamber's assertion that astrological predictions are seldom fulfilled by offering a long list of successful prognostications. Almanacks, he admits, are sometimes in error, but now that Tycho Brahe and Edward Wright have made certain astronomical corrections, they will be more accurate.[58] The ninth chapter opens with one of Heydon's frequent diatribes on Chamber's unacknowledged borrowings and proceeds to treat of the validity of prognostications. Heydon says that Chamber does not understand necessity and never mentions contingency; he seriously doubts Chamber's comprehension of logical principles. He agrees with Pontano that the will is subject in part to the complexions and that the stars form these complexions. Sense data, he insists, have no place in astrological predictions, for sense deals with the present and astrology with the future. This argument is continued in the tenth chapter, where Heydon writes that astrological predictions resolve the minds of men and are hence of great benefit. Though the motions of the stars are necessary, their influences are varied according to inferior mutations, and so the celestially necessary becomes the terrestrially avoidable.

In his eleventh, twelfth, and thirteenth chapters, Heydon uses the conventional method to controvert Chamber's arguments about twins, the attitudes toward astrology of ancient philosophers, and the historic hostility of emperors toward the art. He notices that there were five emperors who opposed astrology and more than three times that number who were

---

[58] *Op. cit.* (London, 1603), pp. 190-206. See Heydon's letters to Camden on astrology in *Gulielmi Camdeni et illustrium virorum ad G. Camdenum epistolae,* ed. T. Smith (London, 1691), pp. 128-131.

patrons of the art. In the following chapter, Heydon charges Chamber with obfuscation and tries to refute his statement that the fool goes to the astrologer whereas the wise man trusts God. The adherence of Thales and Eudoxus to the doctrines of astrology are considered in the fifteenth and sixteenth chapters, and Heydon attempts to argue that Chamber is wrong in saying that they were not apostles of astrology. In the latter chapter, Heydon writes that there were astrologers in Greece before Thales, who was much anterior to Eudoxus. Heydon is particularly annoyed with Chamber's seventeenth chapter, in which it had been argued that astrology was the least noble of all forms of divination. The fact that astrology has endured, whereas other forms of divination have perished, proves to Heydon the essential nobility of that art. Are the mathematics of the astrologer, he asks, less tangible, less concrete than the guts of animals? Are not the senses employed in the study of the stars? Are not the stars nobler objects than the intestines and food of animals?

Heydon uses the eighteenth and nineteenth chapters to reply to the arguments drawn from the contradictions of astrologers and to attack Pereyra's reasons for the astrologer's occasional success. The essential difficulty, Heydon writes, is not the confusion of the astrologers, but the confusion of Chamber, who borrows liberally from Pico della Mirandola and does not understand what he borrows. Heydon now confronts Pico in the person of Chamber and challenges his arguments with technical data and authoritative references. He then turns to the four reasons offered by Pereyra for the occasional successes of astrologers. Pereyra and Chamber had written that this success might arise from a pact with Satan, and Heydon asks about the Biblical accounts of stellar foreshowing and wonders if Satan, the father of lies, can tell the truth. The second explanation offered by Heydon's opponents was that God occasionally made use of the astrologer for divine ends. If this is the case, says Heydon, the astrologer ought to be reverenced as the instrument of God's wisdom; he adds that in light of what Chamber has said about the diabolical origins of astrology this is a very impious explanation. Pereyra and Chamber had also said that the astrologers delivered their prognostications in such riddles that the truth might occasionally be read into them. There is a jargon, Heydon declares, for all professions; these men, he thinks, should listen to the next physician they see examining a flask of urine. Finally, Pereyra and Chamber had asserted that many astrological successes arose from the simplicity of the astrologer's clients, who unwittingly fulfilled the predictions. Heydon thunders in his usual cumbersome fashion: "But that the imagination of a dull credulous fellowe, can make the Astrologers predictions to fall out true, in such externall accidents, as either befall himselfe, or others, or the world in generall, is so dull a conceipt, as may hardly be thought to flowe from a man of any witte."[59]

In the last chapter of his book, Heydon makes a long face over Chamber's homily against astrologers. He selects various rhetorical flourishes of Chamber for comment and continues to develop his thesis that Chamber, like the other opponents of astrology, was utterly ignorant of the methods and purposes of the stellar science. He peers at Chamber's character and laments his lack of charity and his unchristian malice; he observes that the moral nature of Chamber was infinitely more decayed than that of many of the astrologers whom he had attacked. Appended to this piece of rodomontade is a chronological outline of the development of astrology and a list of famous astrologers that begins with Adam in 3032 B.C. and extends to Tycho Brahe and Axelsön of A.D. 1602. There is little doubt that Heydon's purpose was a sincere one and that he was more learned than Chamber in astrological matters. At times one is even forced to admire Heydon's skillful sophis-

[59] *Ibid.*, p. 396.

try, but his method and matter are far too heavy for the tastes of the public that the opponents of astrology were trying to reach.

Heydon's confutation was, of course, eventually answered by Chamber's friend Carleton, but long before the answer was printed, the most engaging of all attacks on astrology was written by John Melton. Melton's *Astrologaster or the Figure-Caster* was published in 1620; it was written with a definite flourish, and though the formal arguments were trite and time-worn, the topical allusions and the stylistic vigor of the book give it an interest that is wanting to most of these treatises.

The *Astrologaster* opens like a fourteenth-century allegory with the description of a splendid and variegated garden in which the author finds himself. As he saunters along the garden paths, he draws many moral and philosophic lessons from the trees and flowers, which are to him as emblems. His reveries are broken by the arrival of a party of twenty women, who pass chattering through the garden and are followed by an elderly man. Melton stops the ancient and asks where the company is going; the old squire replies, providing us undoubtedly with the name of a fashionable astrologer.

The Party to whom they come, is a Bird, of whose kinde, I think there are but few living, for he professeth himselfe to be a Wise-man; and the cause of their comming, is to be resolved either of Money, Silver-Spoones, Rings, Gownes, Plate, or Linnen they have lost: some, to know how many Children they shall have; some, how many Husbands, and which shall love them best: others, about businesse; but in generall, all of them to know something, which indeed at the last comes to nothing. And I my selfe (like a Holy-day-foole) have beene there at the least halfe a score times, onely to give my money away, to bee laught at. Yet I have words ynough: for he will promise more then twentie Courtiers, talke more for halfe a Peece then halfe a score Lawyers, and lye more then twentie Chronologers; yet with some tricke, or evasion, hee will come clearely off, without being suspected for an Imposter, especially if he have some man in hand he thinkes he dare worke on, as he hath done me for example.[60]

The old man informs Melton that having had his purse stolen at Pauls Cross, he went on the advice of a friend to Dr. P. C. in Morefields. After many visits and the payment of numerous fees, the astrologer told him that he had identified the thief but that nothing could be done because the cutpurse had fled into the Lowlands.

Melton decides, however, to call on an astrologer. He is admitted to the house and led upstairs by a small boy.

Before a Square Table, covered with a greene Carpet, on which lay a huge Booke in *Folio,* wide open, full of strange Characters, such as the *Ægyptians* and *Chaldaeans* were never guiltie of; not farre from that, a silver Wand, a Surplus, a Watering Pot, with all the superstitious or rather fayned Instruments of his cousening Art. And to put a fairer colour on his black and foule Science, on his head hee had a foure-cornered Cap, on his backe a faire Gowne (but made of a strange fashion) in his right hand he held an Astro-labe, in his left a Mathematical Glasse. At the first view, there was no man that came to him (if hee were of any fashion) could offer him for his advice lesse than a *Iacobus,* and the meanest halfe a Peece, although hee peradventure (rather then have nothing) would be contented with a brace of Two-pences.[61]

Melton informs the astrologer that he has lost a gold chain of three hundred links at the Kings Bench in Westminster, and the astrologer delivers an oration which is a mock defense of astrology. He says that he knows all that happens in London: what women paint, what clerks take bribes, what drunkards reel from the taverns, and what wives are unfaithful to their husbands. All of this information comes to him through "Di-vine Astrology." He then recites the history of astrology be-ginning with Adam and ending with the moderns: "Was not broad-shouldered *Atlas,* that was bigger then the great Porter, an admirable Astronomer and Astrologer?" He details the

[60] *Op. cit.* (London, 1620), pp. 5-6.   [61] *Ibid.,* p. 8.

doctrine of houses and planets, and relates in a ribald manner his astrological cures for the sick. "Frier *Bacon* was an Asse, Doctor *Faustus* a Foole, *Ripley* an Empericke, and Kelly a Coxcombe to me." After this recital, he assures Melton that his chain will be recovered.[62]

The remainder of Melton's pamphlet is a reply to the mock encomium of astrology that he had placed in the mountebank's mouth. The instruments of astrology, he states, are sheer hocus-pocus and smack of popery; the authorities consulted by the astrologers are obvious atheists. "And as for your knowledge in Astronomie, this is my opinion of you, that you have as much skill of the Poles in Heaven, as you have of the Poles on *Pauls* Steeple."[63] The education of these quacks in medicine, he remarks, is even more limited than their training in astrology, for they have not enough Greek and Latin to read their textbooks. He wonders why the professional astrologers always inhabit the dismal places of the city; there is, for example, the Cunning Man on the Bankside, Mother Broughton in Chicke Lane, Master Olive in Turnbull Street, the "shag-hair'd" wizard in Pepper Alley, and Doctor Forman at Lambeth. Like "Birds of Wonder," they all fly the light of the city.[64] Melton now offers his definition of astrology.

Astrologie is an Art, whereby Cunning Knaves cheat plaine honest Men, that teacheth both the Theory and Practicke of close Cousenage, a Science instructing all the Students of it to lye as often as they speake, and to be beleeved no oftener then they hold their Tongues; that tells truth as often as Bawds goe to Church, Witches or Whores say their Prayers, or never but when the English Nones and Greeke Calends meet together.[65]

He scoffs at the signs of the zodiac; that wilderness of animals illustrates the untruthful fabric of the art. The sheer absurdity of astrology is, he says, shown by the readiness of the astrologue to defend foolish theories like Origen's doctrine of

[62] *Ibid.*, pp. 8-14.
[64] *Ibid.*, p. 21.
[63] *Ibid.*, p. 17.
[65] *Ibid.*, pp. 22-23.

the vitality of planets, the notion that the stars move by their own motive force, and the hypotheses that assign a center to the earth. The variance among astrological authorities proves how silly astrology is, and the layman may perceive this by noticing the disagreements between almanacks. One astrologian will predict thunder and lightning, "When there are no such Inflammations seene, except men goe to the *Fortune* in *Golding-Lane,* to see the Tragedies of Doctor *Faustus.* There indeed a man may behold shagge-hayr'd Devills runne roaring over the Stage with Squibs in their mouthes, while Drummers make Thunder in the Tyring-house, and the twelve-penny Hirelings make artificiall Lightning in there Heavens."[66] Another astrologer predicted a great fire in London for the year 1617, but there were no fires, says Melton, save those kindled by "Venus Nunnes," by the jailer at Old Bailey, by drunkards drinking stale beer, and by sellers of tobacco.

Like all the other English opponents of astrology, Melton admits that there is probably a universal stellar influence; he insists, however, that astrologers who assume more than this overstep their bounds. He makes sport of the twelve houses and their special influences by drawing up a mock analysis of their potencies. He lists various astrological predictions that came true, but demonstrates that they were not fulfilled according to the expectations of either the astrologer or his client. As a case in point, he tells the story of the bishop who was warned that he would die by a fall and thereafter inhabited only the ground floor of his episcopal palace. The fall, however, was his loss of office and his death came from the attendant grief.[67] Melton devotes a large section of his book to astrological doctrine like those of elections which he condemns roundly. Finally, he discusses the astrological amulet which, he says, is the symbol of a satanic compact; it is obviously related to the images of the Papists and is not unlike those set up by Roger Bacon and Albertus Magnus.[68] The last twenty

[66] *Ibid.,* p. 31.   [67] *Ibid.,* pp. 39-43.   [68] *Ibid.,* pp. 59-60.

leaves of the *Astrologaster* contain a condemnation of all forms of divination, which to Melton was a science sprung from Hell.

Unlike Fulke, Howard, or Chamber, Melton possessed a keen sense of satire, and his polemic against astrology comes very close to literary satire. He had not bothered to study the methods of astrology and his technical arguments are, as a consequence, of the most obvious type; but what he lacked in astrological learning, he possessed in wit and laughter, and these qualities, without doubt, were the most effective weapons with which to face pretenses. In spite of his sense of humor, Melton could be deadly serious about some things; his diatribes against Catholicism and his attempts to link it with astrology not only show this facet of his intellectual disposition but constitute for the modern reader a serious blot on an otherwise able performance. One must, however, take Melton in terms of the 1620's, and to men of that age an anti-Catholic bias was a sort of social grace.

The last polemic against astrology before the end of James I's reign was the *Astrologomania* of George Carleton, the official apologist for Chamber. Carleton was one of the best-known ecclesiastics of the day, and Wood describes him as "a person of solid judgement and various reading, a bitter enemy to the papists, and a severe Calvinist." He was the author of Latin verse, of a life of Bernard Gilpin, his former tutor, and of several religious works. His solid judgment and wide reading served him in good stead when he took up his cudgels against the learned Heydon, for Sir Christopher's encyclopedic reading in the science of astrology required a heavily documented reply.

The method employed by Carleton is quite different from that used by other controversialists, for his treatise is an essay against astrology in general and only against Heydon as the immediate representative of that art. There is no attempt on Carleton's part to take up his opponent's arguments seriately and refute them after the fashion of Bellanti or, more immediately, of Heydon. His central theme is a philosophical-theological one, and he controverts Heydon only when his arguments are contiguous to the general theme. From the dedicatory epistle, we learn that the Bishop composed the *Astrologomania* twenty years earlier and permitted it to circulate in manuscript. Its publication in 1624 was prompted by the requests of friends and associates; we learn also that James I's known hostility to all forms of divination encouraged its printing.

Bishop Carleton opens his first chapter by announcing that he cannot say much against astrology that has not already been said, for it has been thoroughly condemned by the "godly in the Church" and the "learned and wise without the Church." He informs us, however, that he will indict the art on the charge of being a branch of demonic magic. He rebukes Heydon for saying that astrology was within the bounds of the natural sciences because it dealt with second causes and for never demonstrating the truth of this thesis. This is deceiving the reader. At other times, Carleton observes, Heydon relates astrology to mathematics and so convicts himself of sail trimming, for there is a great chasm between the natural sciences and mathematics. At still other times Heydon, quoting Aristotle, says that astrology is a median science between mathematics and natural science; Carleton notices this and says that this would not only be impossible, but that Aristotle never made this distinction. With justice he argues that when Aristotle spoke of astrology, he was thinking in terms of astronomy and not of the prognosticating art. Carleton now proves that in the late Elizabethan use of the word, astrology was neither a part of natural science nor of mathematics. In the next chapter, he points out that though the astrologers say that the stars only affect the humors, they do not hesitate to make minute predictions and to boast of those predictions that are fulfilled. He uses the famous prognostication of Gaurico about Henry of France as a case in point, and asks how Gaurico would know that Henry would die of wounds in the head if only the humors were affected by the stars. He faces Heydon's continuous assertion that the opponents of astrology were men who would not tax their brains to learn the art, and lists a distinguished number of scholars, including James I, who mastered astrology in order to attack it.[69] He adds, with the traditional snobbery of the academician, that he knows a number of men who were considered blockish in the universities who now have repute as astrologers.

In the third chapter, Carleton reasons that astrology cannot be proved by the light of nature, and in the fourth chapter, he demonstrates by Scripture and logic that contingency cannot be admitted in astrology, that chance is not the servant of providence, and that any successful prediction must be obtained by satanic aid. To support this last view, he produces the testimony of Ficino that those least skilled in the practices of astrology are often the most fortunate in their prognostications. Carleton says that he has now shown that astrology has no foundation in nature, that the stars are not causes, and that man has no natural means of obtaining foreknowledge. In the following chapter, he assaults Heydon's blundering defense of free will and his unguarded hypothesis that the stars have no power over the regenerate or the wise. It is the study then, says Carleton, "that considereth the fortunes of fooles and wicked."[70] Astrology is for Bishop Carleton the mate of witchcraft and its source is Pandemonium. He attacks, in the sixth chapter, the logic of Heydon's attempt to disprove all arguments against astrology by his own definition of the art, and then he proceeds to destroy Heydon's definition. The Bishop was, without question, a thorough student of analytics, and the merits of his essay rest not on his lamiaphobia but on his skillful mangling of Heydon's *lapsus logicorum*.

Carleton now examines Heydon's thesis that many kings and philosophers of the past were astrologers and turns a se-

[69] *Op. cit.* (London, 1624), pp. 16-17.   [70] *Ibid.,* p. 43.

verely critical eye on the astrological chronology that Heydon
had appended to his book. He examines these data in the light
of historical scholarship and comes to the conclusion that
astrology has never been proved to be either a natural or a
mathematical science, that the most learned among the ancients
were opposed to astrology, and that those ancients who practiced astrology also practiced magic. He strikes Heydon's historical argument a heavy blow by proving that among the
Romans the astrologer had a reputation inferior to that of diviners who took auspices.[71] The eighth chapter is used to examine the operations of the heavenly bodies, and Carleton is
ready to admit the ability of the astrologer to foretell the motions of these bodies and the possible effect of these motions on
the weather. He is not sure that corruptions of the air can be
forecast with certainty, and he denies the ability of the fore-
caster to predict any event that arises from a combination of
natural causes and mortal choice or any happening that occurs
contingently.

Carleton now discusses at great length the relation between
astrology and magic, a relationship that he has indicated re-
peatedly in his treatise. The Bishop admits that many experts,
including the famous scientific thinker Porta, divide magic
into natural and demonic magic; he doubts, however, that the
division is sound and observes that Porta includes a number of
things in his *De magia naturalis* that can hardly be called
natural magic. His method of attack is to go to astrological
authorities like Henry Cornelius Agrippa for references
proving that astrology is the inseparable adjunct of magic.
Working on these assumptions and suggestions, he has, of
course, no difficulty in going back to his original theme of the
demonic inspiration of astrology.[72] The last chapter of Carleton's book is an indictment of Heydon for blasphemy. The
Bishop accuses Heydon of twisting the text and gloss of salient
passages in Genesis, Job, and other Biblical sources to fit his

[71] *Ibid.*, pp. 56-69.   [72] *Ibid.*, pp. 76-96.

personal arguments. The stars, says Carleton, fought against Sisera, but they fought by means of a great rain which caused the river Kishon to overflow. The stars exerted no other force against the unfortunate commander. He reiterates his arguments against Heydon's theory that the blood of Christ removed the influence of the stars from the regenerate, and says that could this impiety be allowed, Christ's blood could not wash away what was not. He taxes Heydon with his inability to grasp the essentials of theology, and declares that Heydon, for this reason, should not complain that others have failed to understand astrology. From the blasphemies of Heydon, Carleton passes to those of astrologers and presents in detailed organization many of the arguments that had pleased theologians of a century earlier. He closes his book with a quotation from the *Daemonology* of King James and a conventional protest against intellectual curiosity: "And so mounting from degree to degree, vppon the slippery and vncertaine scale of Curiositie, they are at last inticed, that where lawfull Artes or Sciences fayles, to satisfie theyr restlesse mindes, euen to seeke to that blacke and vnlawfull Science of Magicke."[73]

We perceive that the English controversy over astrology was not unlike that waged on the continent, save that in England the controversialists were not so erudite as their continental contemporaries and, with one exception, composed their polemics in the vernacular. This is perhaps a clue to the intellectuality of the English Renaissance. In matters of science and even of pseudoscience, the English were seldom as thorough in their investigations as their continental coevals, but they were more ready than the other Europeans to share what they knew with the masses. We perceive also that the attitudes of the proponents and opponents of astrology were not unlike those of the continentals. None of the English opponents of astrology was willing to say that the stars were without influence; at most, they denied that the planets had the governing

[73] *Ibid.*, p. 122.

of the human will and that the influence of the stars could either be measured or predicted. On the other hand, the formal defenders of the art were reasonably moderate. The English proponents distinguish carefully between the base and the upright astrologer; they cling to the doctrine of free will and try to effect a compromise between it and the tenets of astrology. Both parties lament the presence of the charlatan, who, undoubtedly, was the real breaker of the peace and without whom both sides might have lived in unity.

The debate about astrology in England did not end with the death of James I. John Allen,[74] J. Brayne,[75] John Geree,[76] John Gaule,[77] William Rowland,[78] and John Raunce[79] wrote against astrology during the mid-century. Doctor Nathanael Homes did not spare the stargazer in his *Daemonologie and Theologie,* which he published at London in 1650. Homes' work produced a defense from William Ramesey with the title *Lux Veritatis, or Christian Judicial Astrology vindicated and Demonology confuted, in answer to Dr. Nat. Homes* (London, 1651) and may have inspired Hardick Warren's *Magick and Astrology vindicated from those False Aspersions and Calumnies which the ignorance of some hath cast upon them; in which is contained True Definitions of the said Arts and the Justification of their Practise, proved by the authority of Scripture and the Experience of Ancient and Modern Authors* (London, 1651). There were other defenses. In 1660, George Atwel published *An Apology, or Defence of the Divine Art of Natural Astrologie: being an answer to a Sermon preached in Cambridge, July 25, 1652.*[80] The learned divine, Henry More, struck

---

[74] *Judicial Astrologers Totally Routed* (London, 1659).

[75] *Against Judiciary Astrology* (London, 1653).

[76] *Astrologo-Mastix, or a Discovery of the Vanity and Iniquity of Judiciall Astrology* (London, 1646).

[77] *The Mag-Astro-Mancer* (London, 1652).

[78] *Judiciall Astrologie judicially condemned* (London, 1652).

[79] *A Brief Declaration against Judicial Astrologie* (London, 1650); also in Latin in the same year.

[80] Astrology got into the pulpit with Robert Gell's Αγγελοκρατια Θεον, *or a*

at astrology in his *Enthusiasm Triumphatus*[81] and in his *An Explanation of the Grand Mystery of Godliness;*[82] to these remarks John Butler replied in his Αγιαστρολογια, *or the most Sacred and Divine Science of Astrology: i. Asserted, ii. Vindicated, iii. Excused* (London, 1680). More met the challenge of Butler by reprinting the pertinent sections of the *Grand Mystery* in 1681 as *Tetractys Anti Astrologica, or a Confutation of Judiciary Astrology.* Another learned man and divine of the seventeenth century, Thomas Gataker, got involved in a quarrel with the astrologer Lilly and the astrologers themselves were always at strife over the issues of the Civil War. Works on astrology and astrological medicine continued to be written, and he who would learn what writings on the subject of the planets were available to the man of Milton's age may scan the bibliography appended by Lilly to his *An Easie and plain Method Teaching how to judge upon Nativities.* The art lent itself to philosophizing, and one of the most popular books of this sort was Valentine Weigel's *Astrology Theologized,* but for the philosopher's attitude, one may turn to Lord Herbert of Cherbury's *A Dialogue Between a Tutor and a Pupil:* "When it [astrology] is rightly understood and applied, it be not only a lawful, but a most necessary art for a wise man; as long as he takes only general predictions from thence, without presuming to foretell particular and single events, otherwise then, as they depended upon general causes, since they who descend too far into particulars either err or speak truth by chance."[83] Finally, we must remember that Sir Thomas Browne was half converted to the essential tenets of astrology and that John Dryden visited the astrologer and was himself able to cast a figure. In spite of the new astronomy and the rejection of the Aristo-

---

Sermon touching God's Government of the World by Angels (London, 1650); Farmer, *A Sermon preached against Astrology and Astrologers* (Bristol, 1651); T. Swadlin, *Divinity no Enemy to Astrology* (London, 1653).

[81] *A Collection of Several Philosophical Writings* (London, 1662), p. 30.

[82] *The Theological Works* (London, 1708), pp. 240-255.

[83] London, 1768, p. 179.

telian cosmology, astrology continued to thrive. Its grip on the minds of learned men was probably shaken more by the new rationalism and the accompanying theories of the dignity of man that the age of reason brought than by the discoveries of the Royal Society. Its hold on the minds of the lower classes has never been relaxed.

CHAPTER IV

SOME ASPECTS OF THE DISPUTE ABOUT ASTROLOGY AMONG ELIZABETHAN AND JACOBEAN MEN OF LETTERS

WHEN PICO DELLA MIRANDOLA attacked astrology and Ficino repented his youthful devotion to that art, they were both mindful of the philosophical and cosmological implications of their actions. The struggle against Averroism was not yet over, and on the doctrine of astrology one of the basic concepts of the Averroistic universe rested. But astrology shared in more than one heresy, in more than one tangle of philosophies. One of the more important conflicts of ideas in the early Renaissance polarized about the postulates of the cosmos as spirit and as nature. With the recrudescence of the classical themes, a fatalistic stoicism came to be the doctrine accepted by those whose minds were unable to shelter the concepts of the believers in immanence, and for this more tough-minded group, astrology became a most useful implement of both defense and assault. Of these matters and of many others like them, the earlier and more philosophic opponents and proponents of astrology were indubitably conscious.

By the time of the Reformation, astrology was for most men more of a theological than a philosophical question. The opponents of astrology, as has been observed, were partial to arguments from the Scriptures, from canon law and church history, and from the writings of the fathers; the astrologers, when they were able, defended themselves with the same material. We do not wish to suggest that in the new period the purely philosophic bases were forgotten; they had really become fused in the theological arguments. The debate about astrology had

simmered down to a discussion of the nature of God's providence and man's free will, and though we might insert a great
deal of Averroistic or neo-Stoical blasphemy into the argument,
the ultimate sources of these propositions were probably unknown to most of the controversialists. It is, however, in this
period that the main lines of the quarrel are clearly etched.
Many partisans of one side or another are no more than parrots
of Pico, or Pontano, or of some earlier polemicist; but in the
thinking minority, a compromise was effected that suited most
of the opponents of astrology and some of the astrologers themselves. Most of the opponents of astrology were as ready to
admit the reality of an *astrologia naturalis* as they were to grant
that of a *magia naturalis*. The stars, they said (and why should
they quibble with a view that Pico held?), have some sort of
occult influence on the sublunar world. To this influence all
material objects submit. The force of the astral rays is perhaps
undefinable; it is also, without doubt, unpredictable; and it may
certainly be opposed by the more dominant forces of mind and
spirit. These are the attitudes of the opponents of judicial
astrology, for there were no opponents of natural astrology, no
deniers of the general influence of the heavens. Among the
astrologers, on the other hand, there were two views dominant.
The more reasonable type of stargazer, the moderate astrologer,
agreed in part with his opponents, but insisted that there might
be something in the ancient hypothesis which stated that
through further experiment—the word *experiment* was beginning to be popular and talismanic—the science of astrology
would be perfected and the influence of the stars correctly established. Off in a corner, very much by themselves, were the
die-hards, the judicial astrologers. In this band were some very
sincere professionals and many, many charlatans. They believed or pretended to believe that the influence of the stars was
particularized, that they knew the exact powers of Mars, Venus,
or Jupiter; they also said that by means of this knowledge, they
could make predictions about future events. Few members of

this group went the whole distance and insisted on the necessity of planetary forces. They did not deny the powers of providence or of free will completely; they had the Ptolemaic phrases, "The wise man rules the stars" and "The stars incline but do not compel," eternally on their lips. When they spoke in their own defense, they often fought for the virtue of the human mind—did not their predictions enable their clients to fortify their spirits so that their flesh might not be taken unawares? But all the cheats and mountebanks had enlisted in this regiment, and in time, the ill odor of bad company drove out many who were in sympathy with the cause for which it fought.

There is, nevertheless, a certain difference between the expert and the popular view on most questions, and to determine the popular view on astrology during the English Renaissance, we turn to the writings of men of letters of the age of Elizabeth and James. The student will expect to find in their pages no full denial of the astrologer's creed; all of the poets, dramatists, and essayists of the era should believe in the *astrologia naturalis;* some should agree with the theories of the judicial astrologers. The cheat among the astrologers should be the target of the satirists, for the age detested fakes, especially fakes in low social positions. The general attitude of the literary men towards astrology should be more calm, more contained, than that of the controversialists. Poets and dramatists seldom overleap the opinions of their age; seldom are they found in the ranks of the violent partisans. Since the Renaissance believed in astrology, we should not be shocked, as some have been, to discover that Shakespeare or Robert Burton or Sir Thomas Browne inclined to the side of "the superstitious." In order that we may clear men of lesser intellect of the charge of credulity, we turn to the writings of Francis Bacon to see what the father of modern science, the master of the new rationale, had to say about the ancient error of astrology.[1]

[1] I might mention here the titles of the two most important studies of astrol-

Bacon was silent on few subjects, and from time to time he mentioned astrology in uncomplimentary terms; however, it is in the *De Augmentis Scientiarum,* that most mature essay in philosophy, that we come upon his final attitude on the astrologer's art. Bacon has been discussing the special divisions of physics and metaphysics and has considered astronomy as a department of what he calls "concrete Physics"; from this analysis he passes naturally, in the fourth chapter of the second book, to an inquiry into astrology.

As for Astrology, it is so full of superstition, that scarce anything sound can be discovered in it. Notwithstanding, I would rather have it purified than altogether rejected. If however anyone maintains that this science is not based on reason or physical speculations, but on blind experience and the observations of many ages, and on that ground refuses the test of physical reasons (as the Chaldeans professed to do); he may on the same grounds bring back auguries, and believe in divination, entrails, and all kinds of fables; for all these are set forth as the dictates of long experience and traditions passed from hand to hand. But for my part I admit astrology as a part of Physic, and yet attribute to it nothing more than is allowed by reason and the evidence of things, all fictions and superstitions being set aside.[2]

After this promising foreword, Bacon exhibits the "idle inventions" of the astrologers and attacks in turn the notion of planetary hours, the doctrine of horoscopes and the division of houses, and "those fatalities, that the hour of nativity or conception influences the fortune of birth . . . in short, the doctrines of nativities, elections, inquiries." Having announced the precepts of astrology with which he most vigorously disagreed, Bacon mentions the notions of the astrologers which meet with

ogy and English literature in the Middle Ages; they are T. O. Wedel, *The Mediaeval Attitude Toward Astrology* (New Haven, 1920), and W. C. Curry, *Chaucer and the Mediaeval Sciences* (Oxford, 1926).

[2] In the last sentence, Bacon paraphrases the Thomistic objection to the arrogance of the astrologer's claims, but the argument was so frequently in the mouths of the continental polemicists that one doubts that Bacon sought it out in the *Summa.*

his approval and suggests that certain improvements in methodology would make his approval complete. First, he would
eliminate the stars and houses from all astrological calculations
and depend only on the influence of the planets, or, as he says,
"the great guns that strike from afar." "Secondly, the operation
of the heavenly bodies does not affect all kinds of bodies, but
only the more tender; such as humors, air, and spirit; here,
however, the operations of the heat of the sun and heavenly
bodies must be expected which doubtless penetrates both to
metals and to a great number of subterraneous bodies." Bacon
now observes that the influences of the heavens are greater on
the sublunar mass than on the individual parts of that mass;
however, he nullifies this remark by admitting that certain
individual parts of the mass are more susceptible than others
to the influence of the planets. His fourth principle is that
heavenly bodies shed their influence over a broad area of time
rather than in a fixed point of time. Bacon's last emendation
of the rules of astrology is an interesting testimony to the extent of his beliefs.

The last rule (which has always been held by the wiser astrologers) is that there is no fatal necessity in the stars; but that they
rather incline than compel. I will add one thing besides (wherein
I shall certainly seem to take part with astrology, if it were reformed); which is, that I hold it for certain that the celestial bodies
have in them certain other influences besides heat and light; which
very influences however act by those rules laid down above and not
otherwise. But these lie concealed in the depths of Physic, and re-
quire a longer dissertation.

Bacon now talks about the new astrology, or, as he calls it,
"Sane Astrology," which is to be based on scientific principles.
The Baconian astrology does not differ a great deal from that
of the Chaldeans; it is the underlying hypotheses that are altered. The ancients and Bacon both said that the moon had
greater force in Leo than in Pisces, but Bacon shows that this
variation in stellar influence is not caused by the secret powers

of the sign, but results from the fact that the moon in Leo is aided by "her elevation towards the perpendicular and approximation to the larger stars." The new astrology, says Bacon, may be applied confidently to predictions and cautiously to elections. One will be able to predict with a great degree of accuracy "floods, droughts, heats, frosts, earthquakes, irruptions of water, eruptions of fire, great winds and rains, the various seasons of the year, plagues, epidemics, diseases, plenty and dearth of grain, wars, seditions, schisms, transmigrations of peoples, and in short of all commotions or greater revolutions of things, natural as well as civil." Although Bacon had previously criticized the astrologers for particular predictions, he announces that once the foundations of "Sane Astrology" are established, a certain kind of particularized prediction will be possible. One will be able to say, for example, that the season will be especially dangerous to monks and courtiers, or that it will be more ominous for scholars than for soldiers. The new system of astrology, Bacon points out, will also be useful in elections, when the virtues of the planets are of a more lasting nature and when the action they instigate is not immediately accomplished. We might, according to the Baconian theory, predict a good time for planting a field of wheat, but we would hesitate to foretell the taking of a draught of fish. Bacon now suggests four means by which astrology may be purified—they are means suggested by many before him—and concludes this digression on astrology with a Ficinian attack on astrological amulets.

Bacon's position is clear. His attitude towards astrology is so liberal that he can be claimed as a partisan of the art. Pico, writing more than a hundred years before Bacon, had insisted that the influence of the stars was general and that it was derived from the heat, motion, and light of the planets. Bacon goes much farther. The stars, he says, have influences in addition to their light and heat, and though he insists that these forces are general, he thinks that predictions may be made for

particular groups. Pico della Mirandola, even Ficino the credulous, would have considered Bacon a sort of astrological apologist, for in these comments of his the great problem of free will
is never mentioned and the inclination to stray beyond the
honest limits of the *astrologia naturalis* is most strong.

Although Bacon is the pillar in the wastes, he is not the
only learned Englishman of this era to embrace the cause of
the moderate astrologers. If we should scan the roll of Englishmen who wrote during the learned reign of King James,
we should find few scholars greater and few thinkers more
cogent than Robert Burton, Sir Walter Raleigh, and John
Donne. All of these men talked about astrology, and what they
said is extraordinarily pertinent. Raleigh, who wrote about
astrology in *The History of the World,* accepted the moderate
view. The stars, he asserts, have complete power over all the
reasonless things in the inferior world; they have a definite
influence on the disposition of men and signify at their births
the nature of their mortal career. Raleigh admits that the
forces of the planets can be counterbalanced by prayer and
education, but he also feels that they preside over the fates of
most sublunar things.[3] The numerous references to astrological matters in *The Anatomy of Melancholy* and the legend of
Robert Burton's suicide are enough to convince the ordinary
reader of the Oxford polymath's fancy for stargazing. Burton
informs his reader that he was born under Saturn with Mars
in a partile aspect and both planets fortunate; hence, all his
"treasure is in Minerva's tower."[4] These remarks of Burton
recall Ficino's constant complaints about his own saturnine
nativity; and when we come upon Burton's confession of faith
in the stars, we are again mindful of the eclectic Florentine:
"If thou shalt ask me what I think, I must answer, *nam
et doctis hisce erroribus versatus sum,* (for I am conversant
with these learned errors,) they do incline, but not compel; no

[3] *Op. cit.* (London, 1614), pp. 12-15.
[4] *Op. cit.* (Philadelphia, 1853), p. 16.

necessity at all: *agunt non cogunt:* and so gently incline, that
a wise man may resist them; *sapiens dominabitur astris:* they
rule us, but God rules them."[5] We may also summon John
Donne, who has won a vast reputation for his learning in both
the new physics and the new astronomy, to add his testimony
to that of Burton and Raleigh. Surely, the reader thinks, this
cold logician backed by his learning in science and theology
and fortified by the realism that begot his love poetry was a
scorner of the fallacies of astrology. In all of Donne's works
there is no denial of the validity of astrology. A sermon that
Donne preached on Easter, 1623, contains a long passage in the
language of the prognosticators,[6] and though this does not
make Donne an astrological initiate, it suggests that he recognized that this language was intelligible to his congregation.
A more definite astrological pronouncement about the influence of Sirius and comets—matters of common knowledge in
Donne's age—is found in the *Devotions;* nevertheless, Donne's
personal reaction to astrology is elusive, for he writes in conclusion: "No Astrologer tels us when the effects will be accomplished, for thats a secret of a higher spheare, then the
other; and that which is most secret, is most dangerous."[7] Finally, we find mention of the astrological amulet in both
"The First Anniversary"[8] and in "A Valediction: of my name,
in the window," but in neither case can we ascertain Donne's
attitude towards these charms which both Ficino and Bacon
had condemned.

Three of four learned men of letters of the age of James I
lean in the directon of the moderate astrologers; the fourth
member of this group is more reticent, but he does not attack
astrology and he uses lore raked from its teachings to elaborate
his earlier verses and to illustrate the prose of his period of
devotion.[9] What can we make of this? By the time that the

[5] *Ibid.,* p. 130.   [6] *LXXX Sermons* (London, 1640), p. 177.
[7] *Op. cit.,* ed. Sparrow (Cambridge, 1923), p. 55.
[8] *Poetical Works,* ed. Grierson (Oxford, 1912), I, 243.
[9] In his *Daemonologie* (*Works,* London, 1616, pp. 100-101), King James per-

note

writings of all of these intellectuals were printed, the new astronomy had banished the ancient notion of the incorruptibility of the superlunar heaven, and the Ptolemaic doctrine of the spheres was completely unhinged, but, in spite of the new findings, these giants of the Jacobean era remained true, after their fashions, to the antique dogma of the astrologers.[10] An absolute explanation is impossible. Perhaps they could not divorce themselves from the notions of youth; perhaps they thought as Heydon did when he wrote:

> For whether any of their opinions be true, or whether they be false, whether they be (as Tycho would have it) but one continued orbe, or many, or whether (as *Copernicus* saith) the sun be the center of the world, and the earth be in the Sunnes place . . . the Astrologer careth not. For so that by any of these *Hypotheses,* he may come to the true place, and motion of the Starres, this varietie of opinions, whether such things be indeede, and in what order they be, is no impeachment to the principles of arte.[11]

The scholar cannot account for the continued triumph of astrology during the seventeenth century any more readily than he can explain its eventual decline; but knowing that some of the greatest thinkers among the literary men of this age attached their faith to some of the astrologer's "superstitious" notions, he cannot become so disturbed about the astrological inclinations of lesser minds that he is driven to apologize for them.

To most authors of the English Renaissance, the science of astrology was a storehouse of rhetorical ornament. Sixteenth-century England produced no great astrological poets like

note

mits *astrologia naturalis* but condemns that "second part" which trusts "so much to their influence, as there by to fore-tell what Common-weales shall florish or decay: What persones shall be fortunate or unfortunate: What side shall winne in anie battell etc." F. G. Marcham in "James I and the 'Little Beagle Letters,'" *Persecution and Liberty: Essays in Honor of George Lincoln Burr* (New York, 1931), says that James liked to turn astrologer and write in astrological jargon (pp. 321-322).

[10] Most of these writers fit into the third class of astrological believers described by Andrew Willet in his *De animae natura et viribus* (Cambridge, 1585), pp. 87-100.

[11] *Op. cit.,* p. 371.

Pontano, Lorenzo Bonincontri, and Basino da Parma; but its poets had, like Petrarch or even Ficino in his private correspondence, a liking for the astrological figure or allusion, a penchant that they shared, of course, with the writers of both France and Italy. Now the use of an astrological trope by a literary man does not prove that he believed in astrology; it does, however, suggest the milieu in which he lived and worked. The effectiveness of a literary ornament depends, after all, on its intelligibility to readers, and the frequency with which one comes upon astrological references in the writings of Renaissance literary men, together with the technical nature of many of these allusions, suggests that the Renaissance public was as familiar with the astrologer's theories and jargon as the modern public is with the methods and language of psychologists. Hence, we shall not attempt to decide which Elizabethan and Jacobean literary men believed and which did not believe in astrology; on the contrary, we shall simply let these writers speak for themselves, and place what they have to say in appropriate pigeonholes.

Perhaps the most frequently used astrological trope of the Renaissance is some variation of the expression, "Oh, my stars." Sometimes the stars are thanked; sometimes they are cursed; sometimes they are cajoled; sometimes they are threatened. Allusions of this type are numerous but meaningless to the reader who is searching for an attitude; piled together, however, they make an impressive showing and suggest that the age was not only credulous but, like all other credulous periods, desperate. On occasions the tune is altered. The expression "planet struck" becomes the pardoning phrase for a *gaucherie* or moment of mental aberration; Robert Armin uses this phrase to suggest the effect on a young man of the sight of a pretty woman,[12] but the expression is used often enough

[12] *The Historie of the two Maides of More-clacke* (Students' Facsimiles, 1913), sig. C1r; see Dekker, *Works*, ed. Rhys (London, 1887), p. 325; *The Wisdom of Doctor Dodypoll* (Students' Facsimiles, 1912), sig. C2v; Jonson, *Works*, ed. Gifford-Cunningham (London, 1904), I, 82.

to become stereotyped. The technical terminology of the astrologer was also made subject to the rhetorical requirements of the man of letters. The cynical Bosola congratulates Antonio on being "Lord of the ascendant" with the Duchess of Malfi,[13] and Chapman's Savoy says of a rival:

> Nor do I like that mans Aspect, me thinkes,
> Of all lookes where the Beames of Starres have carved.[14]

At times one comes upon the compounding of an astrological reference into a graceful simile like Dekker's "Lovers watch minutes like astronomers,"[15] whereas at other times the allusion is so recondite and the simile so twisted that the effect is almost incongruous.[16] Finally, the astrological figure is occasionally used to describe an action or explain a situation; warriors are said to assail each other like "tilting stars" or a husband and wife are likened to a conjunction of friendly or unfriendly planets.[17]

Astrological figures were not, of course, used exclusively by serious poets or writers of tragedy. Nashe, spending a dry Lent among the salt fish of Yarmouth, complains that he has settled under "that predominant constellation of Aquarius,"[18] and Fletcher's Petruchio insists that some "dog-star, bull, or bear-star" reigned when he took his wife.[19] The sign *Virgo* caused no end of mirth. The relations between Virgo and Saturn, the planet of old men,[20] were as laughable in the sixteenth century as the January-May fables of the fourteenth century. There were, of course, some other humorous interpretations; Bilbo of

[13] Webster, *Works*, ed. Lucas (London, 1927), II, 54.
[14] *Works*, ed. Shepherd (London, 1873), II, 192; *Lear*, Act II, scene 2, ll. 111-113; *Richard III*, Act V, scene 5, ll. 20-21. I have used the Cambridge Shakespeare throughout.   [15] *Op. cit.*, p. 117.
[16] Harvey, *Works*, ed. Grosart (London, 1884), II, 184, 227, 327.
[17] *The Weakest Goeth to the Wall*, ed. Greg (Malone Society Reprints, 1912), sig. D2v; Thomas Hughes, *The Misfortunes of Arthur, Dodsley's Old English Plays*, ed. Hazlitt (London, 1874), IV, 265; Dekker, *op. cit.*, p. 194.
[18] *Works*, ed. McKerrow (London, 1910), III, 154.
[19] *Works*, ed. Waller-Glover (Cambridge, 1905-12), VIII, 49-50.
[20] *The Wit of a Woman*, ed. Greg (Malone Society Reprints, 1913), sig. Fr.

The Merry Devil of Edmonton shakes his head over a girl whose sign, as he puts it, is no longer in Virgo.[21] An extended rhetorical quotation of this type is placed by Marston in the mocking mouth of Maquarelle, the bawd of *The Malcontent:*

note

> O! beleeve me a most secret power, looke yee a Chaldean or an Assyrian, I am sure t'was a most sweete Jew tolde me, court any woman in the right signe, you shall not misse: but you must take her in the right veine then: as when the signe is in Pisces, a Fishmongers wife is very sociable; in Cancer, a Precisians wife is very flexible; in Capricorne, a Merchants wife hardly holdes out; in Libra, a lawyers wife is very tractable, especially, if her husband bee at the terme: onely in Scorpio t'is very dangerous medling. . . .[22]

Besides providing the Elizabethan and Jacobean men of letters with rhetorical devices, the art of astrology produced a theme for the conceit-hungry sonneteers. The English prototype of the astrological sonnet is the twenty-sixth sonnet of *Astrophel and Stella.* Only fools, says Sidney, can doubt astrology, can doubt that "those bodies high raigne on the low." If he were not convinced of the truth of astrology by other reasons, he would be converted by the two stars in Stella's face. Closely related to Sidney's astrological sonnet is Shakespeare's fourteenth sonnet, which may have been written with Sidney's verses in mind. Shakespeare says that he cannot read the stars, yet he thinks that he has "astronomy." It is not the kind of astronomy, he explains, that tells of good and evil fortune, "of plagues, of dearths, or season's quality"; however, by the constant stars of his friend's eyes, he can prognosticate the friend's fate. A different type of astrological sonnet is found in Barnes' *Parthenophil and Parthenope.* In this sequence, the unfortunate lady is drawn through the signs of the zodiac in a series of twelve sonnets.[23] This was a convention popular with both the

---

[21] Dodsley, *op. cit.,* X, 233.
[22] *The Plays,* ed. Wood (Edinburgh-London, 1934), I, 202; Greene, *Works,* ed. Grosart (London, 1881-83), II, 35; *All's Well,* Act II, scene 1, ll. 53-56; *The Winter's Tale,* Act I, scene 2, ll. 200-204.
[23] *Elizabethan Sonnets,* ed. Lee (Westminster, 1904), I, 187-192.

French and Italian poets of the era; Gilles Durant, the reader recalls, wrote a *Stances du Zodiaque,* which was highly popular. In 1595, Chapman brought out his "Amorous Zodiac" in his *Ovid's Banquet of Sense,* and shortly before that date Drayton devoted the forty-seventh "amour" of his *Ideas Mirrour* to an account of the voyage of the sun through the zodiac, where its normal course is altered by the influence of a "faire planet." Another type of astrological sonnet is found in Alexander's *Aurora,*[24] Fletcher's *Licia,*[25] and Constable's *Diana.*[26] This third type of sonnet lists the powers of all the planets and tells of their influence on the sonneteer's beloved; the theme may have been suggested by Sidney's sonnet, but it has a neoclassical provenience, and we may find the motif elsewhere in Renaissance literature, for example, in John Lyly's *The Woman in the Moon.*

To pass from a consideration of the purely rhetorical use of astrological lore to the conscious use of the astrologer's doctrine as an explanation of the relationship between man and his cosmos or as an apology for man's character and activities is to realize the amazing currency of this type of learning in Renaissance England. That there was a definite sympathy between the heavens and sublunar creatures was, of course, common knowledge. The notion of a general celestial influence on man and his world is a part of most literary men's philosophy,[27] and it was quite in keeping with this idea to indicate such common examples of this irresistible force as the pull of the moon on the tides or the vitalizing force of the sun on plants or minerals.[28] To a reader of astrological literature, this is an

[24] *Works,* ed. Kastner-Charlton (Edinburgh, 1929), II, 499.

[25] *Elizabethan Sonnets,* II, 47.

[26] *Ibid.,* II, 102; see Smith's *Chloris,* XXVIII, *ibid.,* II, 339.

[27] Drayton, *Works,* ed. Hebel (Oxford, 1931), I, 147.

[28] Heywood, *Works,* ed. Pearson (London, 1874), I, 64; III, 163, 233; *A Midsummer Night's Dream,* Act III, scene 1, ll. 201-204; *Troilus and Cressida,* Act III, scene 2, ll. 184-185; *The Winter's Tale,* Act IV, scene 4, ll. 105-106; *Sonnets,* XXV; P. Fletcher, *Works of Giles and Phineas Fletcher,* ed. Boas (Cambridge, 1908), I, 136; Harvey, *op. cit.,* II, 61, 106.

old argument; it is the argument with which almost every defense of astrologers or manual of astrology began. The literary
men knew, moreover, the whole sequent argument, the whole
irrefragable chain of logic. The planets influence the elements
and in this way come to the sovereignty of the humors; the
resulting complexion establishes the character of star-cursed
man. The Elizabethan and Jacobean writers were charmed by
this idea; it was, of course, their basic psychology. We can
find poetic evidences of it almost everywhere, but in Drayton's
Endimion and Phoebe we discover the whole philosophy
wound up within the compass of a dozen lines:

> And that our fleshly frayle complections,
> Of Elementall natures grounded bee,
> With which our dispositions most agree,
> Some of the fire and ayre participate,
> And some of watry and of earthy state,
> As hote and moyst, with chilly cold and dry,
> And unto these the other contrary;
> And by their influence powerfull on the earth,
> Predominant in mans fraile mortall bearth,
> And that our lives effects and fortunes are,
> As is that happy or unlucky Starre,
> Which reigning in our frayle nativitie
> Seales up the secrets of our destinie,
> With frendly Plannets in conjunction set,
> Or els with other meerely opposet.[29]

Drayton's lines epitomize the astrologer's theory, but for
the ordinary man of the Renaissance, no epitome was needed.
The frequency with which the stars are praised or blamed as
intruders in mortal affairs has already been described as a
rhetorical device; if, however, the scholar studies these references, he notices that there are many adjectives, many epithets
which suggest that for men of this age the force of the stars

[29] *Op. cit.,* I, 147; Greene, *Plays and Poems,* ed. Collins (Oxford, 1905), II, 254;
Works, ed. Grosart, XI, 127; Ford, *Works,* ed. Dyce-Bullen (London, 1895), III,
164-165.

was ineluctable. When the planets have been bestowers of benefits, of those gifts of Fortune that were in their keeping, they are described as "blessed stars," "lucky stars," "happy stars," "smiling stars," or "fair stars."[30] Since the donatives of such stars were invariably pleasant, it seems to have become a custom to salute one's friends with some astrological phrase of good will; in John Fletcher's *The Two Noble Kinsmen,* for example, one of the queens blesses Theseus with the phrase, "To thee no star be dark."[31] The sixteenth century seems not, however, to have been a happy century; it seems to have shared like all ages before and and since in the cosmic surplusage of human woes. It is undoubtedly because of this pessimism that one finds the stars continually blamed for their malevolence. The epithets of praise that were thrust upon the planets have been mentioned, but more frequently does one find epithets of censure and more often do these qualifiers suggest the passion that clouds the hearts of frustrated mortals. One cannot pause to notice all the poetic curses hurled against the planets, but we find them frequently labeled as "planets of mishap," "malignant and ill-boding stars," "cruel stars," "ill planets," "unlucky stars," "damned and accursed planets," or "low'ring stars." Other qualifiers regularly tied to the planets are "unkind," "sour," "malicious," "wrathful," "oppressive," "tortuous," and "malevolent."[32]

[30] *Jeronimo,* Dodsley, *op. cit.,* IV, 393; Brandon, *The Virtuous Octavia,* ed. McKerrow (Malone Society Reprints, 1909), sig. E5v; *All's Well,* Act I, scene 3, ll. 249-252; Heywood, *op. cit.,* IV, 43; Middleton, *Works,* ed. Bullen (London, 1885), II, 54; J. Fletcher, *op. cit.,* V, 346; VI, 380; IX, 38; *The Tragedy of Locrine,* ed. McKerrow (Malone Society Reprints, 1908), sig. F2r. There was always the love of parody, too, so in J. Fletcher's *The Noble Gentleman,* Longovile sighs, "I thank my Stars I am a whoremaster" (*op. cit.,* VIII, 178).

[31] *Op. cit.,* IX, 304.

[32] Greene, *Works,* ed. Collins, I, 180; Drayton, *op. cit.,* I, 170; Marston, *op. cit.,* I, 158; Peele, *Works,* ed. Bullen (London, 1888), I, 188; Dekker, *op. cit.,* p. 316; Daniel, *Delia,* XXVII; P. Fletcher, *op. cit.,* II, 181; Lodge, *The Wounds of Civil War;* Dodsley, *op. cit.,* VII, 181; Machin, *The Dumb Knight, ibid.,* X, 151; *The Tragedy of Locrine,* sig. B3v; *The Tragedy of Tiberius,* ed. Greg (Malone Society Reprints, 1914), sig. H3r; J. Fletcher, *op. cit.,* VI, 354; VIII, 257; IX, 82; Jonson, *op. cit.,* I, 40; Smith, *Chloris, Elizabethan Sonnets,* II, 339; *The Tragedy of Caesar*

Though these frequently repeated epithets suggest something of the temper of the age, they tell us little or nothing
about the extent of this literary faith in astrology. Like the
rhetorical uses of astrological doctrine, this material does little
more than indicate the nature of the philosophical backdrop
that was in everyone's mind. We can, however, come a little
closer to perceiving the texture of this curtain by examining
the literary references to the influence of the natal stars, to the
powers of the stars on specific days and hours, and to the absolute necessity of the stellar decrees and the relationship between
the sidereal messengers and the regiment of fate and fortune.
From these matters, which are essentially philosophic, we may
pass to a survey of the nature of the technical facts of astrology
known to Elizabethan and Jacobean men of letters. With this
information before us, we should be able to come to a comprehension of the attitude towards astrology and astrologers in
Renaissance England, and we should also perceive how well
the literary attitude coincides with that of the special pleaders.

The unfortunate, but highly popular, Captain Stukeley,
finding himself at the end of his adventurous rope, turns to
his followers and, according to Peele, addresses them in this
fashion:

> But from our cradles we were marked all
> . . . to die in Afric here.[33]

The audience was apparently not disturbed by this unchristian
yet strangely Calvinistic sentiment, for, without doubt, most of
them felt that like Stukeley they, too, were star-marked in their
cradles. The formal opponents of astrology all declaimed
against this notion of the lasting influence of the birth star, but
among ordinary people of the period, the idea would not down,
and the literary men, especially the playwrights, made as much
capital of it as they could. Tamburlaine, we recall, talks con-

---

and Pompey, ed. Boas (Malone Society Reprints, 1911), sig. A4v; I *Henry VI,* Act I,
scene 1, ll. 23-24; Act IV, scene 5, l. 6. See the rather interesting use in *The
Duchess of Malfi (op. cit.,* II, 92).   [33] *Op. cit.,* I, 291-292.

tinually about his fortunate birth under a strong constellation,[34] and Robert Greene, who did not name his little son
"Fortunatus" for the sake of euphony, refers constantly in his
writings to the influence of the natal star.[35] These men are, of
course, not isolated in this attitude, for the nativity scheme is
commonly mentioned as the explanation of the good and bad
qualities or the successful and unsuccessful careers of men.[36]

We must, however, distinguish between literary references
to the predictions of birth constellations and those which refer
to a momentary good or bad fortune arising from the disposition of the stars. Allusions to the problem of elections, or the
selection of a proper hour and day for the transaction of some
business, are almost as frequent as those to the stars of birth.
Men of the Renaissance were most mindful of the propitious
hour. Ficino, we recall, spoke constantly of the hours and
days in which his planet was unfavorably placed. The planet
Mercury, for example, was most influential on Wednesday at
the first and eighth hours and had Saturn, Jupiter, and Venus
as friendly planets. Though there were other things to consider, a native of Mercury would fare best on Wednesday at
one of the two mentioned hours provided that a friendly planet
was in a favorable aspect and all unfavorable stars were declining. A native of Mercury would consult his astrologer to learn
what Wednesday in a given month was most fortunate and on
that day he would sign a contract or start on a journey or en-
gage in some other important business project. Since many

[34] *Op. cit.,* ed. Ellis-Fermor (London, 1930), pp. 81, 94, 99-100, 142, 238;
Marlowe's very competent knowledge of astronomy is observable in *Faustus.*
[35] *Works,* ed. Collins, I, 120; *Works,* ed. Grosart, II, 40-41, 176; IV, 115; VII,
201; IX, 52.
[36] Heywood, *op. cit.,* III, 54; Dodsley, *op. cit.,* VII, 185; X, 151; Webster,
op. cit., III, 85; Ford, *op. cit.,* I, 189; Dekker, *op. cit.,* p. 16; Drayton, *op. cit.,* II,
59; J. Fletcher, *op. cit.,* V, 342; VI, 354, 380; Munday, *Fidele and Fortunio, The
Two Italian Gentlemen,* ed. Simpson (Malone Society Reprints, 1909), sig. F4v;
Jonson, *op. cit.,* I, 92; II, 13; Spenser, *Faerie Queene,* Bk. I, canto 1, s. 27; Bk. II,
canto 2, s. 2; Bk. II, canto 6, s. 44; *All's Well,* Act I, scene 1, ll. 204-215; *Twelfth
Night,* Act II, scene 5, ll. 184-187; *Much Ado,* Act II, scene 1, ll. 348-350; *Pericles,*
Act III, scene 1, ll. 31-34; *Richard III,* Act I, scene 3, ll. 229-230; Act IV, scene 4,
l. 215; *The Two Gentlemen of Verona,* Act II, scene 7, l. 74.

Englishmen of this age seem to have gone to astrologers for advice of this sort, it is not surprising to find the literary men talking about this practice. In *The Tragedy of Tiberius,* Vonones, caught in a tangle of misfortune, cries out:

> Curss'd bee the houre, and curssed bee the lampe
> Which gives the influence to my haplesse being.[37]

Captain Stukeley, who seems to have been given to astrological complaints, notices that his band of adventurers arrived in Lisbon in a "fatal hour,"[38] and one comes upon a similar idea with a iatromathematical connotation in the second part of *Tamburlaine.*[39] Ben Jonson, who went deeply into all sciences, even when he knew them to be spurious, writes a speech of this sort in astrological terms for *The Magnetic Lady:*

> I wished you stay, sir, till tomorrow, and told you
> It was no lucky hour: since six o'clock
> All stars were retrograde.[40]

Now a man might take a literary oath by the stars; he might believe in the influence of the stars on sublunar creatures, on the day of his birth, and on specific moments in his life; he might believe all of these things and still be an opponent of judicial astrology though not a foe of natural astrology. The hard-bitten judicial astrologer went farther than this, although under the lash of the polemicists he was coming to admit the power of free will, for like Pontano and all the astrologers before and after him, the Renaissance astrologue believed, in the bottom of his heart, that the stars were the ministers of fate or fortune or providence or whatever unseen power it was that ruled the world and all that it contains. There is no use, these men would say, in struggling against the stars, for what they have decreed is final. This major premise had been accepted by most of the Averroists and by the Paduan heretics, and it

[37] *Op. cit.,* sig. H3r.
[38] *Op. cit.,* I, 291.   [39] *Op. cit.,* pp. 273-274.
[40] *Op. cit.,* II, 434; Drayton, *op. cit.,* I, 186; Middleton, *op. cit.,* II, 54; *Twelfth Night,* Act I, scene 4, ll. 35-36.

was inevitably insinuated, in a pious fashion, by all the great astrologers. For this reason, Pico della Mirandola expatiated at length on the nature of fate and fortune; and Pontano, when he rode to the defense, came armed with the new doctrine of the *fortunati*.

England, though not yet much given to abstract speculation, had heard of all these matters. This knowledge was by no means esoteric; it was the possession of the crowd. As we read through the pages of the literary texts of the Elizabethan and Jacobean period, we are impressed by the number of times that the notion of fate, fortune, destiny, and the powers of the planets are knotted together. To the philosopher, to someone like Alberti or Politian or Bruno, there was an essential difference between fate and fortune, but to the poet of the English Renaissance, with the exception of a few careful inquirers like Chapman and Jonson, these hidden powers upon whom the careers of men were based were one and the same thing. To gain further knowledge of this aspect of Renaissance thinking, the student may study the poetry of Shakespeare, who was more given to speaking about the stars and their services and disservices to men than most of his literary fellows.[41]

We usually feel that Shakespeare is most himself in the sonnets, and we are, consequently, inclined to consider any declaration that he makes in them as essentially what he thought. It is fortunate to discover that there is a certain amount of astrological material within the limits of these verses. The nature of the fourteenth sonnet, the answer to Sidney's "Astrologie," has been noticed; however, it is followed, as is often the case, by an echoing sonnet, a familiar verse which begins with an astrological motif.

> When I consider everything that grows
> Holds in perfection but a little moment,

[41] Thousands of words have been written on Shakespeare and astrology; the most recent paper is Moriz Sondheim's "Shakespeare and the Astrology of His Time," *Journal of the Warburg Institute*, II, 243-259.

> That this huge stage presenteth nought but shows
> Whereon the stars in secret influence comment;
> When I perceive that men as plants increase,
> Cheered and check'd even by the self-same sky . . .

With the themes of two of the earlier sonnets to lead him, the reader is not surprised to find fortune and the stars linked in the twenty-fifth sonnet.

> Let those who are in favour with their stars
> Of public honour and proud titles boast,
> Whilst I, whom fortune of such triumph bars,
> Unlook'd for joy in that I honour most.

This marriage between fortune and the stars, is, of course, not unknown in Shakespeare's plays. Hamlet's remarks about those who have the "stamp of one defect, being nature's livery, or fortune's star"[42] are illustrative of the sixteenth-century concept of the union between nature, the stars, and fortune. Henry VI makes plans to conquer "Fortune's spite" by living in a lowly condition; by protecting himself, he says, he will also protect his people from the malice of his "thwarting stars."[43] Here one finds an example of the astrologers' often-repeated theory that when Fortune exalts the humble or hurls down the great, she does it by means of the stars. Perhaps the best commentary on this idea is found in Prospero's well-known speech:

> By accident most strange, bountiful Fortune,
> Now my dear lady, hath mine enemies
> Brought to this shore; and by my prescience
> I find my zenith doth depend upon
> A most auspicious star, whose influences
> If now I court not but omit, my fortunes
> Will ever after droop.[44]

[42] *Op. cit.*, Act I, scene 4, l. 32.

[43] III *Henry VI*, Act IV, scene 6, ll. 19-29; Warwick, replying to this speech, brings in the Renaissance notion of the relation between virtue and fortune.

[44] *Op. cit.*, Act I, scene 2, ll. 178-184. Shakespeare was enchanted by the "tides in the affairs of men" notion, but we do not know that he thought these tides were caused by the stars.

In various places in other plays of Shakespeare, we find sympathetic characters flatly assuming that the stars dominate the flesh and perhaps the spirit of man. Lear—and we must admit that Lear is superstitious—swears by "all the operation of the orbs from whom we do exist and cease to be,"[45] and towards the end of his tragedy, he cries out:

> It is the stars
> The stars above us, govern our conditions;
> Else one self mate and make could not beget
> Such different issues.[46]

There are, of course, the "star-crossed lovers" of *Romeo and Juliet* and Romeo's "inauspicious yoke of stars";[47] there are, also, the interestingly parallel careers of the twins Viola and Sebastian; and there is the prayer of Timon in which the sun is invoked to grant "several fortunes" to twins of "one womb" whose procreation, gestation, and birth "scarce is dividant."[48] Though we can find denials of this point of view—for Shakespeare, like Cicero, reports all attitudes—the idea reiterated throughout the plays is that man is subject to the stars "as plantage to the moon." Duke Vincentio probably announces Shakespeare's world-weary opinion in his consolatory speech to Claudio:

> Reason thus with life:
> If I do lose thee, I do lose a thing
> That none but fools would keep. A breath thou art
> Servile to all the skyey influences,
> That dost this habitation where thou keep'st
> Hourly afflict.[49]

[45] *Op. cit.,* Act I, scene 1, ll. 113-114.   [46] *Ibid.,* Act IV, scene 3, ll. 34-37.
[47] See also Act I, scene 4, ll. 107-110; Act V, scene 1, l. 24.
[48] *Op. cit.,* Act IV, scene 3, ll. 1-8.
[49] *Measure for Measure,* Act III, scene 1, ll. 6-11. See also *Pericles,* Act I, scene 1, ll. 10-11; Act II, scene 1, ll. 1-4; Act V, scene 3, ll. 9-10; *Antony and Cleopatra,* Act III, scene 13, ll. 145-147; *Coriolanus,* Act II, scene 2, ll. 116-118; *Hamlet,* Act I, scene 1, l. 162; Act II, scene 2, l. 141; *Winter's Tale,* Act I, scene 2, ll. 363-364, 425-426; Act II, scene 1, ll. 105-108; *Cymbeline,* Act V, scene 3, ll. 3-4; I *Henry*

From Shakespeare we may turn to some of his important coevals, but we do not turn to a new attitude on astrology. Robert Greene does not hesitate to announce that for him there was a definite relationship between the stars and fortune.[50] In *Tullies Love,* for example, Greene takes the view that the stars can force variable fortune to be constant,[51] but he more often suggests by words placed in the mouth of a character that to struggle against the dictates of the stars is impossible.[52] Marlowe, like his friend Greene, accepted the idea of an alliance between fortune and the stars, and gave this doctrine embodiment in the character of Tamburlaine, who, we remember, talks constantly and confidently of his fortune and his good stars. The foolish Cosroe, who still cherishes his illusions about Tamburlaine, says to his ministers:

> Nature doth strive with Fortune and his stars
> To make him famous in accomplished worth.[53]

The example of Shakespeare, Marlowe, and Greene is echoed by Francis Beaumont and John Fletcher in many of their plays. In *The Maid's Tragedy,*[54] Philaster ascribes his "weak fortunes" to his "weak stars"; in *The Coronation,*[55] Arcadius blames his "unlucky Stars" for his fate; and in *The Prophetess,*[56] we come upon a discussion of the powers of the stars to alter fortune. Chapman,[57] Drayton,[58] Ford,[59] Heywood,[60] Lodge,[61] and many other writers[62] adopt the same theory and

---

VI, Act I, scene 1, ll. 52-56; III *Henry VI*, Act V, scene 6, ll. 78-79; *All's Well,* Act II, scene 3, ll. 27-28; *Timon,* Act IV, scene 3, ll. 107-109.

[50] *Works,* ed. Collins, II, 60; *Works,* ed. Grosart, VII, 81-82.

[51] *Ibid.,* VII, 189-190.

[52] *Ibid.,* II, 122; IV, 92, 118.   [53] *Op. cit.,* p. 94.

[54] *Op. cit.,* I, 82.   [55] *Ibid.,* VIII, 257.

[56] *Ibid.,* V, 331; see also V, 350; VIII, 268, 294.

[57] *Works,* ed. Shepherd (London, 1873), II, 302.

[58] *Op. cit.,* I, 267.   [59] *Op. cit.,* I, 228.

[60] *Op. cit.,* III, 54.   [61] Dodsley, *op. cit.,* VII, 185, 195.

[62] Webster, *op. cit.,* II, 76, 119-120; Middleton, *op. cit.,* III, 12, 49; Brandon, *op. cit.,* sig. E5r; Dodsley, *op. cit.,* X, 132, 151, 182; *The Tragedy of Caesar and Pompey,* sig. A4r; *A Pleasant Comedie of Faire Em* (Students' Facsimiles, 1911), sig. C3v.

force us to believe that for most men of the Age of Elizabeth
and James the influence of the planets was at one with that of
fate and fortune.

The philosophy of the literary men of the English Renaissance was in many ways the philosophy of the moderate astrologers. The stars, according to the poets and dramatists, had
an irresistible force which is joined to the powers of fortune
and cannot be overcome. Since this is the case, a man would
do well to learn about his natal stars, and it might be to his
advantage to consult the stars in matters requiring careful decision. The sixteenth-century English men of letters are, however, chary of going the full distance; they do not come out
stoutly for the full claims of the judicial astrologers. Most of
these writers are, then, somewhere between Chamber and Heydon in their views; they believe more than the former but not
so much as the latter.

As most of the Elizabethan and Jacobean authors accepted
the basic tenets of the moderate astrologers, it is not surprising
to discover that they all seem to know something about the
technicalities of astrology. The Ptolemaic cosmology, in spite
of Kepler and Copernicus, was still the cosmology of most educated Englishmen; from Ptolemy one might learn about the
powers of the planets.[63] Robert Greene used a Greek and Latin
text of Ptolemy's *De praedictionibus astronomicis, cui titulam
fecerunt quadripartium,* which was published at Basel in 1543,
besides Pontano's *Ægidius dialogus* and the *Astronomicon* of
Manilius for the learned references in his *Planetomachia*.[64]
Spenser, who regretted, according to Harvey, his lack of astrological learning, had a reasonable knowledge of sixteenth-century astrological technicalities.[65] It is quite unfair to compare

[63] See Hugh Dick, *The Doctrine of the Ptolemaic Astronomy in the Literature
of the English Renaissance,* Cornell University MS Dissertation. Professor Camden's
papers listed in Chapter III throw a great deal of light on this question.

[64] D. C. Allen, "Science and Invention in Greene's Prose," *Publications of the
Modern Language Association,* LIII (1938), 1013-1018.

[65] Hugh De Lacy, "Astrology in the Poetry of Edmund Spenser," *Journal of English and Germanic Philology,* XXXIII (1934), 520-543.

the knowledge in this field of a literary man with that of a professional astrologer, but I suspect that Jonson, Drayton, and perhaps Harvey could have held up their end in a conversation with some of the best astrologers in the kingdom.

In the Renaissance, astrological learning was a part of any national culture. Those Englishmen who could not read the many learned handbooks on the art of prognosticating published in Latin or some continental language could study Humphrey Baker's *A briefe and short Introduction upon Judiciall Astrology,* which was published at London in 1557. If one wanted something with a foreign flavor, there was G. C.'s translation of Dariot's *Ad astrorum judicia facilis introductio,* Fabian Wither's version of Jean de Hayn's *Introductiones apotelesmaticae,*[66] and Thomas Kelway's Englishing of Oger Ferrier's *Les jugements astronomiques sur les nativitez,* a highly popular continental manual. There were, naturally enough, other sources of information. A very popular book during the whole of the sixteenth century was Godfridus' *The Boke of Knowledge of thyngs unknouen apperteynge to Astronomye;* another book that informed the ordinary reader about astrology was the famous *Kalendrier des Bergiers* of Guy Marchant, which appeared in English in 1503 as the *Kalendar of Shyppars.* Besides special treatises on astrology and general works of knowledge which contained astrological sections, there were hundreds of almanacks and prognostications which went a long way toward salting the mind of the Englishman with astrological theories and spicing his language with the jargon of astrologers.

It is not an accident that the mythological tale of Endimion was popular in Renaissance England, for it was an age enamored of the moon. Sometimes that satellite was thought of as the chaste and fair Cynthia, the symbol of the throne; some-

[66] To this translation, which he published at London in 1598, Wither prefixed an epistle defending astrology and appointing the stars agents of providence. God uses the stars to warn men that they may "flye unto hym, whoe alone cann turne the same awaye."

times it was the inconstant and immoral mistress under whose countenance Falstaff and his fellows stole and made puns. It was the planet nearest the earth; it marked the boundaries of the corruptible and the incorruptible; and its powers were visible to all men. Horatio, the neo-Stoic, talks about "the moist star upon whose influence Neptune's empire stands";[67] and this special function of the moon was the subject of innumerable memoirs by scientists as well as of many poems by men of letters. But the moon's sway over the tides was equaled by its force in the brains of men; in *Lanthorne and Candle-Light,* Dekker observes that in England the word "Moone-man" means "mad-man."[68] In the main, however, the moon was thought of as a humid, altering planet which left such a mark on women that it was assigned to them as their governing star,[69] and the English writers were never weary of calling their readers' attention to this. Greene, for example, refers often to the inconstancy that the moon breeds in its tender subjects, and the heroes of his romances comment unendingly on choleric man, who is faithful under the moon, and phlegmatic woman, who is false under even the dominance of Mars.[70] One need not search the literature of the Elizabethan and Jacobean period for allusions to the powers of the moon; it would be not unlike searching for hay in a haystack. From Drayton's *Endimion and Phoebe,* we may borrow some lines that summarize the story of the moon and her powers:

For of the seaven sith she the lowest was,
Unto the earth she might the easiest passe;
Sith onely by her moysty influence,
Of earthly things she hath preheminence,
And under her, mans mutable estate,
As with her changes doth participate;

[67] *Hamlet,* Act I, scene I, ll. 118-119.
[68] *Works,* ed. Grosart (London, 1884-86), III, 258.
[69] For astrological references on the power of the moon read Firmicus Maternus, *Matheseos,* ed. Kroll-Skutsch (Leipzig, 1897), III, 13, and Pontano, *De Rebus Coelestibus* in *Opera* (Venice, 1518-19), III, 155-157.
[70] *Works,* ed. Grosart, II, 180, 221, 223-224; IV, 132.

And from the working of her waning source,
Th' uncertaine waters held a certaine course . . .
And unto her of women is assign'd,
Predominance of body and of mind,
That as of Plannets shee most variable
So of all creatures they most mutable.[71]

To the Renaissance, Saturn, the birth star of Ficino and Burton, was the most awe-inspiring of all the planets, for it stirred up the black bile and begot in men a double melancholy which under some circumstances produced the scholar and poet and under other circumstances the malcontent and madman.[72] As a consequence of this special force, Saturn left his impress on many Renaissance writings and on works of art like Dürer's "Melancolia." Shakespeare's Don John, we notice, cannot believe that the cheerful Conrade was born under Saturn, for being a true saturnist himself, he thinks that a man of his humor cannot hide his basic characteristics. In general, most Elizabethan sons of Saturn are alike, and the planet is usually spoken of as "sullen," "angry," or "lumpish," qualities it shared with its natives. Sometimes, however, we hear of the double nature of the planet.

For though they faine their *Saturne* melancholy,
Of sowre behauiors, and of angry moode:
They faine him likewise to be iust and holy.[73]

Saturn was not a planet unopposed; the Renaissance astrologer, like the Renaissance statesman, knew something about compromise. When Greene in *The Planetomachia* represents Venus and Saturn in dispute, he is portraying the established

---

[71] *Op. cit.*, I, 139-140.

[72] Pontano, *op. cit.*, III, 158-161; Maternus, *op. cit.*, III, 2; Simon Brosserius, *Totius philosophiae naturalis epitome* (Paris, 1536), p. 54v; Alfonso di Fonte, *Somma della natural filosofia*, ed. di Ulloa (Venice, 1557), pp. 67-68; Ptolemy, *De praedictionibus astronomicis*, ed. Pontano (Basel, n.d.), p. 184; Ptolemy, *Quadripartium*, ed. Melanchthon (Basel, 1543), pp. 28, 98-99.

[73] Elizabeth Falkland, *The Tragedy of Mariam*, ed. Dunstan (Malone Society Reprints, 1914), sig. H4v.

astrological theory that Venus and her consort Mars are most
hostile to Saturn. Venus, said the astrologers, is a moist planet
and Saturn a dry planet; Venus is feminine, Saturn masculine;
Venus governs the air and water, Saturn the earth. The natives of these two planets were, as a result of these hypotheses,
opposed to each other in temperament and the opposites of
each other in appearance, and the literary men saw to it that
the hostility between these planets and their natives was fully
exploited.[74] Since, however, the two planets were enemies of
each other, their influences ameliorated each other;[75] Fletcher
makes amusing profit of this fact in *The Sea Voyage:*

> I give my judgement thus, for your aspect,
> Y'are much inclin'd to melancholy: and that tells me,
> The sullen *Saturne* had predominance
> At your nativity, a malignant Planet,
> And if not qualified by a sweet conjunction
> Of a soft and ruddy wench, born under *Venus,*
> It may prove fatal.[76]

Planets other than Venus could alter the baleful influence of
Saturn, and the poets usually knew this astrological fact. One
of the mitigating planets was Jupiter, whose influence was always tempering.[77] Drayton tells how Jupiter calms "Saturnes
rage,"[78] and Greene likewise describes the lenitive effect of
Jupiter.[79] Sometimes the unfortunate planet Saturn, like all
the other planets, gained added influence by entering a heavenly house sympathetic to its special powers. The twelfth
house, which, according to Maternus, was called "Malus Dae-

[74] For Venus' powers see Pontano, *op. cit.,* III, 164-166; Maternus, *op. cit.,* III,
6; di Fonte, *op. cit.,* p. 71; Ptolemy, *Quadripartium,* pp. 29, 101-102; Brosserius,
op. cit., p. 55r.

[75] See Pontano, *Opera* (1505), sig. B7v.

[76] *Op. cit.,* IX, 35-36.

[77] For Jupiter's influence see Pontano, *op. cit.,* III, 161-163; Maternus, *op. cit.,*
III, 3; Brosserius, *op. cit.,* p. 54v; Ptolemy, *Quadripartium,* p. 29; di Fonte, *op. cit.,*
p. 69.

[78] *Op. cit.,* II, 495.

[79] *Works,* ed. Grosart, VI, 46; for Jupiter's influence on Saturn see Maternus,
op. cit., VI, 3, 9, 15, 22.

mon" by the Romans,[80] was most hospitable to Saturn. The later astrologers called the twelfth house the "House of Death" and observed it carefully when they were prognosticating for someone who was going to the wars or for someone who was seriously ill. With this knowledge before us, it is easy to perceive what Spenser is talking about when he informs the reader of the *Faerie Queene* that Phantastes was born when Saturn sat "in the house of agonyes."[81] At other times the baneful powers of the planet are augmented by conjunction with another planet or by the proximity of sympathetic signs. Drayton tells, for example, of a luckless child born when Saturn was in the ascendant and the moon was dominant in an earthly triplicity. The earthly triplicity, Taurus, Virgo, and Capricorn, would add its dulling effect to the earthy qualities of Saturn and the enfeebling forces of the moon; however, as any astrologer knew, a child born during the conjunction of Saturn and the moon had very little to expect of life,[82] so the added misfortune of the triplicity was quite unnecessary.

The planetary infatuation between Venus and Mars was also known to Renaissance literary men, who had long been acquainted with the mythological romance of these immortals. According to the astrologers, Venus was one of the most gregarious planets, for it was the friend of all the other stars save Saturn; on the other hand, Mars had no friends except Venus. Children born with Mars in the ascendant were cursed with evil natures, but when Venus was in conjunction with Mars,

---

[80] *Op. cit.*, II, 19; for an interesting anecdote see Lilly, *Easie and Plain Method teaching how to judge upon Nativities* (London, 1658), p. 473.

[81] *Op. cit.*, Bk. II, canto 9, s. 52.

[82] Maternus says that such a native will either die as a minor or live to be a suicide (*op. cit.*, IV, 2). One remembers that Marlowe's Mycetes was born during a conjunction of Saturn and the moon and lacked the mitigating powers of Jupiter, Mercury, or the sun in his horoscope; for this reason he was weak and foolish and an easy prey to Tamburlaine (*op. cit.*, pp. 69-70). At times, of course, the temptation to invent a horoscope was great and one finds Middleton doing something of this sort when he associates Saturn in the fifth house with pocket-picking (*op. cit.*, III, 192).

these qualities were often altered and sometimes dignified.[83]
Chapman versified this doctrine in his *Andromeda Liberata:*

> For when in heaven's blunt angles shine his flames,
> Or he, his second or eight house ascends
> Of ruled nativities, and then portends
> Ill to the then-born; Venus in aspect
> Sextile or Trine doth, being conjoined, correct
> His most malignity; and when his star,
> The birth of any governs, fit for war,
> The issue making much to wrath inclined
> And to the venturous greatness of the mind,
> If Venus near him shine, she doth not let
> His magnanimity, but in order set,
> The vice of Anger making Mars more mild
> And gets the mastery of him in the child.[84]

The astrologers also felt that a day on which Venus, the feminine planet, and Mars, the male planet, were conjoined was a
favorable occasion for a marriage, and Firk mentions this fact
when the wedding plans are made in *The Shoemakers' Holi-
day.*[85] Venus, of course, was the bestower of especial favors
when she was in union with some exceptionally benign planet
like Jupiter; consequently, Spenser does not err when he finds
such a conjunction in the horoscope of Belphoebe.[86] Ptolemy
commends highly the characters of mortals born under such
a conjunction; they are, he says, filled with many virtues; they
are "honesti et laudati."[87]

In these ways the Renaissance men of letters made use of
the data that the astrologers had gathered. Few are the occa-

---

[83] For the influence of Mars see Pontano, *op. cit.,* III, 163-164; Maternus, *op. cit.,*
III, 4; Ptolemy, *Quadripartium,* pp. 29, 100-101; Brosserius, *op. cit.,* p. 54v; di
Fonte, *op. cit.,* p. 69. Shakespeare jests on the power of Mars when he makes
sport of Parolles' lack of valor in war by saying that he was born under Mars
retrograde (*All's Well,* Act I, scene 1, ll. 196-206).

[84] *Works,* ed. Swinburne (London, 1875), p. 188; Greene, *Works,* ed. Grosart,
II, 223-224.

[85] Dekker, *op. cit.,* p. 73; Maternus, *op. cit.,* VI, 5.

[86] *Faerie Queene,* Bk. III, canto 6, s. 2.

[87] *De praedictionibus astronomicis,* p. 190; see also Pontano, *op. cit.,* III, 204-205.

sions on which one suspects that the poet has turned to some astrological treatise to read up on the virtues of some planet or conjunction; the references of this type are fairly spontaneous in tone and are seldom inaccurate. The writers knew a great deal about the moon, Saturn, Venus, Mars, and Jupiter; they refer less often to Mercury and to the sun,[88] although they regularly comment on the latter planet in a physical sense. As important, however, for an understanding of the place of astrology in sixteenth-century literary thought as the comments on individual stars are the extended passages in which the forces of all the planets are described. Such catalogues appear in the type of astrological sonnet written by Alexander and Constable, and we come upon other passages of this nature in Drayton's *The Shepherd's Garland*[89] and in Phineas Fletcher's *The Apollyonists*.[90] Nicholas Breton, as we might expect, knew about the powers of the planets and made whimsical use of this knowledge to suggest what occupations were best suited to their natives.[91] We must, however, read Lyly's *The Woman in the Moon* to see how astrological learning of this sort can be skillfully wound into a dramatic fable. Early in this play Nature calls upon Pandora and praises her in terms that recall the astrological poems of the sonneteers. The planets, however, rebel at Nature's partiality to Pandora, and, on the advice of Saturn, resolve to dominate her. First, Saturn fills her with his melancholy mood; then, Jupiter, enforcing his "influence to

---

[88] For the influence of the sun see Pontano, *op. cit.*, III, 154-155; Maternus, *op. cit.*, III, 5; for Mercury see Pontano, *op. cit.*, III, 166-168; Maternus, *op. cit.*, III, 7; for interesting references see Fisher, *Fuimus Troes: The True Trojans*, Dodsley, *op. cit.*, XII, 473; *The Pedlar's Prophecie*, sig. B3v; P. Fletcher, *op. cit.*, II, 38; *Wily Beguiled*, Dodsley, *op. cit.*, IX, 278; *The Tragedy of Tiberius*, sig. N2r; *The Tragedie of Caesar and Pompey*, sig. F4r; Wilkins, *The Miseries of Enforced Marriage*, Dodsley, *op. cit.*, IX, 557; Marston, *op. cit.*, II, 210; Drayton, *op. cit.*, I, 368; Falkland, *op. cit.*, sig. H4v; Jonson, *op. cit.*, II, 313; Spenser, *Faerie Queene*, Bk. VII, canto 7, s. 50-54; *Titus Andronicus*, Act II, scene 3, ll. 30-39; *Timon*, Act IV, scene 3, ll. 107-109; *Troilus and Cressida*, Act I, scene 3, ll. 86-118; *The Winter's Tale*, Act IV, scene 3, ll. 24-26.
[89] *Op. cit.*, I, 67.   [90] *Op. cit.*, I, 180-181.
[91] *Works in Verse and Prose*, ed. Grosart (London, 1879), II, 28.

the worst," makes Pandora ambitious and disdainful. Mars has no difficulty in making her "churlish," but the sun, being of a universally benign nature, brings it about that she is

> . . . loving, liberall and chaste,
> Discreete and patient, mercifull and milde,
> Inspired with poetry and prophesie.[92]

Venus now nullifies the chastity bestowed by the sun, and makes Pandora witty, quick, and amorous; to these dubious qualities, Mercury adds deceit, prevarication, and eloquence. Pandora is now endowed with many conflicting vices and virtues and so, like her sisters, she must become Cynthia's daughter.

To this constant literary discussion of the celestial powers we may add the frequent literary employment of astrological terms as a further proof of the sixteenth century's familiarity with the art of the stars. The words *aspect, conjunction,* or *opposition* appear often with an astrological implication; the term *ascendant* is most usual, and the word *retrograde* occurs regularly to indicate a declining state of affairs.[93] We come also upon the use of astrological trade terms like *trigon, triplicity, quartile, sextile, combustion,* and other expressions of this nature, but they appear rather infrequently.[94] The "figure" or celestial diagram drawn up by every professional astrologer prior to the determining of a definite prediction is mentioned by a number of writers. Jonson's Subtle employs his time "erecting figures," and Surly scornfully designates him as "the Faustus that casteth figures."[95] Antonio, the unfortunate hero of *The Duchess of Malfi,* "sets a figure" for his son's birth and makes a fatal forecast.[96] Since London was a city of signs (Othello stayed at the Sagittary in Venice), the zodiac and its

[92] *Works,* ed. Bond (Oxford, 1902), III, 256.
[93] Lodge, *op. cit.,* Dodsley, *op. cit.,* VII, 185.
[94] *The Pedlar's Prophecie,* sig. D1v; II *Henry IV,* Act II, scene 4, ll. 286-289; Greene, *Works,* ed. Collins, II, 98.
[95] *Op. cit.,* II, 7, 59, 427.   [96] *Op. cit.,* II, 59-61.

animals were familiar to most Englishmen. Barnes' use of
these signs in his sonnets is, of course, typical; and we must not
forget that one of the most popular school texts of the period,
the *Zodiacus vitae* of Marcellus Palingenius, though not astrological in content, used the zodiacal signs to mark its major
divisions. The most familiar use of the twelve signs in the
English poetry of the Renaissance occurs in Spenser's pageant
of the months,[97] but the astrological learning of the average
Englishman is better suggested by the humorous errors of Sir
Andrew Aguecheek and Sir Toby Belch about the anatomical
province of the sign Taurus.[98] References of these types are
not infrequently found in the literature of the reigns of Elizabeth and James; they are not exactly recondite references, but
they suppose a definite familiarity with the essentials of astrology on the reader's part. Ben Jonson, as was his custom, set all
his readers on their heads with remarks about almutens, Platic
aspects, Hyleg, and Alchochoden,[99] but Jonson was not the
man to be contented with ordinary matter. The other writers
of the period had neither his intellectual pride nor intellectual
curiosity.

The literary men's knowledge of technical astrology did not
end with these matters. The astrologer talked at length about
eclipses, although he was not certain of their sublunar effects.
Shakespeare's Gloucester follows the usual pessimistic attitude
of the astrologers when he comments drearily upon the results
of an eclipse,[100] and Othello reverses the ordinary attitude when
he insists that an eclipse should follow his crime.[101] The influence and effects of comets were universally known; the manuals of astrology were filled with accounts of the evil and
noxious rays of the bearded monsters. In Pontano's edition of
Ptolemy, the novice in astrology could learn that a comet, de-
pending on its celestial locus, forecast the death of kings and

[97] *Faerie Queene*, Bk. VII, canto 7, s. 32-44.
[98] *Twelfth Night*, Act I, scene 3, ll. 133-143.
[99] *Op. cit.*, II, 296, 322.
[100] *Lear*, Act I, scene 2, ll. 112-121.   [101] *Op. cit.*, Act V, scene 2, ll. 99-101.

princes, the alteration of governments, the advent of devastating pestilences, and the incursion of enemy hosts. In Pontano's commentary on this section, the student might also read over an impressive list of fatal comets and discover that a burning star hung over the army of Tamburlaine as it swept into Western Europe.[102] The amateur of comets might follow the trails of these celestial threateners through numerous books; some of these books like Libau's *De universitate et rerum conditarum originibus*[103] bore very innocent titles. Serious scientists of the age sought to explain the cause of the comet's deadly influence. Scipion du Pleix, who was acquainted with the findings of Copernicus and of other scientific giants, inserted an explanation of the comets' insidiousness in his *La physique ou science des choses naturelles;*[104] and Bernardo Telesio, sometimes called the father of modern science and a writer upon whom Bacon leaned most heavily, printed a solemn account of a similar nature in his *Varii de naturalibus rebus libelli.*[105] The comet was a favorite emblem for preachers declaiming about the wrath to come, and if we turn to Bishop Frederick Grau's *Of all blasing starrs in generall, as well supernatural as naturall,* we can read that God produces comets so that man may be forewarned to meet "his fatherly mercie."[106] An Englishman, however, had no need to read about comets, for a very handsome one appeared in May, 1582, and, according to Camden,[107] produced a perfectly monstrous wind and hailstorm in Norfolkshire. It is undoubtedly to this comet that Henry Howard refers when he tells the following story to illustrate the courage and common sense of Elizabeth:

I can affirme thus much, as a present witnesse by mine owne experience, that whē divers (upon greater scrupulosity then cause)

---

[102] *Op. cit.,* p. 163.
[103] *Op. cit.* (Frankfurt, 1610), pp. 445-449.
[104] *Op. cit.* (Lyons, 1620), p. 278.   [105] *Op. cit.* (Venice, 1590), p. 3v.
[106] *Op. cit.,* ed. Fleming (London, 1577), sig. B2v.
[107] *Annales Rerum Anglicarum et Hibernicarum Regnante Elizabetha* (London, 1615), pp. 329-330.

went about to disswade her maiesty (lying then at *Richmond*) from looking on the Comet which appeared last: with a courage answerable to the greatnesse of her state, she caused the window to be set open, and cast out this word, *Iacta est alia, The Dice are throwne.* Affirming that her stedfast hope and confidence was too firmly planted in the providence of God, to bee blasted or affrighted with those beames which eyther had a ground in nature whereupon to rise, or at least no warrant out of Scripture, to portend the mishaps of Princes.[108]

When the valiant queen of England talks like Caesar at the Rubicon before she opens her shutters on a comet, one is not surprised to find that the literature of her reign and that of her successor is filled with references to these stars with curled manes. The comet, though oftentimes used in rhetorical figures,[109] appears most regularly as a symbol of unspeakable horror and ill-fortune.[110] Not all writers, however, limit themselves to general references to comets, for nearly every man of letters seems to have known something about the special ills attending the appearance of these wonders. In "The Miseries of Queen Margarite," Drayton describes the attitude of the English commonalty during the occurrence of a comet and includes in his description an account of the evils that befall a country under a comet's glare:

> As when some dreadfull Comet doth appeare
> Athwart the heaven that throwes his threatning light,
> The peacefull people that at quiet were,
> Stand with wilde gazes wond'ring at the sight,
> Some Warre, some Plagues, some Famine greatly feare,
> Some falls of Kingdomes, or of men of might.[111]

[108] *Op. cit.*, p. 77.

[109] Webster, *op. cit.*, I, 173, 187, 189; Chapman, *Works,* ed. Shepherd, III, 319; Drayton, *op. cit.*, I, 74; J. Fletcher, *op. cit.*, VI, 390, 395; VII, 32; VIII, 111; *Pericles*, Act V, scene 1, l. 87; I *Henry IV*, Act III, scene 2, ll. 46-47.

[110] *Elizabethan Sonnets*, II, 394; Heywood, *op. cit.*, V, 54; *The Tragical Reign of Selimus*, ed. Bang (Malone Society Reprints, 1908), sig. C4r; J. Fletcher, *op. cit.*, III, 246; IV, 260; Greene, *Works,* ed. Grosart, V, 189; Drayton, *op. cit.*, I, 74; III, 76; *The Taming of the Shrew*, Act III, scene 2, ll. 97-98.

[111] *Op. cit.*, III, 76.

Most poets were not so eclectic as Drayton in their descriptions of comets and think of these celestial wanderers as harbingers of war[112] or as signs of sequent danger to the state.[113] Since the realm was usually in most danger during an interregnum, the appearance of a comet was feared especially as the precursor of the king's death. "When beggars die," says Shakespeare, "there are no comets seen,"[114] and sets the text in this matter for most of his fellows. It became a sort of dramatic convention to exhibit a comet of the stage variety before the death of some royal member of the dramatis personae. Tourneur's Lussurio, for example, looks at a comet, which appears in the last act of *The Revenger's Tragedy*, and utters a speech to gladden the heart of an astrologer:

> I am not pleased at that ill-knotted fire,
> That blushing, staring star. Am I not duke?
> It should not quake me now. Had it appeared
> Before, it I might then have justly feared;
> But yet they say, whom art and learning weds,
> When stars wear locks, they threaten great men's heads.[115]

Such then is the nature of the astrological learning of the Elizabethan and Jacobean men of letters, and in a way it indicates the popularity of this type of information among the ordinary citizens who were the writers' customers. When the technical astrological information of these men is added to

---

[112] Rowley, *The Noble Soldier* (Students' Facsimiles, 1913), sig. D3v; *The Tragedy of Tiberius*, sig. D4v; Jonson, *op. cit.*, III, 68.

[113] I *Henry VI*, Act I, scene 1, ll. 1-5; Act III, scene 2, ll. 31-32; J. Fletcher, *op. cit.*, VI, 17; *The Tragedy of Caesar and Pompey*, sig. B2v.

[114] *Julius Caesar*, Act II, scene 2, ll. 30-31.

[115] *The Best Plays of Webster and Tourneur*, ed. Symonds (London and New York, 1903), pp. 427-428. In Heywood (*op. cit.*, VI, 354), who was as learned in these matters as Drayton or Middleton, one comes on a rare reference to the benign influence of westering comets. For comets and kings see Webster, *op. cit.*, I, 144; Heywood, *op. cit.*, II, 212; *The Death of Robert Earl of Huntington*, Dodsley, *op. cit.*, VIII, 279; Wilkins, *op. cit.*, Dodsley, *op. cit.*, IX, 557; *Lust's Dominion; or The Lascivious Queen*, Dodsley, *op. cit.*, XIV, 175; T. D., *The Bloody Banquet* (Students' Facsimiles, 1914), sig. G3v. For the theory of a comet's origin, see Ford, *op. cit.*, II, 75; for the notion that their influence was quite subsequent to their appearance, see Greene, *Works*, ed. Grosart, II, 150; V, 36.

their philosophic attitude towards astrology, we get a sum that indicates a definite and widespread belief in the art. The fervor with which individual literary men embraced these doctrines is difficult to determine, but we can no longer say that it was accepted by only the credulous, the unenlightened, and the superstitious. There were, of course, certain objectors and certain objections. Petrarch, to mention an early, but important, figure, uses astrological references by the dozen, but he had no respect for the astrologer. Many of the English poets did not differ greatly from their Italian forerunner. They are sure that the stars have a definite influence over the character and actions of men; some of them agree with the moderate astrologers who said that this influence could be altered by education, food, climate, or the will; all of them join in attacking the activities of the unscrupulous professional astrologer. The basic attitude of the literary men of the English Renaissance is perhaps best represented by that of Doctor John Dee, Elizabeth's astrologer; in his remarks on the three enemies of astrology, Dee observes that there are those who expect too much of the art and those who grant it too little, who allow only a general and limited virtue to the planets. The last enemy is, unfortunately, the worst.

The third man is the common and vulgar *Astrologian,* or Practiser, who being not duly, artificially and perfectly furnished: yet, either for vain glory, or gain: or like a simple Dolt, and blind Bayard, both in matter and manner erreth: to the robbing of those most noble corporall Creatures, of their Naturall Vertue: being most mighty: most beneficiall to all elementall Generation, Corruption and the appurtenances: and most Harmonious in their Monarchie.[116]

It was at Dee's "third man," the vulgar astrologer, that most of the shafts of the literary men were leveled, but before we look at this target, we should notice some aspects of the moderate view as they appear in the literature of this period.

[116] *Op. cit.,* sig. G3r-G3v.

The Renaissance man of letters did not always place everything at the charge of the stars; like the earlier opponents of
astrology and the later moderate astrologers, he admitted that
other factors united with the stars to shape the characters of
men. The Moore in Peele's *Battle of Alcazar* attributes his ill-
fortunes to his stars, his mother, his nurse, the four elements,
and "all causes that have conspired in one."[117] In his *Mundus
Alter et Idem,* Joseph Hall complains of the regiment of fools
who would tie a man's manners so closely to the stars that
nothing is left to "mans owne power, nothing to the parents
natures, nothing to nurture and education."[118] Like Hall, Robert Greene, in spite of his astrological learning, continually insists that the decrees of the planets are not final, that there is
"no necessitie in their influence."[119] He tells, for instance, of
the sagacity of the great Amazon Queen, Penthesilea, who by
knowing the causes of eclipses saved her army from being infected by the fears of the astrologers.[120] In another place, however, Greene talks of a wise father who had the horoscope of
his son scrutinized by an astrologer and then thwarted the predictions of the stars "by pollicie."[121] The moderate astrologers
recommended their art to just this end. In the plays of Shakespeare we find several characters who inform us that there
is no necessity in the stars. Cassius' grammar-school maxim is
known to everyone, but Helena is, without doubt, closer to the
notions of the Elizabethan age when she gives her answer to
men of Cassius' kidney.

> Our remedies oft in ourselves do lie,
> Which we ascribe to heaven. The fated sky
> Gives us free scope, only doth backward pull
> Our slow designs when we ourselves are dull.[122]

[117] *Op. cit.,* I, 287-288.
[118] *The Discovery of a New World,* ed. Brown (Cambridge, Mass., 1937), p. 11.
[119] *Works,* ed. Grosart, IX, 189.
[120] *Ibid.,* VI, 207-208; also III, 68.   [121] *Ibid.,* V, 185-186.
[122] *All's Well,* Act I, scene 1, ll. 231-234; see also Lyly, *op. cit.,* II, 433; *Tancred
and Gismunda,* Dodsley, *op. cit.,* VII, 92.

In none of these literary attitudes is there a denial of the essential doctrines of astrology. The poets say that the stars do not control all things or that the influence of the stars may be altered; they do not deny that the stars are causes. Even Cassius does not question the powers of the stars; he simply shelters them from mortal contumely. There are, however, among the fictions of Elizabethan and Jacobean literary men a limited number of characters who do not believe in astrology. One of these realists is Shakespeare's Edmund. The world, says Edmund, blames its disasters on the stars and accounts for its monstrous citizens by insisting on "an enforc'd obedience of planetary influence":

> An admirable evasion of whoremaster man, to lay his goatish disposition on the charge of a star! My father compounded with my mother under the dragon's tail; and my nativity was under *Ursa major;* so that it follows, I am rough and lecherous. Fut, I should have been that I am, had the maidenliest star in the firmament twinkled on my bastardizing.[123]

In John Fletcher's *Love's Cure,* we meet a character similar to Edmund, one Alguazier, who insists on the virtues of free will, but who elects to use his free will to follow the inclination of his stars.[124] A third reviler of astrology is D'Amville of *The Atheist's Tragedy,* who like Alguazier is chiefly interested in the gold standard and who insists that it is money and not the stars, those agents of God, that controls the destinies of men.[125] Finally, there is Chapman's Byron. We remember the scene in *Byron's Conspiracie* where the protagonist goes to the astrologer La Brosse, and, learning that he is doomed by the stars, strikes the stargazer down. To the audience he says:

> Spight of the Starres, and all Astrologie,
> I will not loose my head: or if I do,
> A hundred thousand heads shall off before.
> I am a nobler substance then the Starres,

---

[123] *Lear,* Act I, scene 2, ll. 137-145; also Act I, scene 2, ll. 112-121, 152-163.
[124] *Op. cit.,* VII, 193.   [125] *Op. cit.,* p. 323.

And shall the baser over-rule the better?
Or are they better, since they are the bigger?
I have a will, and faculties of choise,
To do, or not to doe this: the starres have none,
They know not why they shine, more then this Taper,
Nor how they worke, nor what: ile change my course,
Ile peece-meale pull, the frame of all my thoughts,
And cast my will into another mould:
And where are all your Caput Algols then?
Your Plannets all, being underneath the earth,
At my nativitie: what can they doe?
Malignant in aspects? in bloudy houses?
Wilde fire consume them; one poore cup of wine,
More then I use, that my weake braine will beare,
Shall make them drunke and reele out of their spheres,
For any certaine act they can enforce.[126]

This is a brave speech, but in the sequel play Byron does "loose" his head.

Now all of these opponents of astrology are not out-and-out villains, but they are all skeptics, all fellow realists. They are Marlowes, Harriots, and Warners; they insist on facts and common sense; they refuse to accept the notion that all first principles are based on intuition; they are the ancestors of the masters of modern scientism. The Renaissance could see where men of this type were going and what would happen to civilization should they reach their goals; hence the Renaissance, which was still somewhat medieval, was both fearful and suspicious of them. Lafeu tells one all about these Edmunds and D'Amvilles, these scientists and Puritans, in a rather trenchant speech: "They say miracles are past; and we have our philosophical persons, to make modern and familiar, things supernatural and causeless. Hence it is that we make trifles of terrors, ensconcing ourselves into seeming knowledge, when we should submit ourselves to an unknown fear."[127] The literary men of the Renaissance knew what happened to such peo-

[126] Op. cit., II, 224-228.　　　[127] All's Well, Act II, scene 3, ll. 1-6.

ple; eventually these freethinkers met bad ends. Unfortunately they often involved others in their personal catastrophes. In general, the writers who served under Elizabeth and James did not question the basic doctrines of astrology and were doubtful of those who did; however, like John Dee and sensible astrologers everywhere, they had small love for the professional astrologer who insisted on the accuracy of his predictions. Astrology, said these men, is an exact science, but its devotees are inexact; only too often they are rank amateurs. These men, the satirists pilloried in the mock almanack and prognostication. There was another group, however, against whom the men of letters sharpened the barbs of their arrows; this group was composed of fakers, of mountebanks, and of charlatans who used the science of astrology as a shears with which to fleece the poor, the ignorant, and the credulous members of the English nation.

Against the whole tribe of stargazing scoundrels, the Renaissance men of letters poured out the vials of their wrath. The fact that their anger was directed against a certain type of astrologer and not against astrology is suggested by Tomkis' play, *Albumasar,* the *ur*-type of Dryden's *Mock Astrologer,* which was presented before James at Cambridge in 1614. *Albumasar* tells the familiar story of the old man who wishes to marry a young woman and hires a false astrologer to aid him to attain his end. The play is an attack on astrologers of Albumasar's type, just as *The Alchemist* is an attack on charlatans like Subtle, but in spite of this intention, there are several places in the play where Tomkis not only speaks approvingly but poetically of astrology.[128] We imagine that Tomkis and his fellows thought of astrology much as Phillip Stubbes did in 1583, when he discussed it in *The Second Part of the Anatomie of Abuses:* "I neither condemne astronomie nor astrologie, nor yet the makers of prognostications, or almanacks for the yeere. But I condemne the abuse in them both, and wish they were

[128] *Albumasar: A Comedy as it is Acted at the Theatre Royal in Drury-Lane* (London, 1747), pp. 23, 58.

reduced to the same perfection that they ought, and to be used to the same endes and purposes which they were ordeined for."[129]

With few exceptions, the writers of the English Renaissance portray the astrologer as a rogue; sometimes, as in Webster's bedlam scene,[130] the follies of the professional astrologer are shown through the lenses of madness. Jonson hated the astrologer with a grand passion. Subtle, we recall, is an astrologer as well as an alchemist; Practice of *The Magnetic Lady* is an amateur steeped in Allestree; and Merefool of *The Fortunate Isles* is deceived by an astrologer. In spite of these and other attacks on astrologers, the great Ben was able to cast a figure and was not above cozening a lady in the suburbs by pretending to be an astrologer.[131] The false astrologer does not come single spy into Renaissance letters, for in Fletcher's *The Bloody Brother*,[132] we come on a battalion of them. The five rascals of this piece—Norbrett, LaFisk, Rusee, DeBube, and Pipeau— converse in the most complicated of astrological jargons which suggests that the author of this scene knew both astrology and astrologers. Like Jonson, Joseph Hall could not countenance the cheating astrologer. In the *Mundus Alter et Idem,* he consigns the astrologers to the hamlet of Lyers-bury in Theevingen; and in the seventh satire of the second book of the *Virgidemiarum,* he satirizes the whole tribe in a fashion that recalls the more sprightly minds among the polemicists. Some of the most conventional of Hall's jibes are echoed by Taffata in Lodowick Barry's *Ram-Alley* when he comments on these mountebanks who never have five shillings, yet who venture to tell others where to seek money. They forecast the deaths of other men, says Taffata, and do not foresee that they themselves shall be hanged for pilfering table-cloths.[133] None of

---

[129] *Op. cit.,* ed. Furnivall (London, 1882), p. 62.

[130] *Op. cit.,* II, 95.

[131] *Notes of Conversations with Ben Jonson made by William Drummond of Hawthornden,* ed. Harrison (London, 1923), p. 14.

[132] *Op. cit.,* IV, 295-299.   [133] *Op. cit.,* Dodsley, *op. cit.,* X, 284.

these remarks is fire new, for Ficino had said the same thing in the preface to his projected attack on astrologers. Almost all English writers of this era agree with these declarations, and the author of the late interlude *The Conflict of Conscience* was not unmindful of this tradition when he represented the character Hypocrisy as an astrologer, and made him, as Shakespeare made Autolycus, a native of Mercury.[134] This was a personification that was applauded for the next hundred years.

We should be highly pleased if we could feel that this literary attack on the dishonest astrologer was begotten by the nobility and moral purpose of the men of letters. In some instances this was without question the case; Hall and Jonson often moved their pens according to the dictates of what they felt to be their public duty. Other writers may have had other motives. The astrologer deceived and prospered; the literary man labored and starved. The success of the rascally astrologer burdened the literary men's sense of distributive justice. The astrologer in Lyly's *Galathea* is no thing of virtue, but he fares well. The astrological brothers whom Nashe castigates in *Have With You to Saffron Walden* succeeded after their own light, although Nashe's *Pierce Penniless*[135] would have us believe otherwise. Greene is vastly annoyed because the professional astrologer was honored[136] and visited by great throngs of women,[137] and Sincerity, a character in the late morality, *The Three Ladies of London,* admits that she would have had a much better living, had she been an astrologer.[138] But it is probably Donne, in his poverty-ridden eleventh elegy, who perhaps best expresses the annoyance of literary men with the bank balances of astrologers:

> Or let mee creepe to some dread Conjurer,
> That with phantastique scheames fils full much paper;
> Which hath divided heaven in tenements,

---

[134] *Ibid.,* VI, 46-47.
[135] *Op. cit.,* I, 196-197.
[137] *Ibid.,* VII, 139.

[136] *Works,* ed. Grosart, IV, 217.
[138] *Op. cit.,* Dodsley, *op. cit.,* VI, 287.

And with whores, theeves, and murderers stuft his rents
So full, that though hee passe them all in sinne,
He leaves himselfe no roome to enter in.

Such is the literary opinion of astrology and the astrologer, and it does little more than reflect the position of the moderate astrologers, the attitude that they had taken for more than a century. The great mortal mass, since it was much below the literary men in intelligence, must have found the ideas of the extreme astrologers very attractive. It was on this mass that these astrologers and their imitators among the charlatans fattened, and it was against this class of astrologers that the Elizabethan and Jacobean men of letters cried out. Nevertheless, astrology, "Divine Astrology," was sacrosanct, and enjoyed for many years its pleasant speculations on the mountain of the muses.

CHAPTER V

ELIZABETHAN AND JACOBEAN SATIRES ON THE ALMANACK AND PROGNOSTICATION

THOUGH Elizabethan and Jacobean men of letters agreed for the most part with the views of the moderate astrologers, they united like so many fox-hunting squires to ride down the pretenses of the extreme school of judicial astrologers. To them the sillinesses and deceits of this group, which included so many rogues and malefactors, were documented by the almanacks and prognostications with which the stalls of the booksellers groaned. The writers of this age thought of the almanack and prognostication with mixed feelings: it was a thing of eternal humor as it had been to Pico, Turnebé, Montaigne, and others before them; and it was, too often, the sole furniture of many private libraries, the untrustworthy source of faith and learning for numerous foolish and simple Englishmen.

That it was the superstitious and the untutored who were the regular purchasers of these catchpenny publications is suggested by the reliance of Shakespeare's mechanic actors on an almanack[1] and by a similar instance in *The Witch of Edmonton*.[2] Jonson sends the childish Abel Drugger to consult Subtle about the rubrication of his almanack,[3] and draws the picture of Sordido, who is one of the prognostication-trusting farmers of Fulke or Perkins brought to life.[4] Though the almanack is

---

[1] *Midsummer Night's Dream*, Act III, scene 1, ll. 52-56.
[2] Ford, *op. cit.*, III, 198.　　　　[3] *Op. cit.*, II, 17.
[4] *Ibid.*, I, 76-77. Sordido's renunciation (p. 105) is interesting: "Tut, these starmonger knaves, who would trust 'hem? One says 'dark and rainy,' when 'tis as clear as crystal; another says, 'tempestuous blasts and storms,' and 'twas as calm as a milk-bowl? here be sweet rascals for a man to credit his whole fortunes with! You sky-staring coxcombs you, you fat-brains, out upon you; you are good for nothing but to sweat night-caps, and make rug-gowns dear! You learned men, and have not a legion of devils 'a vostre service! a vostre service!' by Heavens, I think I shall die a better scholar than they: but soft, how now sirrah?"

frequently mentioned as the vade mecum of fools, it is more
regularly described as misleading or untruthful. When in *The
Purple Island* Phineas Fletcher paints the portrait of Superstition, he notices that "her onely bible is an Erra Pater,"[5] and
Erra Pater was a fabulous Hebrew astrologer over whose name
prognostications were issued during the whole century. In
Philomela, Greene remarks that woman's flattery is like the
sayings of the almanack-makers, who proclaim "that for a most
faire daye that prooves most clowdye";[6] and Joseph Hall, in
the preface to his satires, remarks that if everyone's taste were
satisfied in art, the state of literature would be like that of the
weather should "every almanack be verified."[7] Webster, whose
skill in astrology has been recognized, describes a lying character as an almanack-maker,[8] and places the following words
about the cheating astrologers in the mouth of the supposedly
honest conjurer employed by Brachiano:

> . . . besides these
> Such a whole reame of Almanacke-makers, figure-flingers,
> Fellowes indeed that onely live by stealth,
> Since they do meerely lie about stolne goods
> Thei'd make men thinke the divell were fast and loose,
> With speaking fustian Lattine. . . .[9]

An amusing scene, concerning the nature of the almanack and
prognostication and the trust of the intellectually immature in
it, occurs in the second *Returne from Parnassus* play; the can-
didate, who has the significant name of Immerito, is questioned
by Sir Raderick about his knowledge in astronomy, which is,
of course, his knowledge of almanacks.[10] If we desire, however, a full-length photograph of the prognosticator, we turn

[5] *Op. cit.,* II, 96; see also Marston, *op. cit.,* III, 218.
[6] *Works,* ed. Grosart, XI, 120; see also VIII, 127.
[7] *Satires,* ed. Warton-Singer (London, 1824), p. xciv; for other references see
Middleton, *op. cit.,* II, 131; V, 80; Heywood, *op. cit.,* IV, 9; Rowley, *op. cit.,* sig.
F4r; Chapman, *Works,* ed. Shepherd, I, 141; III, 23.
[8] *Op. cit.,* I, 168.   [9] *Ibid.,* I, 132.
[10] *Op. cit.,* ed. Macray (Oxford, 1886), pp. 114-117.

to Sir Thomas Overbury's character of "An Almanack-Maker,"
and there we find references not only to the insolent vapidity
of the prognostication, but also to the astrologer's poetry, which
has a "worse pace than ever had Rochester Hackney."

We have already observed that Jonson had no regard for the
cheating astrologer, and so we should expect him to level his
acid-tipped pen at the writers of prognostications. In this ex-
pectation we are not disappointed. Oliver Cob, the bruised
water-carrier of *Every Man in His Humor,* is disgusted with almanacks for the good lower-class reason that they indicate the
fasting days.[11] Truewit, in *The Silent Woman,* proposes to eliminate Morose by printing a false almanack which would cause
him to take the air on coronation day and be slain by the noise
of the cannonading.[12] Compass of *The Magnetic Lady* makes
fun of the almanack-makers and their books by questioning
Practice, who reads these works assiduously, confesses and
prays according to their directions, and makes love and selects
his mistresses by the calendar's listing of favorable and unfavorable days.[13] Looking over the masques, we discover that
Jonson did not hesitate to attack the almanack-makers before
their royal clients. The chauvinistic inclination of some of the
English astrologers is mimicked in Johphiel of *The Fortunate
Isles,* who tells Merefool of one who is busy writing a confutation of a French almanack.[14] The ingredients of a prognosticator are listed in *Mercury Vindicated from the Alchemists.*

Then another is a fencer in the mathematic, or the town's
cunning-man, a creature of art too; a supposed secretary to the
stars; but indeed a kind of lying intelligencer from those parts. His
materials, if I be not deceived, were juice of almanacs, extraction
of ephemerides, scales of the globe, filings of figures, dust of the
twelve houses, conserve of questions, salt of confederacy, a pound
of adventure, a grain of skill, and a drop of truth.[15]

[11] *Op. cit.,* I, 32.
[12] *Ibid.,* I, 409.
[13] *Ibid.,* II, 404.
[14] *Ibid.,* III, 194.
[15] *Ibid.,* III, 99.

Besides allusions of these types, which suggest the attitude of the writer toward the almanack and its composer, there are, of course, innumerable occasions when the reference is quite casual. Rosaline refers to the almanack, for instance, when she calls Katherine "my red dominical, my golden letter,"[16] and Autolycus, warning of punishment, plans it for "the hottest day prognostication proclaimes."[17] Like other of the dramatists, Webster was quick to see the popular appeal of almanack metaphors. George of *Anything for a Quiet Life* speaks of a woman standing "like your Fasting-days before Red letters in the Almanack,"[18] and in the same play, the barber remarks that since his almanack says that "the Sign is in Taurus,"[19] he would not dare to cut his own throat. In Marston's *Parasitaster,* Herod suggests that Dondolo's wit, like last year's almanack, is out of date;[20] and in Fletcher's *The Chances,* one of the characters compares himself to the astrological man found in the early leaves of most almanacks.[21] References of these types are not uncommon in this era; they appear almost as frequently as the conventional astrological allusions. The almanack and prognostication is not seriously attacked by the men of letters; it is simply a good subject for a jest whenever one needs one.

Since the prognostication is attacked in most of the formal polemics against astrology and not vigorously defended by even the moderate astrologers, since it is often the subject of humorous and sometimes of sarcastic literary references, and since it was burlesqued and parodied for several centuries, we should pause to survey the history and nature of the victim of so much mirth before we chronicle the early years of the mock prognostication. To compile a history of the English almanack is one of the most difficult of tasks, for the almanack is an excellent example of the type of printed paper that is seldom preserved. With rare exceptions, it was a work valuable for only

---

[16] *Love's Labour's Lost,* Act V, scene 2, ll. 44-45.
[17] *The Winter's Tale,* Act IV, scene 4, l. 815.
[18] *Op. cit.,* IV, 117.   [19] *Ibid.,* IV, 104; see also II, 81, IV, 204.
[20] *Op. cit.,* II, 150.   [21] *Op. cit.,* IV, 213; see also IV, 184.

one year, and at the end of that period it was probably read to tatters. Those almanacks and prognostications that are now preserved have often survived through the accident of being bound with other books, and there is no great collection of these works in any library to which a student may go to study the evolution and development of this type of book in England. Fortunately, however, Mr. Bosanquet has canvassed a vast number of collections for his admirable bibliographical study of these little books, and any survey of the almanack and prognostication must be based on his labors.[22]

Although the manuscript almanack was not unknown in the Middle Ages, Bosanquet was unable to find any works of this nature published in England before 1492. The earliest almanacks and prognostications were not compiled by Englishmen, but were put together by continental astrologers and translated by some servant of the English printer who brought them out. For the first forty years of the sixteenth century, the most popular foreign prognosticators were the Laets, Thibault, and Parron. The Laets, who founded a dynasty, are most interesting for they composed at least half of the almanacks printed in England between 1492 and 1550. These men were Flemings, and for more than eighty years they followed the profession of almanack-maker and prognosticator. The first member of the family to compile these books was John Laet, who was succeeded by his son Jasper and his grandsons Jasper II and Alphonsus. All of the Laets advertised themselves as doctors of physick and astronomy, departments of learning that were, of course, complementary. Unlike the printing practice of the continent, which favored the broadside almanack and prognostication, the English translations of the Laets' almanacks were usually uttered in quarto or octavo. The title page

[22] *English Printed Almanacks and Prognostications* (London, 1917); "English Printed Almanacks and Prognostications. Corrigenda and Addenda," *The Library*, 4th Series, VIII, 456-477; "English Seventeenth-Century Almanacks," *ibid.*, X, 361-397; see also H. R. Plomer, "English Almanacs and Almanac-Makers of the Seventeenth Century," *Notes and Queries*, 6th Series, XII, 243, 323, 383, 462.

of these books was ordinarily followed by a description of forthcoming eclipses, by a seasonal prognostication indicating the floods and droughts to be expected, by a forecast of the weather attendant on each lunar phase, and by an announcement of wars and plagues. The latter sections of these books were usually filled with predictions for individual rulers, nations, and principal cities. In 1520, Jasper Laet I made the following prediction for England: "The moost noble and plentifull kyngdome of Englonde this yere shall suffre damage in their bestis & fruyt. A litil murmour shalbe in the comon peple yt lightly shalbe layd downe. The eclyps of the moone was in the opposicion signe of Englond."

The year 1545 saw the publication of a prognostication and almanack by Andrew Boorde. Boorde, who has got greater fame for his work on medicine and the humor of some of his proposed remedies, states carefully that he is an Englishman. This announcement leads Bosanquet to believe that Boorde was the first Englishman to compose an almanack, but we feel that were this the case, Boorde would not hide his light under such a modest bushel. Perhaps Boorde realized that he would have many foreign competitors and was simply playing the old game of "Englishmen for my money." It is in the preface to this work, which exists as a one-leaf fragment in the Bagford collection, that Boorde admits that prognosticating is against the laws of God and the Realm and indicates that he is thinking in terms of the act of 1541 against "fond and fantastical Prophecies"[23] which may have made Englishmen chary about issuing prognostications under their own names. The example of Boorde and the laxity with which laws against prophets— as long as their predictions did not threaten the throne—were

[23] Numerous laws against prophecy were passed during the century, but it is difficult to decide whether or not the astrologer was included in the bill. The law of 1541 was repealed in 1549, but there were discussions in Commons and another act was issued in the same year. Commons discussed bills in 1554 and 1558 and passed a further act in 1562. Face threatens Subtle with the act of 1541 in *The Alchemist* (op. cit., I, 255-258).

enforced probably encouraged other English astrologers to come forward in print.

Practically all of the extant almanacks written by English-men were printed in London although many of them were calculated for the meridians of other English cities. Among the first astrologers to adopt this custom was Anthony Ascham, whose almanack for 1548 was computed for the city of York. Ascham limited his prognostications, however, to the nature of the weather and the types of expected diseases, and so escaped the main burden of astrological iniquity; he also began his year in January and by this set a precedent for subsequent English astrologians, who were not always skilled in astronomy. With the opening years of Elizabeth's reign, numerous English almanack-makers competed with one another for the pennies of their countrymen. Among these astrologues were Cuningham, who issued almanacks and prognostications in 1558, 1559, 1560, 1561, 1564, 1565, 1566; Vaughn, who printed his compilations in 1559 and 1561; Low, whose almanacks were published in 1558, 1559, 1560, 1563, 1564, 1565, 1566, 1567, 1569, and 1574; and Securis, who issued his compositions in 1562, 1563, 1564, 1566, 1568, 1569, 1570, 1573, 1574, and 1579. Most of these names are familiar to the reader of the English polemics against astrology, but Securis, who was a favorite of Gabriel Harvey,[24] is probably the most original of all these compilers; for, as Bosanquet observes, he always adds something to his prognos-tication of special interest to his readers. In 1564, for example, he informs his purchasers that rhubarb, senna, and manna may be taken at any time without danger; in 1569 he prints the baneful verses of Regiomontanus for 1588; and in 1568 he plays heretic to the best astrological principles when he writes, "I saye al dayes are good to a good man, after a certaine respecte and meaninge." This last remark of Securis might suggest a trend which moved towards Heydon's eventual assumption

[24] *Op. cit.*, II, 131; for a reference to the astrologer Kett see II, 169.

that the regenerate were immune to the hostile influences of the stars.

Before passing to a further phase of the almanack industry in the reign of Elizabeth, we may pause to look through the pages of Securis' *A New Almanacke and Prognostication for the yeare of our Lord God MDLXXI*, a typical example of this form of Elizabethan reading matter. The prognostication begins with the golden number, the circle of the sun, the epact, and the dominical letter; these conventional announcements are followed by a list of the principal feasts, an explanation of the signs, and the astrological man in all his nudity and zodiacal splendor. Securis predicts the eclipses and advises on physick. The reader is warned against purging and blood-letting in very hot or cold weather; he is told that the body must not be touched with a surgical instrument when the sun, moon, or lord of the ascendant is in the sign governing the affected part. Under no circumstances should one phlebotomize in Gemini, Leo, the last half of Libra, the first twelve degrees of Scorpio, Taurus, Virgo, and Capricorn, or in the two days anterior or posterior to the change of the moon. Clysters and gentle purgations, Securis informs his clients, may be used at all times, and blood may be let at any time, of course, in diseases arising from a fullness of blood. After this medical lore come Securis' predictions for the year. During the first six months of 1571, many oppositions to the moon weakly placed in the first degree of Libra and the concourse of planets in the west angle of the heavens indicate that many people of the common sort will lose their possessions through fire, robbery, and war. The fact, however, that Saturn is retrograde in Scorpio and that Mars is combust with Jupiter dominant may alleviate these stellar visitations. There will be, nevertheless, many diseases among men and cattle; rivers will run low; the air will be corrupt; there will be great winds with little rain; and the people will be unstable and inconstant. The last half of the year, according to the predictions of Securis, is to be even drearier. Droughts, inconstant weather, agues, murder, robbery, and open, assault fill the calendar from July to December. Cities like Constantinople, Venice, Milan, York, and St. Andrews, and countries like France, Scotland, and Holland that are under the dominance of Cancer are direfully threatened. Saturn, Securis thinks, will bring a scarcity of fruits and corn, a provocation to war, torrential rains, and, in the latter part of winter, many shipwrecks. Women, writes Securis, will bear children before term, and there will be difficulty with ambassadors; Mars will cause the death of many in middle age, incite servants to vex their masters, and bring a great scarcity of water; and Venus, since she is *in domo cadente,* will cause many to give themselves to acts of lechery. This melancholy, but safely trite, series of predictions is followed by several pages of quotations from the fathers and the Scriptures on the proximity of Judgment Day. One can only surmise the reason for this. Perhaps Securis wished to give his prognostication a tinge of sanctity; perhaps he was fanatically religious in the fashion of the later preachers of doom.

Securis was, of course, not the only interesting almanack-maker of this period. Francis Cox, whose misfortunes have been related, was one of his contemporaries, and Bomelius, who ran into various difficulties in England and eventually became the favorite magician of Ivan IV, was another. In 1571, however, two printers, Richard Watkins and James Roberts, received a patent for the printing of almanacks and prognostications, and their first publication seems to have been Thomas Hill's almanack and prediction for 1572, which bears the imprimatur "Cum privilegio Regiae Maiestatis." After this date Watkins and Roberts became the official publishers of these compositions and printed the works of Hill, Securis, Low, Mounslowe, and other astrologers who predicted during the early part of Elizabeth's reign. As these almanack-makers died, their places were taken by newcomers like Hartgill, Norton, Harvey, Forster, Frende, Gray, and Dade, who made their appearances between 1580 and 1590, and by Watson, Westhawe, and others who began to compile almanacks between 1590 and 1600. With the death of Watkins in 1599, the partnership of Watkins and Roberts was dissolved, and though Roberts assigned his rights to other printers during the remainder of Elizabeth's reign, he lost his patent upon the accession of James, who granted the privilege of publishing these books to the Stationers' Company. In 1616 a second and broader patent was granted the Stationers and this new writ protected their monopoly for the whole of James' reign.

Of the new group of almanack-makers, the most popular and most individual in the compilation of prognostications were Buckminister, Forster, and Frende. Buckminister began to put together almanacks in the early 1560's and followed this profession for at least thirty-five years. He had strong protestant inclinations, and in his almanack for 1590 he apologizes for listing the saints in his calendar and says that they are certain persons "who have lyved long heretofore, and whereof some have been famous for Learnyng and good lyfe, and have also confirmed their Doctrine by tormentes and death." These names he adds to his work only "as notes and markes of some certaine matters." Like some of his competitors of whom Overbury spoke, Buckminister was something of a poet. Bosanquet attributes two anthems in Sternhold and Hopkins to him,[25] and he was the author of a patriotic hymn which began with the words, "O Lorde preserve our gratious Queene." In some of his later almanacks and prognostications, he cannot resist the poet's temptation to see himself in print and so he slips his verses in with his predictions. In his almanack for 1589, one finds these admonitory lines:

> Awake for shame, why snort you thus and sleepe?
> Why lye you styll when tyme it is to ryse?
> Why cause you not this slome away to creepe?
> Why doth it styll thus lurke within your eyes?

[25] *English Printed Almanacks and Prognostications*, p. 44.

Awake I say, ye worldlynges nothing wyse,
Destruction and wrath els sodenly wyll come:
Awake therefore and shake away this slome.

The career of Doctor Richard Forster has been related, but
he is especially interesting as an almanack-maker because he
seems to have written for an upperclass clientele. In 1575 he
published an *Ephemerides Meteorographicae,* which he dedicated to Robert, Earl of Leicester. This work is written entirely in Latin and contains a brief history and panegyric of the
astrological and astronomical sciences. It is a work of some
technical completeness, and its contents are quite beyond the
intellectual grasp of the ordinary purchasers of the vernacular
prognostications; nevertheless, it contains the conventional
predictions about the weather and diseases that one is accus-
tomed to find in all the other almanacks. Gabriel Frende, the
third member of this group, we learn from his almanacks,
was a practitioner of medicine and astrology. Frende seems to
have been compiling almanacks as early as 1583 and to have
lived at Canterbury. A special feature of Frende's almanacks
is the interleaved blank pages that were provided for the purchasers' notes, and Bosanquet declares that the 1587-1592 series
which are preserved in the library of Canterbury Cathedral
contain copious notes and faithful observations on the accuracy
of Frende's forecasts of the weather. Like Buckminister,
Frende also courted the muse, but he was by no means an
important contender for a place on Parnassus, as a few lines
from his prognostication for 1589 will prove:

Thou hast my gesse at dayly weather,
Here present in thy viewe,
My credite shall not lie thereon,
That every word is true:
Yet some to please I thought it best
To shewe my mynde among the rest.

Frende is probably better at prose than at verse, for, in the
main, he always adopts an easy, familiar tone in voicing his

predictions which suggests that he thought of himself as the immediate neighbor of most of his clients. At times, however, Frende is quite disturbed by the wicked practices of vulgar charlatans who steal the bread from the mouths of serious and sincere practitioners of the astrological arts. On these occasions he dips his pen in gall and writes with that peculiar joy that invaded the bosom of an Elizabethan when the summons to controversy was given. The acid side of Frende is illustrated by some of his remarks in his 1589 prognostication.

But this caveat by the way, that whosoever ventureth thus to Purge and Cleanse the body without the counsell of an expert and honest Phisition, may chaunce to be sicker, and worser of his phisicke, then of his former uncleaness: wherefore I would advise everyone that hath need o the Phisitions helpe, yf he have any care of his owne sounde welfare, to seeke to such as are learned, and advised in their profession, and to let all other Dogleaches, Horse-leaches, lacklatten Dotterelles, ignoraunt cooseners, and deceyuyng mates, passe to such places and workes, as are more fitte and decent for them, then the least phisicall inspection, or Chyrurgicall instru-ment, whereunto in trueth, they are even as fitte and meete as an asse to the Harpe, accordyng to the common proverbe. Well, I besieche God reforme them, that they may one day see their owne follyes, and abuses: and in the meane tyme I pray God all honest, and well disposed persons may take heede of them so, that they be never untangled, or mangled by them, or any such.

At the death of Queen Elizabeth, the English almanack and prognostication was completely standardized; it could almost be compiled by formula. The composition always began with the golden number, the circle of the sun, the dates from Crea-tion and the Conquest, and the principal holidays. Advice on the proper times for planting, castrating, and bloodletting fol-lowed, and if his portrait had not been published earlier in the octavo, the zodiacal man was now added. After this matter, the astrologer printed his calendar and his notices of special astronomical spectacles like eclipses. The almanack always

concluded with the compiler's predictions for each season and
month of the year. Since the authors of burlesque almanacks
always base their satire on the prognostication, and since only
one of them parodied the full scope of the serious almanack, a
liberal number of illustrations drawn from the almanacks of
the year 1603 will enable the reader to comprehend the targets
at which the burlesquers fired.

The astrologers Walter Gray, William Mathew, and Doctor
John Dade issued calendars and prognostications for the year
of Elizabeth's death. Walter Gray's almanack is distinguished
by small woodcuts delineating the monthly activities of man
and by a prose style of some vigor. His prognostication for the
summer of 1603 shows that he was possessed of a fairly salty
vocabulary.

The Sunne on the 12. of June being at the uttermost bound of
his Northerne progresse, even with the period of his accesse to
Cancer: This Sommer quarter began, wherein there is great hope
of pacifycation of former discorde, though rumours serving, as
dreadfull dreames, may cause an impression of feare to stay intended
iorneyes. Some Southerne shire will receive quiet by a great Magis-
trate, or Prince of the same clyme: whose wasted partes, yieldes
gaine to neerer neighbours: So as Venus now seemes to lull Mars
asleepe more pleasing and mutually embraced, then seemly applauded: which seemes peppered with pestiferous sickenes of deadly
qualitie: besides other, of longer continuance more painefull than
dangerous: as aches in the head, ioynts, thighes, and huckle boanes,
the heavens often raging with thunders and overblowing windes,
threatens scarsitie towards the North. The Sunne now the xiii of
September peysing the day with the night in equall ballance, when
he entered the first minute of Libra, a signe equinocticall, and the
daily house of Venus: who now within the reach of his beames,
there associate with Mercury, one of the Plannets, signifying rayne,
where weake and in combustion: with other (causes too long to
recite) threatens, glymmers, and sights in the ayer: great and stout
windes, and stormes of divers being: as hayle, rayne, and snowe:
towards the end of this quarter, an hard frost to ensue: yet not

much offensive to seede, plants, and graine now set or sowne though otherwise hurtfull, to such thinges as are nowe to be gathered, with divers such maladies mentioned before, as now to raygne, as melancholy passions, causing griefes of the hart and breast, toyes of the mind &C. Some braules presently quieted, are now to revive, and eftsoons to be suppressed by Schollers and grave men: whose well employed censures, will countervaile their endevours with condigne merrit, and generall applause.

Another almanack for 1603 was composed by William Mathew, who describes himself as a practitioner of Ryegate in the county of Surrey. His prognostications, which are rectified for his own city and for the southern parts of England, are also hallowed by appropriate quotations from the second chapter of St. Luke. Mathew's almanack is not especially unusual; it does, however, provide the reader with rules for judging the course of a disease by the phases of the moon. If the illness began on the third day of the moon, the patient may "with due regarde in Phisick" be recovered; if the patient sickened on the seventh day, he has no more than three months to live; if the disease started on the sixteenth day, the patient shall be "in great danger of death if he take the open ayre"; and if the illness commenced on the twenty-third day, "after a few dayes he shall dye." Mathew's prediction for the summer is shorter than Gray's; it is also different.

Concerning the disposition of the weather, I doe gather it will be a reasonable hotte Summer, because I doe finde in the ascendent Leo, a hotte and a fierie signe, the Sunne entering into the xi house, Mercurie in the xii house, Venus placed in Leo in the ascendent. The Moone in the x house, Iupiter and Saturne being retrograde, being placed in the fift house in Sagittarie, and Mars entering into the fourth house, so that the weather will be very hotte, which will breede strange and burning Feavers amongst young children, and many dye thereof.

With the summer predictions of Gray and Mathew, one may compare that of Dade, whose prophecy is much more

dreadful than that of either of his competitors and who seems
to have been of a very saturnine complexion. After praying that
God would grant the English comfort during the cold of the
winter and salvation for their souls, Dade describes a very
pessimistic spring and then writes almost cheerfully of the
summer:

> Summer (accounted the third part of the yeere Astronomicall)
> beginneth at the Sunnes ingresse into the first minute of Cancer, at
> which time he is in his neerest proximitie to our verticall point,
> making his greatest declination towards the North from the Equi-
> noctiall, causing the Summer or Estivall Solstice, which shall be
> this yeere on Monday the xi of June.
> Touching the condition and state of the weather, herein it may
> be seene in the dayly inclination of the weather.
> The sicknesses of this time are divers and greevous, threatned
> as well to men as to women, as burning agues, Plurisies, Frensies,
> hotte Apostumes divers paines in the head, noysome Sweatings,
> sundrie inflammations, besides the Pestilence in divers places, and
> Pestilentiall Fevers, with some strange and new infirmities, proceed-
> ing especially of hotte and chollericke humors, wherewith many
> shall bee vexed, and not a fewe bereft of their lives this quarter.

The learned almanack-makers, we notice, are united in
their pessimism although they seem to disagree in everything
else. It is characteristic of predictors to announce only the evil
and the dire, but we feel that they should agree on the first
day of summer. The generalness and commonplaceness of
these prognostications are their second common characteristic,
and one that the authors of the burlesque almanacks were
quick to exaggerate for the amusement of the reader and the
humiliation of the astrologers. Neither Gray nor Mathew nor
Dade employ the literary frills and poetic devices that some of
the other astrologers employed; without doubt it was this pre-
tension to polite letters that annoyed the satirists as much as
anything else and brought down their wrath on the heads of
the astrologers.

If we wish to observe the vice of style among the fashioners of almanacks, we can turn for an example to the prognostication published in 1604 by Thomas Johnson. In many ways Johnson's almanack is quite conventional, but the author, a native of Loughborough, was addicted to sprinkling his pages with homemade verse and delivering his premonstrations in a form of rich, purple prose. Before Johnson announces his forecast for the year, he provides himself with a literary loophole.

As touching other events, whereof some perchaunce may expect at mine hands, I stand doubtful, for if they proove not as ye Oracles of Appollo then are we censured by the contempt: if they proove true, (nay it may be too true) then stand we in danger of checke, according to the old verse.

The time never was, neither ever I thinke will be,
That truth unshent should speake in all things free.

So that whether we hit the marke or misse it, although there can come no hurt any way, yet doe wee purchase displiasure: But by your patience.

Johnson, like other astrologers of this date, seems also to feel that he should defend astrology, and devotes a leaf of his little octavo to a list of ancient predictions that were fulfilled. He also likes to write jingles that he hopes will enable his clients to keep various matters in mind; and though none of these verses was good enough to make the professional poets envious, they are not so much inferior to those of rimers like Taylor. A mnemonic rime for Hilary Term indicates the limits of Johnson's poetical powers.

The twentie three of January,
If it doe not on Sunday fall:
Begins our Tearme of Hillarie,
Prepare therefore you Clyants all.
Uppon the twelfth of February,
This tearme doth end most usually.

All of these matters are simply prologues to Johnson's black but general prediction for the year. Johnson reads in the stars that there will be an inordinate number of adulterers, that men will lose money through the dishonesty of servants, that many merchants will become bankrupts, and that there will be great pestilences in Frankfort and Vienna, cities comfortably distant from Jacobean London. From these utterances, Johnson turns to his seasonal predictions, which incline toward the flowery side of rhetoric. His prognostication for summer is introduced in these words: "Man hath but a space and everie flower a time to fade: The Sunne (the eye of the worlde) hath his boundes & limites which he cannot passe, for being mounted up on high so farre as he may, must likewise descend. . . ." The general predictions for the seasons are followed by monthly prophecies and admonitions; Johnson's advice for March is characteristic of his hortatory manner.

Use meates of good digestion, and such as ingender good bloud, for now man his stomacke may and can digest well, but take heed of great or overmuch feeding. The wether being temperate, & the celestial bodies accorded therto, purge, bathe or let bloud, such as are diseased, or likely therto, or full of grose humors, to purge them or to clarifie the bloud. The times serves to enter into dyets, and to prevent and cure whatsoever disease is or may be prevented, or cured. Al kinds of sweet meates and drinkes are now wholesome, in especiall for such as have fleamy stomachs.

IN WORLDLY AFFAIRS

This moneth serveth for making Oyle Conserves of Violets, as also to make white waxe. In the new moone graft any kinde of good fruite, the winde and Weather alwayes regarded, set Quickset, Vines, Willowes, cut hedges and Vines, if the weather in February prooved too extreame. In the wane of the Moone set or sowe Pease, Beanes, Onions, Oates, Parsneps &c. Let dainty husewives set and sowe now all sorts of Hearbes, some fewe excepted. In cold clay grounds, and such as be moist, sowe Barlye at the end of this moneth, set also Mellons, Cowcumbers, Artechockes and such other.

For the closest approach to astrological poetry in Renaissance England, we may cite the almanacks of Edward Pond, who was one of the most prolific and widely read writers of prognostications. Pond seems also to be on the defensive (the attack of Chamber may have had something to do with this), for the prefaces to his almanacks are usually briefs for astrology and the astrologer. His almanack for 1604, for example, begins with an address to the reader in which astrology is praised as an implement of religion. After this introduction, he comes to a castigation of the evil professors of the art, who, he feels, have brought obloquy on the astrologer's profession. These ignorant compilers of almanacks, he says, miss such obvious things as the dates of eclipses and solar aspects and such important things as the exact beginning of the year. Their errors arise from their reliance on foreign almanacks, which they have not enough skill to recalculate for England. These untrained astrologers also use a moon table; but since they omit the moon's latitude of five degrees, her swift and slow motion, and her right and oblique motion in ascension and descension, they are constantly in error. Pond reminds his readers that "the Doctour of all doctours had his backbiters and faultfinders," and urges them not to charge astrology with the errors of these ignorant astrologers. Pond's almanack for 1609 contains a similar defense, but by then Pond had assumed a schoolmasterish manner and lectured his readers on the sublimity of astrology. He represents himself as vexed by the rumors that unkind people invent. Some say that the astrologers coin their predictions; others insist that they follow heathenish rules which no Christian should obey; others—and this is the largest group—declare that the astrologers spent the twelve nights after Christmas lying on their backs and studying the stars; still others whisper that the astrologers conjure and deal wickedly with familiar spirits.

With many such like unchristianlike opinions are wee dayly scandalized by the ignorant multitude, whereof it groweth, that some of us are (uniustly) termed figure-casters, and many people resort unto us, offering great sums of money or other giftes, to tell them of a Silver spone, a Ring, or a Iewell stollen from them, Cattell strayed, and such like, Protesting (if they find us unwilling to heare them) that they will keepe our counsell: thereby confessing that they thinke it evill, or els, why should counsell be kept.

It does no good, Pond writes, to rebuke these simpletons for coming in this fashion to a "Christian professor of lawfull Art," for they just go off to inform their friends that the "professor" has given them substantial information. The news of this gets about and the thief who stole the missing goods becomes frightened and replaces them; the innocent astrologer gets, of course, the credit for effecting the restoration of the stolen property. Pond admits that there are many "Chaldeans" and "Pepper-Alleyans" about, but he insists that they are really devils incarnate. True Christian astrology—the only kind that he prints—is approved by men like Calvin, for it is based "on infallible principles, without which no Science is perfect."

These notes indicate the nature of Pond's character and the problems that he, as an unquestionably sincere astrologer, had to face. There was, however, more to Pond than a salty tongue and a certain amount of scientific indignation. Like many of his contemporaries, he fancied himself as a poet and scatters his halting poesies through his directions for bloodletting and descriptions of eclipses. His almanack for 1604 contains a long verse, a sort of epic version of Aristotle's *De meteorologica,* which makes one think nostalgically of Sir John Davies, Phineas Fletcher, and John Davies of Hereford. We reprint a portion of Pond's lines because they are probably as good as most of Davies of Hereford's poetry and because, to parallel the Johnsonian quip about women preachers, it is not so surprising that an astrologer should write bad poetry as it is that he should write poetry at all. First some Pondian lines on the birth of meteors:

As in our bodies wee may see full plaine,
That fire and ayre, in vitall spirits raigne.
The flesh is earth, the humours waters bee,
So in the bloud, the lowest in degree
Is Melancholy, earthy, seldome good,
And in the midd'st, like Ayre, swimmes purest bloud.
Next watry flegme, and on the top there bubbles
That fyrie Chollor, which so many troubles.
This hotte braind Chollor, quartaine Ague breeds,
And sad Hectique fever, when drynesse exceeds,
So moystures excesse makes dropsie his page,
And hoary fleec'd coldnesse summons old age.
So in the Ayre, by vertue of Heavens light
Are Meteors bredde, apparent to our sight.
As in a bottle glasse, a flame combynde,
Whose mouth in water stands, leaves nought behynde,
But forceably this humour up exhalles,
And there it hangs, within this glazen walles.
Right so the Sunne, two sorts of vapours drawes
From flowrie fieldes, and from the wavering flawes:
The one is thinne, pure, nimble, burning drie,
Th' other hotte and moist, rising heavily.

Then some verses on thunder and the rainbow with the confession of the poet's purpose:

But vapours hotte and drie, with moisture mixt,
Exhald and foulded in a cloude there fixt,
Supprest with heate and moisture, breakes asunder
And makes a roaring noise, which we call Thunder.
Forth of whose crazed sides burstes fyrie flashes,
Whose lightning flames through th' ayre most swiftly dashes

And on a watry cloud, if Sunne doth shine,
The Raigne-bowe then appears, Gods heavenly signe.
Of Sunne and Moone obscur'd I meane to write
Next yeare, when five defects will clipse their light.
O heavenly lampes, your certaine course confirmes
The seasons, yeares, the moneths, dayes and Termes.

This is then the profile of the Elizabethan and Jacobean almanack and prognostication, a work over which many an Englishman pored with the same eagerness and zeal that he gave to the study of Holy Writ and a work which probably had in the long run almost as much influence on the life of the times as the Scriptures. The almanacks which have been described are all of a type; they were small books in octavo and quarto arranged according to a definite formula. There were, of course, other styles, but they were not popular with the almanack reading public. The broadside almanack and prognostication, which was reasonably popular on the continent, had no vogue in England. There was also the perpetual almanack and the almanack compiled for more than one year, works like Digges' *Prognostication of Right Good Effect* and Moore's *A fourtie yeres Almanacke.* There were also almanacks like that printed by Wyer in 1556, which were for the use of illiterates and announced their predictions by means of woodcut symbols. Finally, there were books of a kindred type like the well-known *Kalendar of Shyppars,* which inspired Spenser's *Shepherd's Calendar.* None of these types of almanacks and prognostications was parodied in England, where the satirists vented their ridicule on the annual prediction which was forever coming from the presses.

The burlesque of the almanack and prognostication was not an English innovation; long before the first English satires appeared, continental parodists had battered the almanack with humorous abuse. In Germany comic *lasstafels* appeared as early as 1480; and, in the early part of the sixteenth century certain German astrologers, who had previously been engaged in producing serious prognostications, turned upon their colleagues in satiric burlesques.[26] Among the earliest German

---

[26] See L. Mackensen, *Die Deutschen Volksbücher* (Leipzig, 1927), pp. 51-52; W. Uhl, *Unser Kalender in seiner Entwicklung von den ältesten Anfängen bis heute* (Paderborn, 1893), p. 87; A. Hauffen, *Johann Fischart* (Berlin, 1921), I, 143-154. See also Emil Weller, "Scherzkalender oder Spottpraktiker," *Serapeum,* XXVI

works of this type are the *Practica teutsch doctor Gril von kyttelperg, gepractiziert inn der hochen schul do dy küe auff steltzen geend* and the Swiss *Praktika Doctor Johannis Rossschwanz,* which was plundered by Henrichmann for his *Prognostica* of 1509. Henrichmann's book was frequently reprinted as the appendix to Bebel's *Facetiae,* for Henrichmann had acknowledged Bebel as his master. The *Prognostica* boasts that all its predictions will come true; consequently, most of the predictions are of that general order of common truths that have delighted the makers of facetious prophecies since the beginning of time. The reader is told, for example, that "It shall be better to take money than to spend it" or that "Whoever has no wine shall not scorn to drink water." He also learns that "Women will have weak memories but long hair." Bebel also wrote a *Prognosticon* for 1509, which he asserted was translated *ex Ethrusco sermone.* Another German, Johannes Nas, published a *Practica practicarum* in 1564, which like Henrichmann's book depended to a great extent on a Swiss pattern; subsequent editions of Nas' *Practica,* however, extended the material and added new and more timely sections. These German burlesques and perhaps many others that are no longer extant lay before Johann Fischart when in 1572 he wrote his *Aller Praktick Grossmutter: Ein dickgeprockte Newe unnd trewe, laurhaffte unnd immerdaurhaffte Procdick . . . sampt einer gecklichen und auff alle jar gerechten Lasstafeln.* The substance of Fischart's parody prognostication is not unlike that of the English burlesques; the monthly and seasonal predictions of the serious astrologers are mocked and the vague and carefully generalized statements of the prophets are pilloried in premonstrations like "This year there will be few gulden among the poor." Fischart, as Hauffen has shown, was not completely original, but borrowed from his German prede-

(1865), 236-239. It is highly possible that this type of satire was invented by the professional rhetoricians, for in Ringelberg's *De ratione studii* (Lyons, 1532) there is a chapter on this matter titled: *Ridicula, sed jucunda quaedam vaticinia.*

cessors and from the *Pantagrueline prognostication* of François Rabelais.

The burlesque almanack of Rabelais is, without question, the most interesting and perhaps the most clever example of this form of satire that sixteenth-century France has to offer, but as the English verse parodies of 1544 and 1623 are made out of the ordinary by the large number of prose parodies, so Rabelais' prose satire is extraordinary because of the number of French mock prognostications in verse. Because of their curiousness and because they have all been gathered by Anatole de Montaiglon in his *Recueil des Poesies Françoises des XVe et XVIe siècles*, we may first look over some of these verse burlesques. As an early example of this type of work, we may consider *La grand et vraye Pronostication generale pour tous climatz et nations, nouvellement translatee d'arabien en langue francoyse, et jadis subtilement calculee sur le temps passe, present et advenir, par le grand Haly Habenragel*, a work that Montaiglon dates at about 1530. The author of this work announces with a certain amount of humor that his almanacks are sold *a Callicuth, cheux le seignour de Senegua, a l'enseigne dalz Canibales*, and then writes little verse sections on the dominical letter, the golden number, the moveable feasts, the moon, eclipses, signs, seasons, and months. This technical matter is followed by satirical predictions for trades and announcements of diseases, wars, and truces.[27] Another early verse parody in French was the *Pronostication nouvelle*, which was printed at Lyons in 1545, but which, Montaiglon thinks, was composed twenty years earlier. This burlesque likewise follows the general form of the serious almanack, but it centers its attack of ridicule on the generalness of all astrological predictions. In this fashion the author predicts an eclipse:

> L'eclypse de Lune sera
> En esté ou en temps de ver,

[27] *Op. cit.* (Paris, 1878), VI, 5-46.

> Ou aultrement elle pourra
> Estre en autonne ou en yver.

He announces the widows' lots:

> Jeunes vefves seront vexées;
> Du mal ne fault point enquérir;
> Si d'hommes ne sont confortees,
> En danger seront de mourir.[28]

Other verse satires of this sort collected by Montaiglon are the *Prenostication des anciens Laboureurs,*[29] *La grant et vraye Prenostication, pour cent et ung an, de nouveau composée par maistre Tyburce Dyariferos, demeurant a la ville de Pampelune,*[30] *Le Kalendrier mis par petits vers, composé par maistre Jehan Mollinet,*[31] *Pronostication generalle pour quatre cens quatre-vingt-dix-neuf ans, calculée sur Paris et autres lieux de mesme longitude,*[32] and *La Prenostication de maistre Albert Songecreux, Bisscain.*[33] The last-named verse satire in this group is particularly important because as we look over the list of books in the library that Rabelais furnishes for the Abbey of St. Victor, we come on this title.

The *Pantagrueline Prognostication,* which Rabelais published in 1533 as a prognostication to end all prognostications, is well known to all lovers of the exploits of the heroic Gargantua and his son. The almanack purports to be by Alcofribas Nasier, Architriclin to Pantagruel, and the astrologer likes to invent titles of authoritative works—a trait of literary character which he shares with his creator. In form the *Pantagrueline Prognostication* follows the conventional almanack of the age, but, in keeping with the ethical and religious sides of Rabelais' nature, it has a moral and theological undertone. Rabelais announces, for example, that the governor and lord of the ascendant for the year will be God and that none of the planets will have independent virtues. In a section on the dis-

[28] *Op. cit.,* XII, 148-167.
[29] *Ibid.,* II, 87-98.
[30] *Ibid.,* VIII, 337-346.
[31] *Ibid.,* VII, 204-210.
[32] *Ibid.,* IV, 36-46.
[33] *Ibid.,* XII, 172.

position of the people for the year, Rabelais lashes the rascals
and vices of his time with his usual eagerness. His seasonal
prognostications are of a type to which we shall become ac-
customed, for he says with mock solemnity that the summer
shall be warm with occasional sea breezes and he advises his
readers not to sell their furs during the winter. A second important name in the history of sixteenth-century French literature—that of Bonaventure des Periers—is associated with that
of Rabelais in the war against the almanack-makers. Unlike
the verse satires that Montaiglon assembled, Des Periers' *Prognostication des Prognostications pour tous temps, a jamais,
sur toutes autres veritable, laquelle descœuvre l'impudence des
prognostiqueurs* is not a parody but an attack on astrologers
and almanack-makers in verse. Des Periers laments man's
wicked desire to know the future and informs him that he
does not satisfy this desire by reading prognostications:

> Par ainsi donc, ô monde lunatique!
> Ayes pour tous cestuy seul prognostique:
> C'est que, pour vray, tous tes prognostiqueurs
> Sont et seront ou mocqués ou mocqueurs;
> Et tiens cecy pour un mot bien notable,
> Qu'ilz ne diront rien qui soit véritable
> Pour cestuy an, ny pour l'autre à venir,
> Ny à jamais, s'il t'en peult souvenir.[34]

In spite of the number of Latin astrological poems written
by Italians and the ridicule of almanack-makers in Italian
comedy, the wits of Italy do not seem to have used the prognostication as either a vehicle for satire or a target for abuse.
The exception to this is the *Pronostico dell' anno MDXXXIIII*
of Pietro Aretino, which, though it follows the form of the
almanack, is really a mask for the usual Aretinian libels. The
early part of the *Pronostico* is closer to the pattern of the serious prognostication than the latter parts, which are simply

[34] *Œuvres,* ed. Lacour (Paris, 1856), I, 130-138.

vilifications of the rulers of various states; from this earlier part we may borrow a few illustrative lines.

Il presente anno MDXXXIIII essendo signore dello ascendente il Marchese del Vasto et sedendo nel centro del Zodiaco in mezzo di Fabritio Maramaldo et di Thomaso Tucca, uno quondam buffone et l'altro olim strozziere del Duca di Mantova, molti militi gloriosi (come sarebbe a dire il Duca di Malfi, stallone generale delle donne sanesi) si inclineranno a profumi et a riccami; et per havere Marte quadrato pisciato nello orinale di Venere retrograda, Vittoria Marchesa di Pescara Sybilla haverà per mano del vescovo Jovio parasito apostolico la laurea corona in Ischia.[35]

The jargon of the almanack-maker is here, we note; but since Aretino quarrels only with the worthies of his age, the poor astrologer is spared.

As far as we can ascertain, the English burlesque almanack was utterly uninfluenced by the substance of continental parodies. The writers of polemics against astrology may have suggested some of the matter of these satires by their practice of magnifying the blunders of the prognosticators, but though the English opponents of astrology leaned heavily on their continental precursors, the English compilers of mock almanacks seem to have worked independently. Satirizing the almanack and the matter of the satire may easily have been a sort of reflex action; something that one did with as little effort and thought as breathing. In Marston's *Parasitaster* there is a long almanack scene in the last act, with Herod reading off prognostications that touch characters in the caste like the following one, which is read to Sir Amaros: ". . . heeres likewise prophesied a great skarsitie of Gentrie to ensue, and that some Bores shall be dubbed Sir Amoroso. A great scarsitie of Lawyers is likewise this yeare to ensue, so that some one of them shall be entreated to take fees a both sides."[36] Now this

---

[35] *Op. cit.*, ed. Luzio (Bergamo, 1900), p. 5.
[36] *Op. cit.*, II, 212-213. The English burlesque almanacks have been briefly described by Carrol Camden in "Elizabethan Almanacs and Prognostications," *The*

scene and these speeches which follow the patter of the astrologer so closely may have been a piece of independent parody
on Marston's part; on the other hand, Marston may be delib-
erately imitating, for by the year 1605 the burlesque almanack
and prognostication was an established literary form with the
professional writers.

The earliest English parody is several pages of doggerel
verse which was published in 1544 and which may have been
written in imitation of the French verse burlesques which it
resembles in spirit if not in manner. This work, which exists
only in a unique copy possessed by the Henry E. Huntington
Library, bears a rimed title which reads:

A MERY PRONOSTICACION
For the yere of Chrystes incarnacyon
A thousande fyue hundreth fortye & foure
This to pronostycate I may be bolde
That whā the newe yere is come gone is ye olde.

The hundred and thirty lines that jingle after this title relate,
in an exaggeration of the astrologers' trade language, the proximity of an eclipse, which "shal be sutely, I can nat tell howe
soone," the nature of the four quarters of the year and of the
twelve months, and the diseases, sicknesses, and fates that will
overtake the natives of the various planets. The name of Ptolemy is taken regularly in vain, but the author knows enough
about that authority to mention the *Centiloquium* as a source
for Ptolemy's own doubts about the validity of judicial astrology. *A Mery Pronosticacion* is by no means great literature; in
fact, it does not even compete in esthetic value with the French
rimaille on the same theme. In some respects, however, these

Library, XII, 83-108, 194-207, and F. P. Wilson, "Some English Mock Prognostications," *ibid.*, XIX, 6-43. Mr. Wilson's study has anticipated some of my findings
and at other times presents material that I would otherwise have missed; as a consequence, I have always mentioned this study whenever I am directly indebted to it.
An older study is Cornelius Walford's "Sham Almanacks and Prognostications,"
Book-Lore, II (1885), 67-70.

verses set a pattern for the later prose satires, for they contain
most of the conventional elements: truisms like

> Dyuers dyseases shal rayne this yere
> Some shal dye, and some shal tary here;

non sequiturs like

> Bycause that Saturne is dominator here
> I fynde yt ther shalbe twelue monethes this yere;

and folk jests like

> But I saye yf the nynth daye of Nouembre
> Had fallen vpon the tenth daye of Decembre
> It had bene a meruaylous hote yere for bees
> For then had the Moone ben lyke a grene chese.

Unlike the French, the English did not, apparently, produce many rimed burlesques of this type; in fact, the only
other extant mock prognostication in verse is connected in a
very interesting fashion with *A Mery Pronosticacion*. This first
work, which is an unsigned quarto of three leaves, has long
been thought to want a leaf. This supposition arises from the
fact that the last lines on the verso of the second leaf read:

> Thys is bycause of the Eclyps of the Mone
> Some shal supe theyr potage for lack of a spon
> In the somer tyme shalbe suche an heate;

and the first lines on the recto of the third leaf are:

> For Saturne and Mars haue ful wel discust
> That in the eclyps Mercury is combust.

Allowing for all the vagaries of the anonymous author of *A
Mery Pronosticacion,* we cannot believe that he would inten-
tionally leave an incomplete rime in his verses, and so we
assume that a leaf containing some sixty or more lines of doggerel must have been lost from the unique copy of this satire.
This hypothesis is supported by the second English verse bur-

lesque, W. W.'s *A New and Merry Prognostication,* which was printed in 1623.

This second verse parody is little more than a wordy expansion of *A Mery Pronosticacion;* it follows the same method as the earlier satire, but it is three times the longer. This new magnitude is obtained by adding some new sections and by spending several lines on a notion that the earlier verses dealt with in one line. Between 1544 and 1623 the Stationers' Register lists two nonextant almanack burlesques, *A merry prognostication for the year of our lord God 1567,* which was entered by "J. Dernyll" to William Pickering, and *A new and pleasant prognostication,* which was entered to E. Allde in 1586. The titles of these missing works are quite unlike the titles bestowed by the authors of prose parodies on their works and quite like the titles of the verse satires of 1544 and 1623. Wilson supposes, and we must agree with him, that these vanished works were intermediate steps in the evolution of *A Mery Pronosticacion* into *A New and Merry Prognostication.* But the expanded satire of 1623 also confirms our supposition that a leaf of the 1544 satire is missing, for following the course of the verses of 1544 in their bloated form, one finds the old verses and the rime completed:

> Some say it is by reason of the Moone,
> Many shall sup their Pottage, for lacke of a spoone.
> Others say, because the signes be in such heat
> The people would fare well, if they could get meat.[37]

These lines are part of an extended section on diseases in which undoubtedly are included many of the lost lines of the verses of 1544.

The first prose parodies of the almanack and prognostication appeared in 1591, when three works of this nature were printed. The first of these burlesques is known only by the entry in the Stationers' Register of "A booke entituled Ffraun-

[37] *Op. cit.,* sig. C3v.

cis Fayre Weather" to William Wright on February 25. For a
long time, bibliographers have assumed that this book was
never printed although the pseudonym of its author undoubtedly influenced the coining of another almanack satirist's nom
de plume; recently, however, the sharp eyes of Mr. Wilson
caught an allusion in Florio's *Second Fruits* to those that "pro-
nosticate of faire, of foule, and of smelling weather," and
though this may be just a general reference, it does include all
the pseudonyms of the 1591 authors and suggests that the parody of Ffrauncis Fayre Weather was probably published. The
second prose burlesque, which was reprinted within the year,
has the title, *A wonderfull, strange and miraculous, Astrologicall Prognostication for this yeer of our Lord God 1591. Discouering such wonders to happen this yeere, as neuer chaunced
since Noes floud. Wherein if there be found one lye, the
Author will loose his credit for euer. By Adam Fouleweather,
Student in Asse-tronomy.* This work has long been attributed
to Nashe, thanks to the fact that it was listed as Nashe's in the
sale catalogue of Reed's library and was mentioned as Nashe's
by Collier in his preface to his edition of *Pierce Penniless*. In
three subsequent editions of Nashe's works the prognostication
of Adam Fouleweather has been reprinted, but though he
publishes the work again for the sake of the tradition, McKerrow does not believe that it is by Nashe and offers impressive
arguments to the contrary.[88]

In a preface in which he addresses the reader, Fouleweather
assumes the pious pose that we have noticed before in the technical writings of the astrologers and in almanacks like those
of Pond. As he stares into the future, Fouleweather sees horrible things, which—unless God prevent them—will bring it
about that "many poore men are like to fast on Sondaies for
want of food, and such as haue no shooes to goe barefoot, if
certaine deuout Coblers proue not the more curteous." With
this type of allusion, Fouleweather sets the sociological temper

[88] *Op. cit.,* IV, 476-477.

of most of the mock prognostications, for almost all of these pamphlets were critical first of the economic and ethical short-comings of the times and second of the astrologer and his practices. The early sections of Fouleweather's almanack contain comic accounts of the effects of two eclipses of the moon and one of the sun; the astrologer is not certain of the exact dates of these phenomena, but he is sure that the second eclipse of the moon will occur by the last day of December or not at all. The results of these eclipses are easy to predict. Brewers will water their beer; the rich will prevail in lawsuits with the poor; a variety of religious sects will take issue with one another; the "nuns" in Shoreditch will prosper; certain monstrous children will be born that "shall not knowe their owne Fathers"; butchers will commit murder upon sheep; and "many shall haue more Spruce Beere in their bellies then wit in their heads." The mood of Fouleweather's prognostication is closer to the Rabelaisian parody than to the *Mery Pronosticacion,* but the truisms, folk jests, and *non sequiturs* of the last piece are also present. Like all his predecessors, Fouleweather sprinkles his pages with astrological jargon, and uses, unlike Rabelais, who invented absurd Arabian names, the magic names of Albumasar and Proclus.

The most amusing part of Fouleweather's satire follows the account of the uncertain eclipses and makes sport of the seasonal predictions that one finds in all the serious almanacks of the period. After the pretentious fashion of the astrologers, Fouleweather titles this section, "A declaration of the generall disposition of sundrie conceited qualities incident vnto mens mindes & natures throughout these foure quarters of the yere, by the merrie influence of the Planets, with some other tragicall euents and obseruations worthie the noting, contayned vnder each seperated reuolution." With this section Fouleweather concludes his burlesque, but his mock prediction for summer is quotable as an example of what was done with

those serious predictions for this season that have been cited
earlier.

When the Sunne hath made his course through the vernal signs,
Aries, Taurus & Gemini at his passage vnto the solsticiall estivall
signe Cancer. The third parte of an English yeere called Summer,
taketh his beginning this yere, as Ptolomie sayth, the twelfth of
June, but as my skill doth coniecture, it beginneth when the wether
waxeth so hot, that beggers scorne barnes and lie in the field for
heate and the wormes of Saint Pancredge Church build their bow-
ers vnder the shadow of Colman hedge. The predominant qualities
of this quarter is heate and drynesse, whereby I doe gather, that
through the influence of Cancer, bottle Ale shall be in great author-
itie, and wheat shall doe knightes seruice vnto malte. Tapsters this
quarter shall be in greater credite than Coblers, and many shall
drinke more then they can yearne. And yet because Mercurie is a
signe that is nowe predominant, women shall be more troubled with
fleas then men, and such as want meate shall goe supperlesse to
bedde. Besides, this quarter greate hurlie burlies are like to bee
feared, and greate stratagems like to bee feared, thorough the opposition of Mars and Saturne: for Butchers are like to make greate
hauocke amongst flies, and beggers on Sunne shine dayes to commit great murthers vpon their rebellious vermine, and the knights
of Coppersmiths hal to doo great deedes of armes vpon Cuppes,
Cannes, pots, glasses, and black iacks: not ceasing the skirmish til
they are able to stand on their legges.[39]

The same year that saw the publication of Fouleweather's
humorous prognostication produced another satire by an author
masquerading under the name of Simon Smel-knave, "student
in good felowship." Smel-knave's *The Fearefull and lamentable effects of two dangerous Comets, which shall appeare in
the yeere of our Lord, 1591. the 25. of March. wherein both
man and woman shall find theyr naturall inclination, and
accidentall or necessarie mischiefes.* is embellished with a "figure" drawn from some astrological work and is admittedly in-

[39] *Op. cit.,* sigs. C4v-D1v.

spired by Fouleweather's prognostication. It is, however, to the credit of Smel-knave that though he had "misused" Fouleweather's almanack, his debts to him are never verbal steals; whenever Smel-knave follows the tune of Fouleweather, he has always the good taste to alter the lyric.[40] We mention this matter with some emphasis because the authors of some of the later parodies were not so punctilious, not so mindful of the intellectual property of others.

Smel-knave like Fouleweather is a censor of the age. He denounces hypocritical clergymen and officials hungry for bribes. With the utmost rigor he sketches the unhappy condition of the poor, who shall have no justice because they cannot pay and who, since charity is wanting, will suffer more than other Englishmen from famine and cold. Smel-knave had a little of the Old Testament prophet in him, for he observes that whereas the good suffer, thieves, drunkards, usurers, drabs, and dishonest practitioners prosper and fare well. The text around which much of Smel-knave's satire polarizes is expressed in these words, "To be breefe, the generall disposition of this time is so daungerous, that no man can thrive by trueth, since playne knavery was made a Gentleman."[41]

To mock the professional almanack-maker as much as possible, Smel-knave relieves the prose of his burlesque with verses. Martin Merry-Mate, a devoted friend of Smel-knave, contributes a laudatory poem of fifty lines of rough-hewn verse to *The Fearefull and lamentable effects,* and Smel-knave himself writes a series of gnomic verses on the natives of the planets which he prints in the concluding section of his parody.

[40] Fouleweather had said that Philip and Mary shillings, which had passed for twelve pence would now pass for six pence (A2v), and Smel-knave says that Harp shillings shall not pass for twelve pence (A4v); Fouleweather wrote that there would be storms in houses where the wife wears the breeches (C2r), and Smel-knave has something similar (A4v); Fouleweather tells of children who will not know their own fathers (B2r); so does Smel-knave (B1r). Other conventional matter that they have in common are: the abundance of rye (S. B3v; F. D2v), human caterpillars (S. B3v; F. A3v), and the watering of beer (S. C1r; F. A3v).

[41] *Ibid.,* p. C2v.

Here, for example, is the character of the "Jovialist" as Smel-knave poetically describes him:

> They that are borne,
> Under Iupiter I knowe:
> May perhaps catch corne,
> If they have lande to sowe.
> He that is prodigall,
> And lets his crownes flye:
> If he spare not in time,
> Shall a begger dye.
> Who so marries without money,
> In midst of his dread:
> Shall at night if he please
> Find foure bare legges in his bedde.[42]

A few peculiarities of Smel-knave's almanack remain to be mentioned. In a series of witty comments, he indicates the heated arguments of the time about the relative accuracy of bows and guns; he is willing to prove, he remarks in a pun, that "a Minspie is better than a Muskette."[43] Like other satirists of the prognostication, Smel-knave amuses himself with allusions to astrological authorities, whom he quotes copiously and comically and, of course, with no attempt at accuracy. In the course of his satire, Smel-knave takes the names of John Holy-wood, Haly, Avicenna, Aristotle, Plato, Erra Pater, Galen, Erasmus, Ptolemy, Rabadus, Archelaus, and Albumasar in vain; but he, like Rabelais, is infinitely cheered by a fictitious authority, and so we are referred to Rabbi Salomon's *Nulla-tenus,* "the first Chapter you can find," and the "famous Prognostication" of Doctor Alcander. Smel-knave also shared Chamber's affection for the father of English poetry and Ben Jonson's scorn of scholarly annotators, those swine who continually root in the Muses' garden; the union of these views is seen in this statement: "*Chaucers* bookes shall this yeere, proove more witty then ever they were: for there shall so many

---

[42] *Ibid.,* sig. C3v.   [43] *Ibid.,* sigs. B4v-C1r.

suddayne, or rather sodden wittes steppe abroad, that a Flea
shall not friske foorth, unlesse they comment on her."[44]

If literary thievery is a yardstick of literary success, Smel-
knave's mock prognostication was eminently successful. *The
Penniless Parliament of Threadbare Poets,* which was issued as
an appendix to *Jack of Dover* in 1604 and as a separate publication in 1608, is little more than a reprint of Smel-knave's
burlesque with, as Wilson points out, new opening and concluding paragraphs; and the disguised author of the next
parody almanack, *Platoes Cap. Cast at this Yeare 1604, being
Leape-yeere,* annexed great sections of Smel-knave's burlesque
but sauced them with facetious material that seems to be his
own. Wilson suggests that there seems to be some connection
between the author of this new mock prognostication and the
group of literary professionals to which Dekker belonged; this
hypothesis is supported, after a fashion, by the following lines
from *The Wonderful Year* (1603) from which the title of
Platoes Cap was probably derived: "Platoes Mirabilis Annus,
(whether it be past alreadie, or to come within these foure
yeares) may throwe Platoes cap at Mirabilis, for the title of
wonderfull is bestowed upon 1603."[45] The author of this work
is further linked to Dekker's circle by the fact that Chorlton,
who published *The Black Book* and who sold *Father Hub-
burd's Tales,* was also the publisher of *Platoes Cap,* and by a
further reference to the work in Dekker's *News from Hell,*
where one reads that "Platoe's Cap was not worthy to wipe"
the shoes of the second half of Erra Pater's almanack.[46] Wilson is inclined to think of Middleton as a good claimant for
the authorship of *Platoes Cap,* and we know, of course, that
Middleton and Dekker were collaborating dramatically at this
date. There is one objection, however, to this conjecture, but
we must lay it aside for the moment to describe the nature of
this satire.

The author of *Platoes Cap* follows the pattern of Foule-

[44] *Ibid.,* sig. C2r.   [45] *Op. cit.,* I, 94.   [46] *Ibid.,* II, 104.

weather and Smel-knave and calls himself Adam Evesdropper;
under this pseudonym he writes a pleasant dedicatory epistle
to "all those that are laxative of Laughter" to which his friend
Mihill Mercurie the "Pothecarie" appends a jingle in praise of
the book. This confederacy between the astrologer and the
apothecary is in keeping with the ancient traditions of roguery.
The earlier sections of the satire follow the sun through the
signs and predict what will happen during each of the months.
When the sun is in Libra, one should watch the grocer, the
chandler, and all others who sell by weight; when the sun is
in Sagittarius, the fletchers and bowyers will prosper; and
when it is in Capricorn, old men and old "riueld" women who
have young mates should watch the smoothness of their foreheads. Like Simon Smel-knave, Adam Evesdropper attacks the
vices of his time, the hypocrisies and pretenses, the frauds and
deceits, and, in the fashion of Dekker, the exploitation of the
poor by the rich. As an example of the didactic style of this
satire, of the middle-class decency of its author, we may reprint
two paragraphs on the fortune-hunters of either sex.

This hotte Coniunction being but badly affected, shewes, that
those which were widdowes the last Yeere, will be catcht vp this
yeere, more for wealth and spending-money, than for loue and
honesty, they shall haue many gallant suiters, that will carie all their
Lands vpon their backes, and yet sweare they haue grounds, Backsides, & yards, when they haue no more Ground thā the Kings high
way, no more Backsides than one, and no more Yard, than what
they haue in their Hose and Doublets, and the Taylor deceiues
them of one and a halfe too, to mend the matter, and by that shift
makes the Gallants forsweare themselues.

Thus shall rich Widdowes bee beguild, if they bee not the
craftyer, and what their first Husbands sweate for in honest profitable labours, these their second hotte Louers will sweate out at Dice
in Ordinaries, or in French bals at the Tennis-court, to the rotting
of many fine Cambricke Shirts, and the bandyeng out of taffatie
Elbowes: but polliticke-craftie *Mercurie* euer and anon falling in
among the Bunch of Planets, showes that some *London* Widdowes

will bee subtill ynough for Countrey Gentlemen, and eyther bee made lusty Joynters, or else neuer ioyne battayle with them: their profitable wittes I applaude well, and I hope wittie *Mercurie* will bee good to their mourning Gownes, and not suffer their brittle Sere to repent within lesse than a moneth after their marriage day againe.[47]

The moral vigor of this prose, as well as its prolixity, suggests an associate of Dekker, someone on whom a good deal of the Dekkerian zeal for the right had rubbed off. This might, as Wilson suggests, be Middleton; but this hypothesis is somewhat vitiated by the latter section of *Platoes Cap,* which is borrowed in cold blood from the burlesque prognostication of Simon Smel-knave. To find a reason for this pilfering is most difficult. Perhaps the author of *Platoes Cap* having toiled conscientiously over the early half of his prognostication finished it hurriedly in this fashion to fulfill an agreement with his printer. Perhaps the first section was also filched from a mock almanack no longer extant and fastened to a torso carved from the corpse of Smel-knave's satire.[48] For the moment the

---

[47] *Op. cit.,* sigs. C2r-C2v.

[48] The nature of these borrowings may be suggested by one parallel, and a comparison of the loan with the original will indicate that the printer had more of a conscience than did Adam Evesdropper:

Smel-knave	Evesdropper
Many straunge euents shall happen this yeere, in those houses where *Virgo* is predominant with a Maister, but wants a Mistris to looke narrowly vnto her: for the influence of the Grocers shoppes, beeing eleuated within a fewe sweete degrees, presageth that some shamelesse queanes shall bee still gadding about the streetes for Figges, Almonds, and Comfects, and that without regard of witte or honesty. (B4r)	Many straunge euents shall happen and befall this yeere in those houses where *Virgo* is predominant with a master, but wants a Mistresse to looke narrowly vnto her, for the influence of the Grocers shops being eleuated within a few sweet degrees presageth that some shamelesse Drabbes shall bee still gadding about the streetes for figges, almonds, and Confects, and that without regarde of eyther Witte or Honestie. (D2r-D2v)

Some other parallels are: smell in their nostrils (S. B1r; E. D1v), war between wife and husband (S. A4v; E. C3v), battle between four knaves at cards (S. A4v; E. C3v), the bakers, woodmongers (S. B1v; E. C4r), women . . . long gowns (S. B1v; E. C3v), Barbers (S. A4r; E. C4r), Muscadine (S. A4v; E. D1r), Consumptions (S. B1r; E. D1v), Sing base (S. B1v; E. D2r), Fortune-tellers (S. B4r; E. D2r), venterously disposed (S. C1r; E. D2v), Bakers (S. C1v; E. D2v), Haberdashers (S. A4v; E. D2v).

answer to this problem eludes us, but in spite of the Dekkerian savor of the apparently original part of the parody, we have reason to doubt that the whole work was the product of some member of Dekker's circle. Not many of these men were geniuses, but the least skillful of them borrowed more adroitly.

If we wish to observe a borrower in his full plumage, we focus our gaze upon Anthony Nixon, the author of *The Black Year* (1606), a work that we are forced to register as the burlesque prognostication subsequent to *Platoes Cap,* although its matter is much older. Nixon was an apparently devout man and a most prolific hack. He was the author or copier of a large number of books, among which may be listed *The Christian Navy, The Dignitie of Man,* and *The Three English Brothers.* For a long time it has been known that Nixon was not very scrupulous about the literary property of others and that he had borrowed heavily from Thomas Lodge for his *The Scourge of Corruption.* Nixon seems, however, to have had a penchant for Lodge's work, for an ample portion of *The Black Year* was originally written by Lodge; the whole of Nixon's epistle dedicatory to Francis Coppinger is derived with necessary adjustments from the dedication to *A Fig for Momus,* which supplies matter for other portions of Nixon's supposed satire. *The Black Year* can be divided into three sections: the first section is a burlesque satire, which is simply a mosaic of verses borrowed from Lodge, moral observations drawn from Thomas Wright's *The Passions of the Mind in General,* and prognosticating material from Smel-knave;[49] the second section is a lecture on the decay of the world, which is quite in the

---

[49] An example of Nixon's borrowing from Smel-knave is enough.

Nixon	Smel-knave
Iudas shall this yeare walke about the world, and sell his Neighbour for commoditie to any man: But the Iewes shall bee of other disposition, for having taken out a penie in the shilling these many yeares, they shall nowe with good conscience venture uppon three pence with the advantage. (C4r)	Judas shall walke about the worlde this latter time, and sell his neighbour for commoditie to any man. But the Jewes shall be otherwise disposed, for having taken but a penny in the shilling this six yeere, they shall nowe with a good conscience, venture upon three pence with the advantage. (B3v)

common tradition but for which an immediate source has not been found; and the third section is a diatribe against the Catholic Church, which is borrowed from Henry Smith's *God's Arrow Against Atheists*.[50] All in all, Nixon's *The Black Year* is simply an album of extracts from books that Nixon had about his rooms.

We pause, however, over Nixon's literary plunder because *The Black Year* is a book familiar by title, at least, to students of the Renaissance stage. Nixon speaks, for example, of Marston's *Dutch Courtesan* as being brought in "to corrupt English conditions,"[51] and this reference, while it does not show Nixon as an habitué of the theater, gets *The Black Year* mentioned in all accounts of Marston. More famous still are the connections between this pamphlet and Shakespeare's *Macbeth*. The porter, we recall, speaks of "an English tailor stealing out of a French hose"; and since Nixon writes, ". . . where they were wont to steale but halfe a yard of broad cloath in making vp a payre of breeches, now they doe largely nicke their Customers also in the lace, and take more than enough for the new fashion sake, besides their olde fee,"[52] *The Black Year* has been used as an argument in establishing the date of Shakespeare's play. This conclusion is a caveat for scholars; it italicizes the importance of scrutinizing all ancillary documents.   The

---

[50] Smith's book was published in 1593 and 1600; it was reprinted in the 1604 edition of Smith's sermons. Nixon clips Smith's rhetoric and transposes Smith's references to the margins where they are often printed out of place. Another parallel shows the method.

Nixon	Smith
For tell me I pray you where the Church was visible, when being assembled at Ierusalem, there arose a great persecution against it, insomuch as they were all dispersed and scattered: And where or how was the church visible, when Christ was smitten, and all the rest was scattered, and hid, and concealed themselves. (D4v-E1r)	Let them tell me where the Church was visible, when, being assembled at Jerusalem, there arose a great persecution against it insomuch as they were all dispersed and scattered, as the text sheweth, Acts viii.1. Or let them tell me, where or how the church was visible when Christ was smitten, and all the rest were scattered and hid, and concealed themselves. (*The Works*, Edinburgh, 1867, II, 414)

[51] *Op. cit.*, sig. B2r.

[52] *Ibid.*, sig. C2r.

reference is not, of course, original with Nixon but goes back to Smel-knave's satire of 1591, where we read: "But Taylors by this meanes shall haue more conscience, for where they were wont to steale but one quarter of a cloak, they shall haue due Commission to nick their customers in the Lace, and take more then enough for the newe fashion sake, beside theyr old fees."[53] Tailors seem to have been stealing cloth a good fifteen years before *The Black Year* was pieced together, and so Nixon's book is of little value in establishing the date of *Macbeth*.

As a sort of sop to the virtue of men of letters, *The Black Year* was followed by one of the three most original of mock prognostications and the only one to be acknowledged by its author. Thomas Dekker was not above borrowing, but his *Raven's Almanacke* seems to be completely original. Professor Rupert Taylor suggests that Dekker's book, which was published in 1609, was probably a parody on "The Raven's Almanacke" licensed to Laurence Lyle in July, 1608.[54] Professor Taylor bases his conclusions on the fact that Dekker's similarly named book was not published by Lyle but by Archer. On the other hand, there are a number of reasons for believing that the book licensed to Lyle and the one printed by Archer were the same. It is not unusual, of course, for a book to be entered to one man and printed by another without the transaction being recorded in the Stationers' Register. By this date, as Bosanquet has shown, the monopoly on almanacks was owned by the Stationers' Company; consequently, had "The Raven's Almanacke" entered in 1608 been anything other than a burlesque, it would not have been listed. The full entry in the Stationers' Register reads, "the Ravens Almanacke &c foretelling of A plague, faminc, and Ciuil Warres"; the title page of Dekker's book is *The Ravens Almanacke foretelling of a Plague, Famine, and Ciuill Warre*. All of these facts testify to the identification of the Register notice with Dekker's book.

---

[53] *Op. cit.*, sig. B2r.
[54] *The Political Prophecy in England* (New York, 1911), p. 123.

As a final argument against Professor Taylor's thesis, one may
point out the fact that the title is simply not in keeping with
the conventional titles of serious almanacks which usually combine a scientific with a pious title to lure the pennies of a trust-
ing clientele.

Like the satirical prognostications of Fouleweather and
Smel-knave, *The Raven's Almanacke* follows the form of the
almanack and prognostication but is really an attack on social
abuses instead of a parody on the predictions of astrologers.
The old formulae are repeated; we read the same general and
vague announcements, the same truisms, the same folk jests,
the same appeals to authority, but all of this simply serves as
a vehicle for social satire. In an epistle to the "Lyons of the
Wood (the young Courtiers) . . . the wilde Buckes of the
Forrest (the Gallants and younger Brothers) . . . the Harts
of the field," Dekker, "the new English Astrologer," urges the
young nobles, the younger brothers, the country gentlemen,
and the city tradesmen to beware of folly and of those who
shall attempt to cheat them. This dedication is followed by a
reproduction of the astrological man, who was part of every
serious almanack and prognostication but who had not yet,
interestingly enough, been used by one of the comic prognosticators. In Dekker's book the cut of the famous nude is correctly made, but the side notes have been altered so that Leo
is called Cancer, Scorpio Sagittarius, Taurus Gemini, and so
on through the rest of the signs. To enhance the mirth of the
reader, Dekker comments on the figure.

> At the beginning of eurie Almanacke, it is the fashion to haue
> the body of a man drawne as you see, and not onely baited, but
> bitten and shot at by wilde beasts and monsters. And this fellow,
> they that lye all the yeare long (that is to say, those that deale in
> Kalenders) call the Man of the Moone, or the Moones man, or the
> Man to whom the Moone is mistris. But how rediculous a shape
> do they bestowe vpon the silly wretch? hee standes as if he had
> beene some notorious malefactor, and being stript stark naked, to

goe to execution: do not those Roundels hang about him, shew like so many pardons, tyed to the partes of his body with Labels? or rather does hee not looke (when he lyes along) like a theefe begd for an Anatomy in Surgeons Hall, (so many Barbers figured in those beastes) slashing and slycing, and quartering & cutting him vp? truely he does.[55]

Dekker now descants amusingly on the influences of the signs and describes the twelve months after the manner of the astrologers; he remarks, however, that were he "under the coullors of vulgar Astronomers" he would lead the months into the field each of them wearing "foure unhansome rymes" instead of a plume.

The accounts of months and seasons that follow this introductory matter are not unlike those of Fouleweather and Smelknave. We are told of the avarice of lawyers, the hypocrisies of priests, the infidelities of wives, and the deceits of tradesmen. The Raven's description of summer shows how Dekker differs from the methods of his precursors and approaches the manner of the character writers.

When the heate of the Sunne beames begets golde in the veines of the earth, yet gold when tis brought foorth, shall worke a coldnesse in mens hearts: when Riuers shall swell with Spring-tides, and the Fountaines of Art and learning be drawn drie: when sheep flye to broade trees to defend themselues from ye wrath of heauen vnder their shades, and when innocence is guarded vnder the wings of greatnes from the rage of oppression: whē cuckowes sing merrily, and cuckolds laugh at their owne hornes: when courtiers ride the Wilde-goose Chace, whilst farmers stand by and praise their Horsemanship: when haruesters come singing from the field, because the corne lyes in sheafes: and when Citizens wiues walk to their Gardens, yet bring from thence to their Husbands no Nose-gaies stuck with Rue.[56]

With these matters the traditional part of Dekker's burlesque concludes, but to the prognostications for various seasons Dek-

---

[55] *Op. cit.*, IV, 180.   [56] *Ibid.*, IV, 205-206.

ker adds brief tales that have some connection with the seasonal predictions. To his description of Spring, he appends
the story of how the shoemaker of Ware cured his wife's
shrewish tongue; to his prognostic for fall, he adds the tale of
the lecherous Friar Pedro, that of the usurer of Ravenspurge,
and that of Richard the Ropemaker. These *novelle* occupy the
greater part of Dekker's *Raven's Almanacke,* and we feel that
Dekker was simply combining two popular literary forms to
assure himself a good sale.

Laurence Lyle, who has been mentioned in connection with
the bibliographical problems of *The Raven's Almanacke,* published another burlesque almanack in 1618. For this new work,
The Owle's Almanacke, Lyle, signing himself "L. L.," wrote a
preface in which he commented on the anonymity of the pamphlet and expressed the hope that Sir Timothy Thornhill, to
whom he addressed himself, would not think that the work
was his but rather that the owl had hidden "her broad face
under my Eeves by chance." One should like to see in these
remarks of Lyle an example of false modesty, but since there
is no evidence for this, one is forced to accept his statement as
the truth.

Many years before Lyle published *The Owle's Almanacke,*
a work of this sort was proposed by Pasquil in *A Countercuff
given to Martin,* and one should be happy to find that *The
Owle's Almanacke* of 1618 is a descendant of the Owl's Almanacke planned in 1589. There are, unfortunately, two reasons
that force us to discard this pleasing conjecture. The Owl's
Almanacke of 1589 would, as McKerrow states,[57] obviously
deal with the Martinists and other upstart religionists, and so
we are forced to believe that there is no connection between the
work projected in *A Countercuff* and the mock prognostication
of 1618. The similarity between titles is without doubt purely
coincidental, for we feel certain that the title of the extant
almanack satire is formed by analogy on that of Dekker's alma-

[57] Thomas Nashe, *Works,* I, 60, 74; IV, 45.

nack parody. This assumption is established as a fact by a prefatory epistle, "The Owles Epistle to the *Raven*," with which the almanack opens and in which the Owle relates the story of his voyage to the Court of the Moon. Because of this connection between the two satires, *The Owle's Almanacke* has been attributed by some scholars to Dekker. J. P. Collier, for example, reports in his *A Bibliographical Account* that he had seen a copy of this work in which a notation in an early hand stated that the book was written by Dekker. This inscribed copy has, naturally, been seen by no one else. Wilson, who has been long engaged upon a new edition of Dekker, feels that there is no evidence of either a factual or stylistic nature to warrant the ascription of this book to Dekker, and we find absolutely no reason to question this judgment. The independence of the author of *The Owle's Almanacke* from Dekkerian influence is most amazing because he seems to have been charmed by Dekker's pamphlets. He not only knows *The Raven's Almanacke* but speaks in his satire of "more sinnes" than were mustered together by the *"Bell-man of London,* or *Lanthorne and Candle-light."*[58] Because of this predilection for Dekker's writings, we should expect the Owle to show a Dekkerian influence that might be taken for a proof of Dekker's authorship, but aside from the similarity in titles, there is no other influence.

The Owle's Almanacke is the fullest satire on the almanack and prognostication written during the Elizabethan and Jacobean period. It burlesques all phases and all forms of the professional prognostication, and it is less concerned with social satire and ethical preachments than most of the other parodies of this time. The Owle makes fun of the term dates, of the official chronology of English History, of the annual computations, of the tide tables, of the astrological anatomy, of the calendar, and of the planetary dispositions. In addition to all this, there is a travesty of the conventional health rules and of

[58] *Op. cit.,* sig. C3v.

the premonstrations of plagues, floods, and famines. To this the Owle appends predictions for twenty-seven of the "fundamental trades," and an account of fairs, highways, and good and bad days. This, we know, is the usual *impedimenta* of the serious almanack and prognostication which the Owle has hurled together into one vast jest.

Before we analyze *The Owle's Almanacke* and illustrate his manner with extracts, we should like to notice some peculiarities of his humor that single him out as a wit of some charm. Like all of his contemporaries, the Owle delighted in punning and his puns are, often enough, amusing. The year, he writes, will begin with a *Pax vobis* and end with a *Pox vobis,* or, he tells of the poor defendant whose legal chances are so in the wane that he will shortly be out of his wain. He is fond of mimicking scientific jargon and gives the following unintelligible directions for the making of a moon-dial:

> Take a paire of iron Tongues; pitch them stradling over a kennell; then fasten a Waggon-wheele to the diameter of the Tongues; which done, marke what spoake doth cast the shadow of the Moone into the sinke, directly betweene the bestriders; from which count the spoakes till you come right opposite to the shadow: then dimidiate or part in two equall parts that number, divide it by 3. multiplie it by 7. from which extract the number of the Epact, and the Remanet will be the iust houre of the night. To shew a plat-forme were idle, when the precept is so plaine.[59]

A large portion of the opening section of *The Owle's Almanacke* is given over to a pseudomythological account of the origin of the zodiac which is a clear mockery of the accounts given in formal defenses of astrology and in occasional almanacks. The Owle traces the origin of the zodiac back to the fire-stealer Prometheus, whose introduction of heat and arts brought with it a number of evils that are named abstractedly *Dame Paena* and *Dame Pecunia, Craft* with his pages *Sinon, Davus, Geta, Parasitus,* and *Goodman Dolus.* These creatures,

---

[59] *Ibid.,* sig. C IV.

says the Owle, were followed by *Bribery, Simony, Intemperance,* and the "ill-favor'd facde Beldam," *Deterior Aetas.*

Now issued in from the Reareward, Madame *Vice,* or old *Iniquitie,* with a lath dagger painted, according to the fashion of an old *Vice* in a Comedy, with a head of many colours, as shewing her subtlety, and at her backe two Punkes that were her Chamber-maides, the one called *Too litle* and the other *Too much;* and these two had like Quick-silver eaten the worlds Goodnes to the heart.[60]

Annoyed at this procession from the pages of Ovid and seeing the Age of Gold banished by that of Brass, Jupiter summons Mercury and orders him to bind Prometheus to a rock in the Caucasus. Against Prometheus now appears a whole train of accusers, who abuse him physically and verbally and who are eventually placed in the zodiac by Jupiter. The complaint and vengeance of Virgo are characteristic of those of the others.

Bvt mee thinkes fuming furie should not smoke out of Virgins entrailes, when they haue so many petticoats to smother it: such tendrels of *Venus* groue should not harbour a shadow of reuenge: yea, but looke heere where *Virgo* comes pacing vp the hill, as fast as an Hang-man vp a ladder, at the hope of a good suite, or at least, as fast as her buske will giue her leaue. Well, to bee as breefe as an Apes taile, shee had no sooner got vp the hill, but she begins to chide out these causes of her direfull approach to tongue-tyed *Prometheus;* knocking her fists, as the custome of Shrewes is, where at length her frownes vented this foame. Now thou pilde pilfering knaue, thou maleficious rascall, was the mumps of thy brayne swolne so big, that they must needes breake out into flames, and bring such a smoke into the world, that has infected all our yonsters breath? thou hast taught men (thou captiuated cur) to kindle that quenchlesse fire of tobacco (oh my bodkin! Ile dig out his eyes). In which thou hast robb'd mee of my greatest pleasure; let a fresh bachelour in his new cloths come but towards mee, with intent to draw breath at my lips, why I smell my youth before I come at him; and if he offer me the curtesie, I turne him away with

[60] *Ibid.*, sig. C3r.

a foh, you smell (saue reuerence) of tobacco. If I walke in the streets, and chance to come downe Bucklersbury, oh how the whole Orb of aire is infected with this fume, which so much alters my complexion, that if I should not view my visage, euery houre of the day in the glasse, I durst be sworne that I should not know my selfe, but the worst of all is, that this *Promethean* smoke, melts off the complexion from our coloured cheekes, as fast as we lay it on, I cannot forbeare, the spoyle of that faculty spurs me forward, and forthwith sent shee a red hot spit (as valorously as euer *Tomyris* strucke off *Cyrus* head) into the midst of his belly, that you might well say, that *Prometheus* was no Hypocrite, for you might easily see into him. *Ioue* of pitty, or rather of enuy healed the wound, as strengthning the offender for farther vengeance, but the skarre of the wound remaines in humane portracture, which wee call the Nauell.[61]

The general predictions for the years and the rules for the preservation of health which follow this revision of the Prometheus legend are conventional in tone and not unlike the material that we have encountered in earlier mock almanacks. We read that corn should be cut when it is ripe and the hair sheared when it is too long or too lousy. The diseases incident to winter are hunger and laziness; those peculiar to summer are dry throats and wet backs. The Owle speaks of the inundations to be feared from the eyes of widows who have buried five husbands or from the tears of heirs who have hidden an onion in their hands and gone to the funeral of a rich relative. Like Smel-knave and Fouleweather, the Owle predicts great casualties among sheep, calves, and oxen. Similar witticisms appear in the section of the book devoted to satirizing the fair calendar, highway information, and notices of auspicious days that were regularly printed in the serious prognostication. The reader learns that there is "A Fare on the Bankside when the play-houses haue two penny tenants dwelling in them," that "the way to be an arrant Asse, is to bee a meere Vniuersitie Scholler," that it is a good day when "Attourneyes get no

[61] *Ibid.*, sigs. D2v-D3v.

money," whereas it is on a bad day that the "Cock-pit (is) pluckd downe." With this type of parody *The Owle's Almanacke* concludes, but before this the Owle prints his prognostications of twenty-seven occupations and professions, which are the most interesting and valuable portions of this satire.

The description of the natures of trades and professions was not an innovation in Western letters. Garzoni, who has been mentioned as the compiler of a compendium against astrology, was the author of a quarto-sized *La piazza universale di tutte le professioni del mondo,* which appeared in 1601. In England the practice had begun a vogue with Joseph Hall's *Characters of Virtues and Vices,* and though the form was essentially didactic, it was also, like the Italian method, informative. It is, then, to the character literature that these twenty-seven sections of *The Owle's Almanacke* really belong, for they are in no sense burlesques of the serious almanack and they are obviously written with a literary gusto that is wanting in the satirical parts of the book. The allusiveness and topicality of these sections may be illustrated by the Owle's prediction for the vintners, one of the shortest sections of this type.

A Caske full of comfort for you (crimson-nosd Vintners) that quilt your guests apparell with the best bombast: you shall not neede to take much care for those fellowes that warre so long vnder the Colours of Sacke and Sugar in the Rereward, that now they are like to make an vproare, and cast vp their accompts after the shot: neuer feare any foule play in this case: for when sergeant Grape has arrested any of these Sym-suck-spiggots of an action of liberty, then shall gaffer giddy hale them to prison, where *Somnus* the Iaylor shall shackle their hammes, till the fume of *Bacchus* his anger be ouer, and then you may saue their credits and your owne with a grace. This yeare all the *Catoes* in the world that neuer vsed wine but physicke, shall take it downe at their dyet as liuely as *Tricongius* and all our abstemious youths at the sight of *Qui medice viuit misere viuit,* shall turne pure swash, and visit your Tauernes at midnight. Many Physitions shall set it downe as an *Aphorisme,* that a cup of wine (as the fellow said of butter) shall

be good for any thing: old excellent for old men: It shall inspire
more wit into the Schollers braine, than all the Muses can from
their fountaines: make a Lawyers tongue resound like a mill-clack,
and inrich a Courtier with a nest of complements: it shall make a
Clowne step into the fashion, a begger take the wall of a Gentleman,
and a coward goe into the field with a fencing German: *Nunquam
nisi potus ad arma,* neuer fight but when thou art foxt shall be the
Souldiers motto: *arcana recludit,* wine vntwines hidden mysteries,
shall be the Poets poesie, and a cup of Hipocras shall be the best
stomacher for a sweetheart. The benefit of a good stomacke shall
be the grapes attribute, the exiler of melancholy shall be the tide of
the Vintners hogshead, and the reuiuing of the fly-blowne bloud in
old men, shal be lyens his hor. Diuers friends shall meete iumpe at
a Tauerne, that were almost worneout of memory, then must a
quart of wine play the Embassador to renue the league of friendship
between them. Sack & Claret are like to rise in your houses, if the
parties stomacke be not sound: And sobrieties light shall be cleane
extinguisht with your liquor.[62]

 The Owle's Almanacke, which had established a pattern
for originality and completeness, was followed in 1623 by
W. W.'s *A New and Merry Prognostication,* which has already
been described as an expansion and *réchauffé* of the *Mery
Pronosticacion* of 1544. The same year saw also the publication
of an anonymous prose satire, the *Vox Graculi, or Iacke Dawes
Prognostication. No lesse wittily, then wondrously rectified,
for the Eleuation of all Vanity, Villany, Sinne, and Surquedrie
sublimate, keeping quarter in the Courts, Cities, and Countries,
of all Christendome.* The fowl that is elevated to the authorship of this parody is, of course, part of the ill-omened tradition
to which the raven and the owl belonged, and this relationship
is indicated by a Latin verse on the title page which is patterned
on Vergil's "Saepe sinistra cava praedixit ab ilice cornix" and
reads "Saepe malum hoc vobis praedixit ab aethere Cornix."
The drawing on the title page of this pamphlet is also an

---

[62] *Ibid.,* sigs. G2v-G3r.

imitation, for it is patterned on the title-page illustration of
The Owle's Almanacke. The modification of the Vergilian
line and the imitation of the portrait of the Owle give us a
clue to the nature of the *Vox Graculi,* for like many of its
predecessors, it is not entirely original. Practically all of
Fouleweather's prognostications, and generous portions of *The
Raven's Almanacke,* together with sections of Dekker's *The
Dead Term* are incorporated in this burlesque. The author of
the *Vox Graculi,* however, is more skillful as a borrower than
most of his pilfering predecessors, for whereas some of his
loans are printed in a form that is naked and unabashed, others
are cleverly modified and woven into the texture of apparently
original material. Most of these lifted passages are printed in
the early sections of the *Vox Graculi,* and the last twenty pages
of the satire seem to be completely original. The borrowings
of *Platoes Cap,* which occurred in the end of the book, were
explained as the result of the author's desire to finish his manuscript; the loans in the *Vox Graculi* can obviously not be explained as the result of the author's haste to begin his book.
Until a source for the latter sections of the *Vox Graculi* is discovered, we are forced to consider this material as original, but
we should not be surprised to learn that it is purloined.

Our belief that the *Vox Graculi* is a patchwork, albeit an
able patchwork, of various writers' material is strengthened by
a passage in the center of the book which deviates stylistically
from the earlier borrowed matter and the later pages that are
seemingly original. To add to the peculiarities of this section,
the leaves on which it is printed are oddly signed, and Wilson
has, on the evidence of the matter and a swash letter, come to
the correct decision that here is an example of a manuscript
divided between two compositors. The matter of this section
is, however, much more interesting, for it combines the temper
of some of Jonson's verbal lashings with the tone of the
middle-class moralist, with the commentary of an Orlando
Friscobaldo. One may perceive from this similarity of notions

and intent that there was among the literary men of this era
a definite talent for reform.[63]

The last twenty pages of the *Vox Graculi*—the seemingly
original section of the book—are devoted to a series of mock
predictions for the first six months of the year. Each of these
predictions is preceded by an admonitory poem, and the text
and margin of this portion of the parody are studded with
learned quotations that the author has probably borrowed from
some *polyanthea*. The interesting literary characteristic of this
portion of the book is, as in the case of *The Owle's Almanacke,*
the topicality of the matter; again we find the method of the
character followed so closely that it is difficult to distinguish
between the *Vox Graculi's* predictions for the month and a
character writer's description of a season. As an example of
this literary similarity, we can cite the *Vox Graculi's* prediction for New Year's Day.

The First day of *Ianuary* being raw, colde and comfortlesse to
such as haue lost their mony at *Dice* at one of the *Temples* ouer-night,
strange apparitions are like to be seene: *Marchpanes* marching be-
twixt *Leaden-Hall* and the little *Conduit* in *Cheape,* in such aboun-
dance, that an hundred good fellowes may sooner starue, then
catch a corner, or a Comfit to sweeten their mouthes.

It is also to be feared, that through frailty, if a slip be made on
the Messengers default that carries them, for non-deliuery at the
place appointed: that vnlesse the said messenger, be not the more
inward with his Mistris, his Master will giue him ribrost for his
Newyeares-gift the next morning.

This day shall be giuen many more gifts then shall be asked for:
and Apples, Egges, and Orenges, shall be lifted to a lofty rate; when
a Pomewater be stucke with a few rotten Cloues, shall be more
worth then the honesty of an Hypocrite: and halfe a dozen of
Egges of more estimation, then the Vowes of a Strumpet. *Poets*
this day shall get mightily by their Pamphlets: for an hundred of

[63] Compare: "When children shall fling vp oathes and execrations against the
face of heauen, in the streets, and their Parents sit laughing at their doores, to hear
them so forward of their tongue" with the remarks of the elder Knowell in *Every
Man*, Act II.

Eleborate *Lines* shall be lesse esteemed in *London,* than an hundred of Walfleet Oysters at *Cambridge.*

Be not proude my nimble pated *Mercuries:* you that send forth your *Pamphlets* flutt'ring about the City to fetch in Crownes: for ere this yeares Semicircles meet, (if I ouershoot not my skill in *Astrologie*) *Latine* shal be set at a lower rate, then a Lobster: and *Greeke* stand begging in *Paules* with a Paper on its brest, as a punishment, that it should be so presumptuous, as to begge with an *Heathen* Tongue, in this our *Iewish* Nation; and all this, longe of a malignant Aspect of some pursie Planet, that had rather heare an *Oxe* of his own lowe in his Pasture, then a Scholler declaime of *Hospitality* in his Larder.[64]

The *Vox Graculi* is the last burlesque prognostication to be printed during the reign of King James, but like all its precursors it follows the conventional method of satire. To some degree it parodies the serious almanack and prognostication, for it mocks the penchant of the astrologers for authoritative references, empty generalities, ambiguous announcements, and rugged poetry. Of all the parodies, *The Owle's Almanacke* alone satirizes the full scope of the professional almanack, and *The Raven's Almanacke* is the only satire to make use of the figure of the astrological man. In all of these burlesques, however, the satire is as much directed against man and his follies as against the maunderings of the professional astrologer; often, one feels that the satirist simply conceived of the prognostication as a convenient vehicle for his social censure.

The almanack satire by no means perished with the end of James I's reign, for as it survived in France and Germany in both a humorous and literary form, so was it long popular in England and among English-speaking peoples. In 1626, for example, Nicholas Breton published his last and probably most finished work, *Fantasticks serving for a Perpetuall Prognostication,* which has, in spite of its usual inclusion in the character book genre, many features of the mock prognostication.

[64] *Ibid.*, sigs. G4r-H1r.

Martin Parker, that prolific writer of ballads, was the author of a "Marvellous prognostication," which was entered in the Stationers' Register in January, 1638, by Francis Grove, but which seems now to be lost. The Civil Wars produced new almanack burlesques as they also brought forth biased astrologers and astrological polemics. There are *The Welshman's new Almanack and Prognostication for this present year 1643* and *Wonders Foretold by her crete Prophet of Wales which shall happen this present year 1643*, which nod at the political situation and yet maintain their connections with the tradition of the mock almanack, for the first satire derives from Fouleweather and the second borrows from Melton's attack on astrologers. Another parody prognostication belonging to the same period and political upheaval is a six-page quarto which is titled, *Shinkin ap Shone her Prognostication for the ensuing yeer, 1654, foretelling what admirable Events are like to fall out in the Horizon of Little Britain . . . Printed for the Author, and are to be sold at his shop at the Sign of the Cows Bobby behind the Welsh Mountains.* We cannot find another burlesque prognostication with as engaging a title as Shinkin ap Shone's almanack, but we may mention others like *Now or Never: Or, The Princely Calendar. Being a Bloody Almanack, For the Time present and to come* (1659); *A Merry-Conceited Fortune-Teller: Prognosticating to all Trades and Professions their good and bad Fortune* (1663); *Jack Adams His Perpetual Almanack* (ca. 1664); and *Tim Tell Troth, The Knavery of Astrology discovered in Observations upon every month of the year 1680.*

Two astrologers of the seventeenth century, John Lilly and John Partridge, begot by means of their serious astrological efforts a whole parade of parodies. Lilly, for instance, was the target of many broadsides and satires based on his own predictions; and we can assume that to Lilly is owed the vogue of the mock prognostication during the last half of the seventeenth century. Among some of the more interesting satires on Lilly's predictions are *Strange Predictions* (1652), *Merlinus Democritus; Or, The Merry-conceited Prognosticator . . . By W. Liby, Student in Astrology* (1654), *England's Monethly Observations and Predictions for the Yeare of our Blessed Saviour 1653, fore-told by those two famous Astrologers of our Age, Mr. William Lilly and Mr. Culpeper.* John Phillips, Milton's nephew, entered this discussion in 1660 with his *Montelion,* in which the pretenses of Lilly and other astrologers were mocked; this work seems to have been so successful that Phillips followed it in 1675 with a *Mercurius Verax, Or the Prisoners' Prognostication.* Like Lilly, Partridge also begot a number of satires prior to *Isaac Bickerstaff's Predictions for the Year 1708.*[65] In 1675, for instance, appeared a book ascribed to Partridge and called *The Character of a Quack Astrologer, or the Spurious Prognostication Anatomiz'd with allowance;* this book was followed by more obvious satirical predictions like the *Merlini Liberati Errata* of 1692. By this time, however, the burlesque almanack was an established form of literature, and the astrologers' professional compilations had fathered a child more respectable than themselves.

We have now surveyed the European attitudes toward astrology for almost a hundred and fifty years, and we have discovered that, with slight variations, the opinions on both sides of the question remained virtually constant. In an age that is distinguished by violent upheavals in other spheres of thought, this stability of attitude seems remarkable; but as we consider the matter, we realize that it was because of the revolutionary character of the age that opinions remained unchanged, that no new arguments were invented. The great problems of theology, politics, economics, and social conditions that beset the age required the full attention of the great in-

[65] W. O. Eddy, "Tom Brown and Partridge the Astrologer," *Modern Philology,* XXVIII (1930-31), 163-168, and "The Wits vs. John Partridge, Astrologer," *Studies in Philology,* XXIX (1932), 29-40; B. Boyce, *Tom Brown of facetious memory, Grub street in the age of Dryden* (Cambridge, Mass., 1939), pp. 129-133.

tellectual leaders, who in a more placid era might have found time to consider more thoroughly the question of the validity of astrology. Then, too, the unsettled character of Renaissance beliefs made astrology as necessary to the ordinary man as his daily bread; for when men discover that the beliefs in which they have been brought up are gone, they clutch at straws, and astrology is a very substantial straw. Finally, rationalism —that great product of humanism—did not attain its full stature until the middle of the seventeenth century, when it was systematized by thinkers like Descartes, Spinoza, and Hobbes and it was rationalism that eventually made astrology an untenable faith for the most intelligent section of humanity.

In spite of this constancy of arguments in the controversy about astrology, certain minor variations are obvious. We have noticed that Ficino was a perfect example of the moderate astrologer, who thought that the stars had an influence on the flesh of man, but who eventually refused to assign fatal powers to the planets. Pico della Mirandola, the most accomplished opponent of astrology whom we have encountered, was, we recall, willing to grant that the stars had a general influence, but denied that this influence was particular or predictable. Pontano, on the other hand, believed that the stars provided for the diversity of men's characters and fates, and held that astrology explained all earthly fortuities. This conviction, however, did not blind him to the existence of other causes; and we remember that he was willing to agree with Pico that heredity and environment, or, as he put it, fortune and nature, were important factors in determining the careers of men. Now the curious thing is that the defenders and opponents of astrology in the sixteenth and early seventeenth centuries did not evolve from these men, did not build on them and extend their arguments. As we have said before, the polemicists of the Renaissance borrowed ideas and authorities from these Italians; some of the opponents of astrology did little more than epitomize Pico; but none of them grasped the whole point

of view. It was, in fact, only after a lapse of more than a half
century that the continentals became as liberal as Pico or as
acute as Pontano. Let us scrutinize this conclusion more
closely.

Bellanti, the first opponent of Pico, is a perfect example of
an unregenerate astrologer, who presents all the medieval arguments and has none of Ficino's doubts and none of Pontano's
readiness to see the other side. With Melanchthon, however,
we begin to find the friends of astrology adopting the attitude
of Pontano; they blunt the edge of Pico's argument and of the
arguments of those that echo him by admitting the importance
of free will and by demonstrating that the foreknowledge obtained by the astrologer permits an intelligent employment of
the will. With few exceptions, the later astrologers follow
this pattern. The opponents of astrology also move towards
Pico's admission that the stars have a general influence, and
come more and more to level their attacks at the rascally and
ignorant astrologer rather than at the sincere investigator, who
is trying to correct and perfect the technique of his art. The
later defenders of astrology agree with this attitude and join
their opponents in an attempt to smoke out the charlatans.
The defenders and opponents of astrology finally agreed in so
many things that we sometimes wonder what the quarrel was
about. In the end, however, there was a quarrel and the major
disagreement was this: the opponents of astrology admitted
that the stars had an influence on man, but insisted that it was
impossible to determine what the influence was; the astrologers
said that there were many flaws and fallacies in their art, but
insisted that these difficulties could be removed by experiment
and that in time they could ascertain the exact nature of the
astral forces.

This minor, though ardent, controversy is reflected in the
literature of the English Renaissance, and this mirroring is
important for the historian of culture because it indicates,
better than the formal polemics, the popular attitude toward

astrology. Few of the literary men had read Milich or Pereyra, but they had all listened to discussions of the problem on lower levels, and the dramatists, at least, were ready to provide the public with familiar and intelligible matter. The constant use of astrological allusions, the frequent inclusion of the astrologer's philosophy in works in verse and prose, indicates that the man of letters and his readers believed in the influence of the stars. The fact that the atheistic villains of the stage alone denied the powers of the stars is a significant commentary on the popular opinion. Like both the formal opponents and defenders of astrology, the literary men attacked the cheating and ignorant astrologer, and this fact strengthens our conclusion that belief in the powers of the stars was unanimous, for it is only when there is a confirmed orthodoxy that the unorthodox are persecuted. This attack, as we have seen, was sometimes confined to pure verse satire, to the more rigorous type of character description, and to the portrayal of a thieving astrologer in the cast of a play. The heaviest assault came in the form of the almanack and prognostication parody, which began as a satire on the untruthful predictions of the astrologers, but became shortly a satire on mankind in general and used the manner of the serious prognostication as only a convenient literary form.

APPENDIX

ONE OF THE earliest treatises on astrological medicine in the sixteenth century is Thomas Rocha's *Compilatio quaedam terminorum astronomie. Compilatio quaedam in eligendo tempus corpori humano in exibitione medicinarum ac fleubotomia exequenda utile,* which appeared at Montpellier, where Rocha was a member of the faculty, in 1501.[1] The book, as the title indicates, deals with the determination of the correct moments for administering drugs or opening veins. A second great adept of this period was Augustine Nifo (Niphus), who, we recall, made a reputation among philosophers for his writings on Aristotle and Averroes. In 1504, Niphus published at Venice a work on critical days with the title, *De diebus criticus seu decretoriis aureus liber ad Vicentium Quirinum patritum Venetum.* The first part of this book considers the complicated theories of critical days and brings up a number of controversial problems. In the second book, Nifo expounds the Ptolemaic theory, and discusses the qualities of the planets, the relationship between planets and humors, and the influence of the planets, especially of the moon, in the treatment of various diseases. The third book is given over to prognostics, and special attention is paid to the eclipse of the sun, to comets, and to conjunctions of Mars, Saturn, and Jupiter which have the power to make men ill. The last book instructs the physician on the correct moment for treatment. A purge will be successful when the moon is conjunct with Jupiter, or in Scorpio or Pisces; it is unsuccessful when the moon is conjunct with Saturn or Mars.

An interesting commentary on the methods of astrologers

[1] Reprinted in facsimile by Felix Desvernay at Lyons in 1904.

and an example of the attempt made by reputable astrologers to perfect the *practica* is the *Speculum astrologicum* of the astrologer Johann Essler, which appeared at Mainz in 1508. Essler admits that astrologers have frequently made false predictions, but insists that this is not the fault of astrology but of the ignorance of astrologers, who will not take advantage of the latest findings. They use the star-tables of Ptolemy, for instance, instead of the more accurate tables of Alfonso el Sabio. Essler believes, of course, in the importance of the physician's knowing astrology.

Most important, however, in the history of astrological medicine are the writings of Fredericus Chrisogonus Jadertinus. Chrisogonus was a physician and astrologer and in his preface to his *De modo collegiandi: pronosticandi: et curandi febres. Nec non de humana felicitate: ac denique de fluxu et refluxu maris* (Venice, 1523), he attacks the ancient theories of fever and points out that it is a malady obviously caused by the planets, for he believes that the heavenly bodies bring sickness, recovery, and death. He is quite surprised that physicians of his day still trust the classical theories since they now may make use of the revised astronomy. He illustrates his method with a figure for "Socrates," who took sick on October 9, 1527. He did not, however, approve of alchemy. In Chapter VII, he attacks those "moderns" who ascribe tin to Venus and copper to Jupiter; he proves that the prospects of transmutation are hopeless. The Paracelsians, who believed that all metals arose from sulphur and mercury, are to him the most foolish of men.

Many an astrological work of this period contains a short section on astrological medicine, which is often mentioned in accepted scientific works that are not essentially astrological. Such a section is found in the twenty-sixth chapter of Laurentius Frisius' *Expositio ususque astrolabii* (Strassburg, 1522). This chapter, the longest in the book, is devoted to a study of critical days, and Frisius says that a physician who does not know astrology is no physician. He then explains how one may use the astrolabe in determining these days and so avoid complicated mathematics. Frisius is most famous for his *Spiegel der Artznei,* which he published in 1518 and which was one of the first works on medicine in the vernacular.

One could, however, believe in the importance of astrology in medicine without being a hidebound astrologer. This fact is illustrated by the career of Georg Tanstetter von Rain, who was a friend of Frisius, an editor of Albertus Magnus, and the court physician of Maximilian I. There was a great controversy among astrologers about the prospect of the end of the world in 1524; in this discussion experts like Niphus, Pigghius, Cirvelus, Peranzonus, Scepperus took definite sides. In 1523 Tanstetter brought out his book, the *Libellus consolatorius, quo opinionem iam dudum annis hominum ex quorundam astrologastrorum divinatione insidentem, de futuro diluvio et multis aliis horrendis periculis XXIIII anni a fundamentis extirpare conatur.* Tanstetter relates how frightened men are by the predictions of the coming flood and warns his readers to beware of the predictions of rascally astrologers. He admits that he has issued regular annual predictions, but insists that his prognostications are always made with caution. He tells of one occasion, however, when his name was used on a spurious prediction by a grasping publisher. He then argues on the strength of Biblical authority and of past years when most of the planets were in Pisces that the world will not again be destroyed by water. Tanstetter now makes vast and sweeping predictions as if he had not just been condemning the announcements of other astrologers. In 1531, it was rumored that Tanstetter was dead, so one of his old students, Michael Herus, gave his lecture notes to the scientist-printer Brunfels, who published them in this year as the *Artificium de applicatione astrologiae ad medicinam, deque convenientia earundem, Georgii Collimitii Tansteteri, canones aliquot, et quaedam alia, quorum catalogum reperies in proxima pagella.* Because this book is compiled from a student's notes, it is quite loosely organized and without question often inexact, but it furnishes us with an excellent notion of the type of medical lecture given in the universities of this period. The opening pages are quite conventional: the relations of the planets and the humors, the uses of the astrolabe are thoroughly discussed. This is followed by a compilation from various authorities on crises, the importance of knowing the beginning of the disease, when to expect the crisis, the critical signs, and the causes and courses of a number of diseases. Tanstetter tells how to determine the *dies critici, indicativi, intercadentes sive provocatorii, vacui.* He rejects Galen's theory of *mensis medicinalis,* and gives pages to a discussion of houses, planets, and aspects. He expounds the malign natures of planets and says that a physician whose natal stars are bad can do harm to a patient whose planets are favorable. The hour in which one summons the physician, he declares, should be favorable. He digresses at length on the nature and influence of planets and concludes his remarks with the usual advice on purges, baths, cuppings, hair-cutting, and other medical matters. He supplies the student with moon tables and a tabulation of the powers of planets in various signs.

In almost the same year that Tanstetter's lectures were printed the *Liber de peste, de signis febrium et de diebus criticis* of Antonius Cartagensis appeared. He seems favorably inclined toward many of Pico's arguments, but he sometimes opposes him. He finds astrology useful, however, in determining critical days. The same period also saw the appearance of Manfredi's *Aphorismen* with a preface by the astrologer Schonerus. Schonerus says that the physician who lets blood or compounds medicine when the stars are hostile does his patient a great wrong, whereas the physician who consults the stars does well; on these points it is interesting to find that he respects the authority of Ficino. In 1521, Johann Hasfurtus Virdungus entered the debate about the deluge of 1524 with his *Practica Teütsch über die neüwe erschröckliche vor nie gesehen Coniunction,* and in 1532, he published his *Nova medicinae methodus nunc primum et condita et aedita ex mathematica ratione curandi,* which showed that he was still convinced of the truth of astrology. The first part of this book provides the physician with a foundation in astrology; the second part with traditional matter about complexions, temperaments, planet-sons, sidereal prognosis, clysters, suppositories, fomentations, and other technical forms of treatment. It is more medical than astrological in its earlier pages, but the third part is a study of critical days and the fourth part is a discussion of that great astrological absurdity, the *urina non visa.* The book is a handbook and is frankly written for *tirones et rudes artis medicae.* Another book of this decade was Jacob Scholl's *Astrologiae ad medicinam adplicatio brevis deque convenientia earundem canones aliquot ex probatissimis quibusque et astrologiae et medicinae, authoribus vigilantissime collecti, restaurati et nunc primum in lucem aediti* (Mainz, 1537).

This type of medical theory did not pass without attack, and the assault came from the distinguished Italian physician and Latin poet Girolamo Fracastoro. In his *Homocentrica eiusdem de causis criticorum dierum per ea quae in nobis sunt* (Venice, 1538), he abandons the Galenic theory of the influence of the moon on critical days and says that crises arise from the struggles between the humors themselves. This work—enlightened for its age—was attacked at once by Andreas Thurinus in *Hippocrates et Galeni defensio adversus Hieronymum Fracastorium, de causis dierum criticorum* (Rome, 1542) and Michel-Angelo Biondi in his *De diebus decretoriis, et crisi eorumque verissimis causis in via Galeni, contra neotericos libellus* (Rome, 1544). Biondi, who is well known for his work on physiognomy, says that to attack Galen is to swim against the stream. Not the movement of the humors and their different qualities but the <u>moon</u> also is the *causa efficiens* of acute illnesses and the <u>sun of chronic diseases.</u>

In 1546, Luca Gaurico's book on astrological medicine appeared at Rome. It was titled *Super diebus decretoriis (quos*

*etiam criticos vocitant) axiomata, sive aphorismi grandes utique
sententiae brevi oratione compraehensae.* This work is divided
into twelve tracts, each of which concerns a division in the
science. The first takes up the general value of astrology for
medicine, the history of the doctrine of critical days, the axioms
of Galen, and other commonplace material. The second attacks
Fracastoro's theory of the melancholy humor. The third is a
commentary on the sixty aphorisms of Ptolemy and the fourth
a comment on those of Bellanti and others. The fifth tractate
discusses the sixteen *latera* of Ptolemy and other controversial
matters, and the sixth the doctrine of Paulus Aegineta on critical days. The seventh tract presents the basis of medical astrology, and in the eighth Gaurico presents his own *axiomata*.
The ninth section returns to the doctrines of Ptolemy, the tenth
is a summary of Hippocrates' *De somnis aegrotantium,* and
the eleventh is a commentary on the same author's *Aphoris-
mus V.* In the last essay, Gaurico presents his own interpretation of the pseudo-Hippocratean *de medicorum astrologia.*

The 1550's saw the publication of many works by practical
astrologers that were little more than *rifacimenti* of previous
books. Among these new works are Thomas Bodier's *De ratione et usu dierum criticorum opus recens natum, in quo mens
tum ipsius Ptolemaei, tum aliorum astrologorum hac in parte
dilucidatur* (Paris, 1555). The first part of this work is concerned with Ptolemy's "Super aegrotis criticos dies inspice, ac
Lunae peragrationem in angulis figurae sexdecim laterum ubi
enim eos angulos bene affectos inveneris, bene erit languenti,
contra male, si afflictos inveneris." The latter part is a casebook
of the five preceding years. Another writer of this decade
was Antoine Mizauld, who had previously compiled various
weather prognostications, and who published in 1550 his *Aesculapii et uraniae medicum simul et astronomicum ex colloquio
conjugium.* In 1551 his *Planetologia, rebus astronomicum,
medicis et philosophicis erudite referta; ex qua, coelestium
corporum cum humanis, et astronomiae cum medicina societas,*

et harmonia was printed at Lyons. A most interesting book by Mizauld is his *Harmonia superioris naturae mundi et inferioris; una cum admirabili foedere et sympatheia rerum utriusque,* which appeared at Paris in 1555; it consists of eleven dialogues which expound, after the macrocosmic-microcosmic fashion, the relations between celestial forces and powers and the parts and humors of the body. A book on a similar subject by Mizauld, the *Secrets de la Lune,* was published at Paris in 1571.

One of the first works of this nature printed in the 1560's was the Tübingen oration of Samuel Eisenmenger (Sidocrates), which was published in 1563 with the title *Oratio de methodo iatro mathematikon syntaxeon in qua eam semper medicis veteribus et recentibus usui necessario fuisse ipsorum testimonio ratione et experientia confirmatur et astrologiae fundamenta certissima indicantur.* Eisenmenger's work is a conventional treatise of an astrologer who had already published a prognostication before he brought out his method. At almost the same time, Jean Taisner, whose general treatise on the mechanics of astrology, the *Astrologiae iudiciariae ysagogica et totius divinatricis artis encomia,* had appeared in 1559, published his *Opus mathematicum octo libros complectens . . . omnibus matheseos, cheiromantiae, philosophiae, et medicinae studiosis utiles ac necessarii* at Cologne. This latter work is, of course, a substantial text. A similar manual is Cornelius Schylander's *Medicina astrologica omnibus medicinae studiosis longe utilissima et necessaria, iam denuo multis in locis aucta, una cum practica chirurgiae brevi et facili* (Antwerp, 1570). The opening sections of Schylander's book are devoted to a determination of critical days; the second section concerns astrological diagnosis; and the last section discusses purging and bloodletting. In the main it is an attempt to combine astrology with the normal medical practices of the day. A final work of this nature in the century is the *Ludus iatromathematicus* of Henri de Monantheuil, which appeared at Paris in 1597; in this book the value of all the arts for medicine is described. De Monantheuil insists that a knowledge of the powers of the stars is important for the physician.

The early part of the seventeenth century produced a number of books on practical astrology. A defense of medical astrology appeared in Johannes Asverus Amsingius' *Dissertatio iatromathematica,* which was published at Rostock in 1602. A more important work was J. A. Magini's *De astrologica ratione, ac usu dierum criticorum, seu decretoriorum; ac praeterea de cognoscendis et medendis morbis ex corporum coelestium cognitione* (Venice, 1607). In his preface Magini says that his medical students asked him to write a treatise on astrological medicine, and so he proposes to print an edition of the third book of Galen so that those physicians who turn up their noses at astrology in medicine may see how their god defers to the science of stars. He offers a list of authorities from Hippocrates to his own day who approve of the astrological theory in medicine, and proceeds to his edition which is accompanied by a very astrological commentary. The second half of the book is called "De legitimo astrologiae in medicina usu" and contains the familiar material. Magini is aware that the Church does not approve of astrology and prints in this second section a very amusing evasion.

Astrologiam a sacrosancta Ecclesia condemnari: ideoque boni Christiani officium esse eandem non solum aspernari, sed cane peius et angue fugere. Nam licet merito et sanctissime a Sancta Matre Ecclesia prognosticationes et iudicia nativitatum circa actiones humanas, quae a voluntate nostra, et libero arbitrio dependent, condemnentur; nequaquam tamen illa hanc Astrologiae partem, quae ad sanitatem humani corporis facit, Medico interdixit.

Magini illustrates the conventional contents of the subsequent twenty-eight chapters with about thirty figures supporting his thesis that the nature and course of a disease can be learned from the stars.

Magini's book was followed by a number of very ordinary

works which repeat the traditional matter and only merit bibliographical mention. Ambrosius Floridus brought out a *Tractatus de annis climactericis, ac diebus criticis* at Padua in 1612; Hippolytus Obicius published a *Iatrostronomicon* at Vincenza in 1618; and Johannes Kollner printed a *Tractatus physicus mathematicus* at Greifswald in 1618. In 1622 appeared a fairly mystical work which in some ways is akin to Valentine Weigel's *Astrology Theologized*—this work, the *Introductorium Iatromathematicum* of August Etzler, is filled with many occult notions. Etzler says that the "Verbum Dei" is the basis of all medicine and recalls thereby the notion that Petrarch once expressed that medicine existed undefiled in the mind of God. He lists, like many of his precursors, the secret correspondences between minerals, plants, animals, and stars, and lays special stress on observing the antipathies and sympathies of planets in treating a patient.

In the same year that Etzler brought out his book, Jacques Fontaine published at Lyons a work called the *De astrologia medica liber, in quo ex principiis naturalibus et corpori humano insitis probatur evidentissime vana esse ea omnia quae astrologi iudiciarii de hominum moribus, institutis, morbis, crisibus et illorum morborum curationibus asserverunt.* Sudhoff says that this book is one of the most rational treatises printed, but that it seems to have had little effect in shaping the attitude of the seventeenth century. Fontaine did not deny the influence of the stars, but, on the other hand, he did not consider it very important. The physician, he insists, should observe matters closer at hand. In the letting of blood, the condition of the patient should be observed more carefully than the position of the stars. Fontaine's attitude coincides with that of Sir Thomas Browne, whose rationalism made it difficult for him to believe in stellar influence, yet whose love of tradition made it equally difficult for him to deny that the stars had power.

BIBLIOGRAPHY

PRIMARY SOURCES

ANONYMOUS WORKS

The Tragedy of Caesar and Pompey. Edited by F. S. Boas. Malone Society Reprints. Oxford, 1911.

A Pleasant Comedie of Faire Em. J. S. Farmer, Students' Facsimiles. Amersham, 1911.

The Tragedy of Locrine. Edited by R. B. McKerrow. Malone Society Reprints. Oxford, 1908.

The Historie of the Two Maides of More-clacke. J. S. Farmer, Students' Facsimiles. Amersham, 1913.

A Mery Pronosticacion. London, 1544.

The Pilgrimage to Parnassus with the two parts of The Return from Parnassus. Edited by W. D. Macray. Oxford, 1886.

The Tragical Reign of Selimus. Edited by W. Bang. Malone Society Reprints. Oxford, 1908.

The Tragedy of Tiberius. Edited by W. W. Greg. Malone Society Reprints. Oxford, 1914.

The Weakest Goeth to the Wall. Edited by W. W. Greg. Malone Society Reprints. Oxford, 1912.

The Wisdom of Doctor Dodypoll. J. S. Farmer, Students' Facsimiles. Amersham, 1912.

The Wit of a Woman. Edited by W. W. Greg. Malone Society Reprints. Oxford, 1913.

PSEUDONYMOUS WORKS

Vox Graculi; or Iacke Dawes Prognostication. No lesse wittily, then wondrously rectified, for the Elevation of all Vanity, Villany, Sinne, and Surquedrie sublimate, keeping quarter in the Courts, Cities, and Countries, of all Christendome. London, 1623.

Platoes Cap. Cast at this Yeare 1604, being Leape-yeere. London, 1604. Preface signed "Adam Evesdropper."

FOULEWEATHER, A. *A wonderful, strange and miraculous, Astrologicall Prognostication for this yeer of our Lord God 1591. Discouering such wonders to happen this yeere, as neuer chaunced since Noes floud. Wherein if there be found one lye, the Author will loose his credit for euer. By Adam Fouleweather, Student in Asse-tronomy.* London, 1591.

The Owles Almanacke. Prognosticating many strange accidents which shall happen to this Kingdome of Great Britaine this yeare, 1618. Calculated as well for the meridian mirth of London as any other part of Great Britaine. Found in an Iuy-bush written in old Characters, and now published in English by the painefull labours of Mr. Iocundary Merrie-braines. London, 1618.

SMEL-KNAVE, S. *The Fearefull and lamentable effects of two dangerous comets, which shall appeare in the yeere of our Lord, 1591.* London, 1591.

AGRIPPA, H. C. *De incertitudine et vanitate omnium scientiarum et artium.* Frankfort and Leipzig, 1693.

ALBERTI, L. B. *Opera inedita.* Edited by J. Mancini. Florence, 1890.

———. *Opuscoli morali.* Venice, 1568.

ALEXANDER, SIR WILLIAM. *Works.* Edited by L. E. Kastner and H. B. Charlton. 2 vols. Edinburgh, 1929.

ALSTED, J. H. *Philosophia digne restituta; libri quatuor.* Hebornia in Nassau, 1612.

ANGELI, A. DEGLI. *In astrologos coniectores libri quinque.* Lyons, 1620.

ARETINO, P. *Pronostico dell' anno MDXXXIIII.* Edited by A. Luzio. Bergamo, 1900.

AXELSÖN, K. *Physica et ethica Mosaica, ut antiquissima, ita vere Christiana.* Hanover, 1613.

BABINGTON, G. *Certaine Plaine, briefe, and Comfortable Notes, upon every chapter of Genesis.* London, 1596.

BACON, F. *The Works.* Edited by James Spedding and R. E. Ellis. 15 vols. Boston, 1860-65.

BEAUMONT, F. AND FLETCHER, J. *Works.* Edited by A. R. Waller and A. Glover. 10 vols. Cambridge, 1905-12.

BELLANTI, L. *De astrologica veritate, et in disputationes Joannis Pici adversus astrologos responsiones.* Venice, 1502.

BRANDON, S. *The Virtuous Octavia.* Edited by R. B. McKerrow. Malone Society Reprints. Oxford, 1909.

BRENT, J. *Opera*. Tübingen, 1576.

BRETON, N. *Works in Verse and Prose*. Edited by A. Grosart. 2 vols. London, 1879.

BROSSERIUS, S. *Totius philosophiae naturalis epitome*. Paris, 1536.

BURTON, R. *The Anatomy of Melancholy*. Philadelphia, 1853.

CALDERIA, J. *Concordantiae poetarum philosophorum et theologorum liber*. Venice, 1547.

CALVIN, J. *An Admonicion against Astrology iudiciall*. London, 1563.

——. *Commentaries on the First Book of Moses called Genesis*. Edited by J. King. Edinburgh, 1847.

——. *Opera*. 58 vols. Brunswick and Berlin, 1863-1900.

CAMDEN, W. *Annales rerum Anglicarum et Hibernicarum regnante Elizabetha*. London, 1615.

Guielmi Camdeni et illustrium virorum ad G. Camdenum epistolae. Edited by T. Smith. London, 1691.

CARDAN, G. *Libelli quinque*. Nuremberg, 1547.

——. *Opera omnia*. 10 vols. Lyons, 1663.

CARLETON, G. Ἀστρολογομανια : *The Madnesse of Astrologers. Or An Examination of Sir Christopher Heydons Booke, Intituled A Defence of Iudiciarie Astrologie*. London, 1624.

CHAMBER, J. *A Treatise Against Judicial Astrologie*. London, 1601.

CHAPMAN, G. *The Works: Poems and Minor Translations*. Edited by A. C. Swinburne. London, 1875.

——. *Works*. Edited by R. H. Shepherd. 3 vols. London, 1873.

CHASSENEAUX, B. DE. *Catalogus gloriae mundi*. Lyons, 1546.

CIRVELO, P. *Apotelesmata astrologiae Christianae*. Alcala, 1521.

CONTARENI, G. *De elementis et eorum mixtionibus libri quinque*. Paris, 1548.

COXE, F. *A Short Treatise declaringe the Detestable Wickednesse of Magicall Sciences*. London, 1561.

D., T. *The Bloody Banquet*. J. S. Farmer, Students' Facsimiles. Amersham, 1914.

DEE, JOHN. Preface in Euclid. *Elements of Geometry*. Edited by T. Rudd. London, 1661.

DEKKER, T. *Works*. Edited by A. Grosart. 5 vols. London, 1884-86.

——. *Works*. Edited by E. Rhys. London, 1887.

Des Periers, B. *Œuvres*. Edited by M. L. Lacour. 2 vols. Paris, 1856.

Digges, L. *A Prognostication of Right Good Effect*. Old Ashmolean Reprints III. Oxford, 1926.

Dodsley's Old English Plays. Edited by W. C. Hazlitt. 15 vols. London, 1874-76.

Donne, J. *Devotions Upon Emergent Occasions*. Edited by J. Sparrow. Cambridge, 1923.

———. *Poetical Works*. Edited by H. J. C. Grierson. 2 vols. Oxford, 1912.

———. *LXXX Sermons*. London, 1640.

Drayton, M. *Works*. Edited by W. Hebel. 4 vols. Oxford, 1931.

Drummond of Hawthornden, W. *Notes of Conversations with Ben Jonson*. Edited by G. B. Harrison. London, 1923.

Erasmus, D. *Opus epistolarum*. Edited by P. S. Allen and H. M. Allen. 9 vols. Oxford, 1906-37.

———. *Opera omnia*. 10 vols. Leyden, 1703.

Ficino, M. *Opera et quae hactenus extitere, et quae in lucem nunc primum prodiere omnia, omnium artium et scientiarum, maiorumque facultatum multipharia cognitione refertissima*. 2 vols. Basel, 1561.

———. *Supplementum Ficinianum*. Edited by P. O. Kristeller. Florence, 1937.

Firmicus Maternus, J. *Matheseos*. Edited by W. Kroll and F. Skutsch. 2 vols. Leipzig, 1897.

Fletcher, Giles and Fletcher, Phineas. *Works*. Edited by F. S. Boas. 2 vols. Cambridge, 1908.

Fontaine, J. *Discours de la puissance du ciel sur les corps inférieurs et principalement de l'influence contre les astrologues iudiciaires*. Paris, 1581.

Fonte, A. di. *Somma della natural filosofia*. Venice, 1557.

Ford, J. *Works*. Edited by A. Dyce and W. Gifford. 3 vols. London, 1895.

Frischlin, N. *Carmen de astronomico horologio Argentoratensi*. Strassburg, 1575.

———. *De astronomicae artis, cum doctrina coelesti, et naturali philosophia*. Frankfurt, 1586.

FULKE, W. *Antiprognosticon contra inutiles astrologorum predictiones Nostradami, Cunninghami, Loui, Hilli, Vaghami, et reliquorum omnium.* London, 1560.

———. *Antiprognosticon that is to saye, an Invective agaynst the vayne and unprofitable predictions of the Astrologians.* Translated by W. Painter. London, 1560.

———. *A Most Pleasant Prospect into the Garden of Naturall Contemplation.* London, 1563.

FULLER, T. *The History of the Worthies of England.* 2 vols. London, 1811.

———. *The Holy State. The Profane State.* London, 1648.

FULLER, T. AND OTHERS. *Abel Redevivus. Or, the Dead Yet Speaking.* London, 1651.

GARTZE, J. *Astrologae methodus.* Basel, 1576.

GARZONI, T. *La piazza universale di tutte le professioni del mondo.* Venice, 1601.

———. *Il serraglio degli stupori del mondo.* Venice, 1613.

GAURICO, L. *De eclipsi solis miraculosa in Passione Domini celebrata.* Rome, 1539.

———. *Oratio de inventoribus et astrologiae laudibus habita in Ferrariensis academia.* Venice, 1531.

———. *Tractatus astrologiae iudiciariae de nativitatibus virorum et mulierum.* Venice, 1552.

GEVEREN, S. a. *Of the End of this Worlde and Seconde Commyng of Christe.* London, 1578.

GIUNTINI, F. *De divinatione, quae fit per astra, diversum ac discrepans duorum catholicorum sacrae theologiae doctorum iudicium scilicet Francisci Iunctinus Florentini, ac Ioannis Lensaei Belliolani Professoris Louaniensis.* Cologne, 1580.

GÖCKEL, R. *Acroteleution astrologicum.* Marburg, 1618.

———. *Discursus apologeticus pro astromantia.* Marburg, 1611.

———. *Urania cum geminis filiabus hoc est astronomia et astrologia.* Frankfurt, 1615.

GRAU, F. *Of All Blasing Starrs in Generall, as well Supernaturall as Naturall.* Translated by A. Fleming. London, 1577.

GREENE, R. *Plays and Poems.* Edited by C. Collins. 2 vols. Oxford, 1905.

———. *Works.* Edited by A. Grosart. 15 vols. London, 1881-86.

HALL, J. *Satires*. Edited by T. Warton and S. W. Singer. London, 1824.

——. *The Discovery of a New World*. Edited by H. Brown. Cambridge, Mass., 1937.

HARVEY, G. *Smithus; vel Musarum Lachrymae*. London, 1578.

——. *Works*. Edited by A. Grosart. 3 vols. London, 1884-85.

HARVEY, J. *An Astrological addition, or supplement to be annexed to the late Discourse upon the great Coniunction of Saturn and Iupiter*. London, 1583.

——. *A Discoursive Probleme concerning Prophesies, How far they are to be valued, or credited, according to the surest rules, and directions in Divinitie, Philosophie, Astrologie, and other learning*. London, 1588.

HARVEY, R. *An Astrological Discourse Upon the great and notable Coniunction of the two superiour Planets, Saturne and Iupiter which shall happen the 28. day of April, 1583*. London, 1583.

HAYN, J. DE. *Introductiones apotelesmaticae elegantes in physiognomiam, complexiones hominum, astrologiam naturalem, naturas planetarum, cum periaxiomatibus de faciebus signorum et canonibus de aegritudinibus hominum*. Strassburg, 1630.

HELLER, J. "Prefatio" to John of Seville, *Epitome totius astrologiae* (1548) in Marstaller.

HEMMINGA, S. VAN. *Astrologia, ratione et experientia refutata*. Antwerp, 1583.

HERBERT OF CHERBURY, LORD EDWARD. *A Dialogue Between a Tutor and a Pupil*. London, 1768.

HETH, THOMAS. *A Manifest and apparent confutation of an Astrological discourse, lately published to the discomfort (without cause) of the weake and simple sort*. London, 1583.

HEYDON, SIR CHRISTOPHER. *A Defence of Iudiciall Astrologie, in Answer to a Treatise lately published by M. Iohn Chamber*. London, 1603.

HEYWOOD, T. *Works*. Edited by J. Pearson. 6 vols. London, 1874.

HOWARD, HENRY, EARL OF NORTHAMPTON. *A Defensative against the poyson of supposed prophecies*. London, 1620.

JAMES I. *Works*. London, 1616.

JONSON, B. *Works*. Edited by W. Gifford and F. Cunningham. 3 vols. London, 1904.

LEE, SIR SIDNEY. *Elizabethan Sonnets*. 2 vols. Westminster, 1904.

LEOWITZ, C. *Brevis et perspicua ratio iudicandi genituras, ex physicis causis et vera experientia ex(s)tructa*. London, 1558.

——. *De coniunctionibus magnis insignioribus superiorum planetarum, solis defectionibus, et cometis, in quarta monarchia, cum eorundem effectuum historica expositione*. Heidelberg, 1544.

LIBAU, A. *De universitate et rerum conditarum originibus*. Langen, 1610.

LIEBLER, T. *Defensio libelli Hieronymi Savonarolae de astrologia divinatrice, adversus Christophorum Stathmionem*. Langen, 1569.

LILLY, W. *An Easie and Plain Method Teaching How to Judge Upon Nativities*. London, 1658.

The Lives of those Eminent Antiquaries Elias Ashmole, Esquire, and Mr. William Lilly, written by themselves. London, 1774.

LYLY, J. *The Complete Works*. Edited by R. W. Bond. 3 vols. Oxford, 1902.

MARLOWE, C. *Tamburlaine*. Edited by U. Ellis-Fermor. London, 1930.

MARSTALLER, G. *Artis divinatricis quam astrologiam seu iudiciariam vocant, encomia et patrocinia*. Paris, 1549.

MARSTON, J. *Works*. Edited by H. H. Wood. 3 vols. Edinburgh and London, 1934-39.

MELANCHTHON, P. "Prefatio" to J. Schöner, *De iudiciis nativitatum* (1545) in Marstaller.

MELTON, J. *Astrologaster or the Figure Caster*. London, 1620.

METIUS, A. *Doctrinae sphaericae libri V*. Frankfurt, 1602.

MIDDLETON, T. *The Works*. Edited by A. H. Bullen. 8 vols. London, 1885.

MILICH, J. *Oratio de dignitate astrologiae*. Wittenberg, 1533.

MONTAIGLON, A. DE. *Recueil des Poesies Françoises des XVᵉ et XVIᵉ Siècles*. 16 vols. Paris, 1855-78.

MORE, H. *A Collection of Several Philosophical Writings*. London, 1662.

——. *The Theological Works*. London, 1708.

MORE, T. *L'Utopie. Texte latin*. Edited by Marie Delcourt. Paris, 1936.

MUNDAY, A. *Fidele and Fortunio, The Two Italian Gentlemen*. Edited by P. Simpson. Malone Society Reprints. Oxford, 1909.

NABODE, V. *Enarratio elementorum astrologiae.* Cologne, 1560.

NASHE, T. *Works.* Edited by R. B. McKerrow. 5 vols. London, 1904-10.

NIXON, A. *The Black Year.* London, 1606.

OFFUSIUS, I. *De divina astrorum facultate, in larvatam astrologiam.* Paris, 1570.

PAREUS, D. *In Genesin.* Frankfurt, 1608.

PEELE, G. *Works.* Edited by A. H. Bullen. 2 vols. London, 1888.

PEREYRA, B. *De magia, de observatione somniorum, et de divinatione astrologica.* Cologne, 1598.

PERKINS, W. *Foure Great Lyers, striving who shall win the Silver Whetstone.* London, 1585.

PEUCER, C. *Commentarius de praecipuis divinationum generibus.* Zerbst, 1541.

PICCOLOMINI, AENEAS SYLVIUS. *Opera quae extant omnia.* Basel, 1571.

PICCOLOMINI, ALESSANDRO. *La prima parte dele theoriche o'vero speculationi dei pianeti.* Venice, 1558.

PICCOLOMINI, P. *Parte terza della filosofia naturale.* Venice, 1585.

PICO DELLA MIRANDOLA, G. *Omnia quae extant opera.* Venice, 1557.

PIGGHE, A. *Adversus prognosticatorum vulgus qui annuas predictiones edunt et se astrologos mentiuntur astrologiae defensio.* Paris, 1518.

PLEIX, S. DU. *La physique ou science des choses naturelles.* Lyons, 1620.

PLOTINUS. *Operum philosophicorum omnium.* Basel, 1580.

POGGIO BRACCIOLINI, G. F. *Oratoris et philosophi opera.* Basel, 1538.

PONTANO, G. *Opera.* Venice, 1505.

———. *Opera omnia soluta oratione composita.* 3 vols. Venice, 1518-19.

PTOLEMY, C. *Quadripartium.* Basel, 1543.

———. *De praedictionibus astronomicis.* Basel, n.d.

PURBACH, G. *Theoricae novae planetarum.* Paris, 1553.

RABELAIS, F. *Œuvres Complètes.* Edited by J. Plattard. 5 vols. Paris, 1929.

RALEIGH, SIR WALTER. *The History of the World.* London, 1614.

RANTZAU, H. VON. *Tractatus astrologicus de genethliacorum thematum iudiciis pro singulis nati accidentibus.* Frankfurt, 1602.

———. *Catalogus imperatorum, regum ac principum qui astrologicam artem amarunt, ornarunt et exercuerunt.* Antwerp, 1580.

REISCH, G. *Margarita filosofica.* Translated by G. P. Galluci. Venice, 1599.

RHEINHOLT, E. *Primus liber tabularum directionum discentibus prima elementa astronomiae necessarius et utilissimus.* Tübingen, 1554.

———. *Ptolemaei mathematicae constructionis liber.* Basel, 1549.

RINGELBERG, J. *Institutiones astronomicae ternis libris contentae.* Basel, 1528.

ROPER, W. *The Life of Sir Thomas More.* London, 1925.

ROWLEY, S. *The Noble Soldier.* J. S. Farmer, Students' Facsimiles. Amersham, 1913.

SACRO BOSCO, J. *Spherae tractatus.* Venice, 1531.

SALUTATI, C. *Epistolario.* Edited by F. Novati. 4 vols. Rome, 1891-1911.

SAVONAROLA, G. *Opera singulare del doctissimo Padre F. Hieronymo Savonarola di Ferrara contra astrologia divinatrice in corroboratione de le refutatione astrologice del S. Conte Io: Pico de le Mirandola.* Venice, 1556.

SCEPPER, C. *Adversus falsos quorundam astrologorum augurationes.* Cologne, 1547.

SCOT, R. *The Discoverie of Witchcraft.* London, 1584.

SERVETUS, M. *Apologetica disceptatio pro astrologia.* Edited by H. Tollin. Berlin, 1880.

SMITH, HENRY. *The Works.* 2 vols. Edinburgh, 1867.

SPENSER, E. *Complete Poems.* Edited by R. E. N. Dodge. Cambridge, 1908.

STUBBES, P. *The Second Part of the Anatomie of Abuses.* Edited by F. J. Furnivall. London, 1882.

TAISNIER, J. *Astrologiae iudiciariae ysagogica.* Cologne, 1559.

TELESIO, B. *Varii de naturalibus rebus libelli.* Venice, 1590.

TOMKIS, T. *Albumasar: A Comedy as it is acted at the Theatre Royal in Drury-Lane.* London, 1747.

TYARD, PONTUS DE. *Mantice ou discours de la Verite de divination par astrologie.* Lyons, 1558.

URSUS, N. R. *Fundamentum astronomicum: id est nova doctrina sinum et triangulorum.* Strassburg, 1588.

VESPUCCI, B. *Sphaera tractatus.* Venice, 1531.

W., W. *A New and Merry Prognostication.* London, 1623.

WEBSTER, J. *The Complete Work.* Edited by F. L. Lucas. 4 vols. London, 1927.

WEBSTER, J. AND TOURNEUR, C. *The Best Plays.* Edited by J. A. Symonds. London, 1903.

WILLET, A. *Hexapla in Genesin.* London, 1608.

———. *De animae natura et viribus.* Cambridge, 1585.

WOLF, J. *Admonitio de astrologiae usu* in Leowitz, *Brevis et perspicua ratio.*

SECONDARY SOURCES

ALLEN, D. C. "Science and Invention in Greene's Prose," *Publications of the Modern Language Association,* LIII (1938), 1007-1018.

ALTAMURA, A. *Giovanni Pontano.* Naples, 1938.

BARON, H. "Willensfreiheit und Astrologie bei Marsilio Ficino und Pico della Mirandola," *Kultur- und Universalgeschichte.* Leipzig, 1927. Pp. 145-170.

BOLL, F. AND BEZOLD, C. *Sternglaube und Sterndeutung.* Leipzig, 1931.

BOSANQUET, E. *English Printed Almanacks and Prognostications. A Bibliographical History to the year 1600.* London, 1917.

———. "English Printed Almanacks and Prognostications. Corrigenda and Addenda," *The Library,* 4th Series, VIII (1927-28), 456-477.

———. "English Seventeenth-Century Almanacks," *The Library,* 4th Series, X (1929-30), 361-397.

BOUCHÉ-LECLERQ, A. *L'Astrologie Grecque.* Paris, 1899.

BOYCE, B. *Tom Brown of facetious memory, Grub street in the age of Dryden.* Cambridge, Mass., 1939.

BURCKHARDT, J. *Die Kultur der Renaissance in Italien.* Leipzig, 1928.

CAMDEN, C. "Astrology in Shakespeare's Day," *Isis,* XIX (1933), 26-73.

———. "Elizabethan Almanacs and Prognostications," *The Library,* 4th Series, XII (1931-32), 83-108, 194-207.

———. "Elizabethan Astrological Medicine," *Annals of Medical History,* N. S., II (1930), 217-226.

CASSIRER, E. *Individuum und Kosmos in der Philosophie der Renaissance.* Leipzig and Berlin, 1927. (*Engl. transl.*)

CURRY, W. C. *Chaucer and the Mediaeval Sciences.* Oxford, 1926.

DEFRANCE, EUGÈNE. *Catherine de Médicis, ses astrologues et ses magiciens-envoûteurs.* Paris, 1911.

DE LACY, H. "Astrology in the Poetry of Edmund Spenser," *Journal of English and Germanic Philology,* XXXIII (1934), 520-543.

DELLE TORRE, A. *Storia dell'Accademica Platonica di Firenze.* Florence, 1902.

DICK, H. "The Authorship of Foure Great Lyers (1585)," *The Library,* 4th Series, XIX (1938-39), 311-314.

EDDY, W. O. "Tom Brown and Partridge the Astrologer," *Modern Philology,* XXVIII (1930-31), 163-168.

———. "The Wits vs. John Partridge, Astrologer," *Studies in Philology,* XXIX (1932), 29-40.

GOTHEIN, E. *Die Culturentwicklung Süd-Italiens in Einzel-Darstellungen.* Breslau, 1886.

HARTFELDER, K. "Der Aberglaube Philipp Melanchthons," *Historisches Taschenbuch* (Leipzig, 1889), pp. 233-269.

HAUFFEN, A. *Johann Fischart.* Berlin, 1921.

HELLMANN, G. "Versuch einer Geschichte der Wettervorhersage im XVI. Jahrhundert," *Abhandlungen d. Preussischen Akademie d. Wissenschaften.* Berlin, 1924.

JOHNSON, FRANCIS. *Astronomical Thought in Renaissance England.* Baltimore, 1937.

KNOBEL, E. B. "Astronomy and Astrology," *Shakespeare's England.* Oxford, 1916.

LARKEY, S. V. "Astrology and Politics in the First Years of Elizabeth's Reign," *Bulletin of the Institute of the History of Medicine,* III (1935), 171-186.

LEUBE, H. *Reformation und Humanismus in England.* Leipzig, 1930.

MACKENSEN, L. *Die Deutschen Volksbücher.* Leipzig, 1927.

MARCHAM, F. G. "James I and the 'Little Beagle Letters,'" *Persecution and Liberty: Essays in Honor of George Lincoln Barr.* New York, 1931.

MAGNUS, H. *Der Aberglauben in der Medizin, Abhandlungen zur Geschichte der Medizin IV.* Breslau, 1903.

·⁀ MAURY, L.-F. A. *La Magie et L'Astrologie dans l'Antiquité et au Moyen Âge ou Étude sur les Superstitions Païennes qui se sont perpétuées jusqu'à nos jours.* Paris, 1877.

MERCIER, C. A. *Astrology in Medicine.* London, 1914.

PERCOPO, E. *Luca Gaurico, ultimo degli astrologi; notizie biografiche e bibliografiche. Atti della reale accademia di archeologia, lettere e belle arti,* XVII. Naples, 1896.

———. *Vita di Giovanni Pontano.* Edited by M. Manfredi. Naples, 1938.

PLOMER, H. R. "English Almanacs and Almanac-Makers of the Seventeenth Century," *Notes and Queries,* 6th Series, XII (1885), 243, 323, 383, 462.

POLLARD, A. F. *The Reign of Henry VII from Contemporary Sources.* 3 vols. London, 1913-14.

PROBST, A. *Corneille Agrippa: Sa vie et ses œuvres.* 2 vols. Paris, 1881-82.

SEMPRINI, G. *La Filosofia di Pico della Mirandola.* Milan, 1936.

SOLDATI, B. *La Poesia Astrologica nel Quattrocento.* Florence, 1906.

SONDHEIM, M. *Thomas Murner als Astrolog.* Strassburg, 1938.

———. "Shakespeare and the Astrology of His Time," *Journal of the Warburg Institute,* II (1938-39), 243-259.

STRAUS, H. A. AND STRAUSS-KLOEBE, S. *Die Astrologie des Johannes Kepler: Eine Auswahl aus seinen Schriften.* Munich and Berlin, 1926.

SUDHOFF, K. *Iatromathematiker vornehmlich im 15. und 16. Jahrhundert, Abhandlungen zur Geschichte der Medizin II.* Breslau, 1902.

⁀ TAYLOR, R. *The Political Prophecy in England.* New York, 1911.

✓THORNDIKE, L. *History of Magic and Experimental Science.* 6 vols. New York, 1929-41.

TOFFANIN, G. *Giovanni Pontano fra l'uomo e la natura.* Bologna, 1938.

UHL, W. *Unser Kalender in seiner Entwicklung von den ältesten Anfängen bis heute.* Paderborn, 1893.

⁀ VIGNAL, L. G. *Pic de la Mirandole.* Paris, 1937.

WALFORD, C. "Sham Almanacks and Prognostications," *Book-Lore,* II (1885), 67-70.

✓WEDEL, T. O. *The Mediaeval Attitude Toward Astrology.* New Haven, 1920.

WELLER, E. "Scherzkalender oder Spottpraktiker," *Serapeum,* XXVI (1865), 236-239.

WILSON, F. P. "Some English Mock Prognostications," *The Library,* 4th Series, XIX (1938-39), 6-43.

INDEX

Abraham, 85
Abraham Judaeus, 29
Adam, 19-20, 25, 34, 61, 67, 68, 71, 85, 88, 93, 134, 136
Aegineta, P., 252
Aethiopians, 68 n.
Agriculture, 70
Agrippa, H. C., 51, 56-59, 117, 122, 142; *De incertitudine,* 57-59; *De occulta philosophia,* 57
Alamansor, 79
Alberti, L. B., 37, 42, 165; *Intercoenales,* 40
Albertus Magnus, 24, 138, 249
Albumasor, 24, 25, 30, 60, 79, 90, 95, 220, 223
Alchemy, 49, 115, 248
Alchochoden, 178
Alciati, A., 81
Alexander VI, 91 n., 21
Alexander Aphrodisias, 5
Alexander, Sir William, 176; *Aurora,* 159
Alfonso X, 248
Allde, E., 218
Allen, D. C., 169 n.
Allen, J., 144
Allen, N., 118; *The Astronomer's Game,* 117
Allen, T., 102-103
Almanacks and Prognostications, 113, 120, 126, 132, 138, 170, 186, 190; history of, 193-210; in English literature, 190-193; satire on, 118, 186, 202; satire in England, 215-243; satire in France, 212-214; satire in Germany, 210-212; satire in Italy, 214-215
Almuten, 178
Alsted, J. H., *Philosophia,* 82 n.
Altamura, A., 37 n.
Amadis of Gaul, 124
Ambrose, St., 24, 98
Anabaptists, 74
Angels, 4, 7, 13 n., 15 n., 28, 43, 109
Animodar, 32

Anne of Austria, 52
Antiscia, 30
Antwerp, 253
Apollo, 26
Apothecary, 36 n.
Arabs, 32, 33, 34, 57, 92; Arabian heterodoxy, 5, 10
Archelous, 223
Archer, T., 229
Arcturus, 91
Aretino, P., *Pronostico,* 214-215
Ariosto, L., 37
Aristides, 85
Aristophanes, 4
Aristotle, 23, 28, 38, 41, 62, 68, 70, 78, 83, 99, 107, 140, 223, 247
Armin, R., 156
Ascham, A., 103, 196; *Treatise,* 109
Ascham, R., 103
Ashmole, E., 105 n.
Aspects, 30, 177
Astrolabes, 32, 50
Astrologer, arrogance of, 57, 78, 87; and astronomers, 23, 50, 51-54, 109; disagreements of, 29, 32, 58, 60, 78, 118, 123; false, 102, 105, 115, 182, 201; ignorant, 75, 78, 93, 124, 127, 207, 248; jargon of, 121; satirized in literature, 186-189; scorned by men, 25; why they succeed, 26, 91; why they fail, 59, 78, 109, 119
Astrology, attitude towards, of, Agrippa, 56-59, Axelsön, 91-93, Bellanti, 35 n.-36 n., Calvin, 71-73, Cardan, 81-82, Carleton, 139-143, Chamber, 126-129, Cirvelo, 56, Degli Angeli, 96-99, De Hayn, 55-56, De Tyard, 78-81, Ficino, 6-18, Fontaine, 89-90, Frischlin, 87-89, Fulke, 107-112, Gartze, 83-84, Gaurico, 54-55, Göckel, 94-96, Giuntini, 85-86, Harvey, J., 124-125, Heller, 65-66, Heydon, 129-135, Howard, 112-116, Leowitz, 73-74, Libau, 93-94, Liebler, 82-83, Marstaller, 61-63, Melanchthon, 63-65, Melton, 135-139, Milich, 66, Perkins, 116-122, Pereya,

90-91, Peucer, 66-69, Piccolomini, 70-71, Pico della Mirandola, 22-37, Pigghe, 56, Pontano, 38-45, Rantzau, 84-85, Rheinholt, 69-70, Scepper, 59-60, Servetus, 60-61, Van Hemminga, 86-87, Wolf, 74-78; definitions of, natural, 148, 149, natural and conjectural, 61; natural and artificial, 56; and Genesis, 3, 48, 66, 89, 92, 109, 142; and God, 67, 76-77, 84; and kings, 3, 51-52, 69, 132, 141; and literature, as ornament, 156-159, as source, 169-170, use of technicalities, 177-178, the sonnet, 158-159; and literary men, 182-186; and medicine, 10, 49, 64, 90, 95, 102, 103, 111, 137, 203, 206, 247-255; methods of defence, 54; and myths, 48, 57; and priests, 3, 51, 140, 254; and Satan, 82, 84, 90, 91, 113, 133, 141; and talismen, 8, 10, 76, 138, 152
Astronomers and astrologers, 23, 50, 51-54, 109
Astronomy, 60, 69, 100, 103, 108, 140, 150
Asverus Amsingius, J., *Dissertatio iatromathematica*, 254
Atheists, 65, 84 n.
Atlas, 136
Atwel, G., 144
Augustine, St., 24, 98
Averroes, 5, 23, 247
Averroism, 147, 164
Avicenna, 23, 223
Axelsön, K., 91-93, 95, 134; *Physica et ethica Mosaica*, 91

Babington, G., 71 n.
Babylon, 110
Babylonians, 94
Bacchus, 237
Bacon, F., 112, 149-153, 179; *De augmentis*, 150
Bacon, R., 30, 103, 137, 138
Baker, H., *A briefe and short Introduction*, 170
Barbaro, H., 12, 13
Bardesanes, the Syrian, 80
Barnes, B., *Parthenophil*, 158, 178
Baro, P., 103
Baron, H., 17, 18, 22

Barry, L., *Ram-Alley*, 187
Basil, St., 24
Bebel, H., *Facetiae*, 211; *Prognosticon*, 211
Bellanti, L., 54, 56, 82 n., 85, 122, 139, 245, 252; *De astrologica veritate*, 35
Bellerophon, 79
Bembo, P., 13, 14, 17, 41, 81
Benivieni, G., 12
Bentivoglio, G., 51
Bevis of Southampton, 124
Bezold, C., 52 n.
Bible and Astrology, 48-49, 66, 68, 72, 73, 80, 84, 85, 90, 92, 115, 126, 133, 249
Biondi, M.-A., *De diebus decretoriis*, 251
Boccaccio, G., 48
Bodier, T., *De ratione et usu*, 252
Bodin, J., 82
Bodley, Sir Thomas, 103
Bohemian, 73
Boll, F., 52 n.
Bologna, 7
Bomelius, E., 198
Bonatti, G., 13, 25, 45, 79, 103
Bonaventura, St., 108
Bonincontri, L., 37, 156
Boorde, A., 102, 104 n., 195
Bosanquet, E., 102, 106 n., 118, 194, 195, 196, 200, 229
Bouché-Leclerq, A., 3 n.
Boulogne, 74
Boyce, B., 243 n.
Brahe, T., 73, 91, 132, 134, 155
Brandon, C., *Octavia*, 161 n., 168 n.
Brayne, J., *Against Judiciary Astrology*, 144
Brenlanlius Britannus, 35
Brent, J., 71 n.
Breton, N., 176
Brosserius, S., 172 n., 173 n., 175 n.
Broughton, Mother, 137
Browne, T., 104, 145, 149, 255; *Pseudodoxia*, 107, 129
Brunfels, O., 249
Bruno, G., 5, 165
Buckminister, T., 117, 198
Burckhardt, J., 51 n.
Burneston, 103
Burr, G. L., 155 n.

Burton, R., 149, 154; *The Anatomy*, 153
Butler, J., 145

Caesar, J., 85, 180
Caesar and Pompey, tragedy, 161 n.,
    168 n., 176 n., 181 n.
Caius, J., 104
Calderia, J., 61 n.
Calendars, 63, 73, 84, 93, 201
Calvin, J., 71-73, 208; *Contre l'astrologie*,
    71; *An Admonicion*, 71
Calvinism, 112
Calvinist, 139, 162
Cambridge, 103, 104, 106, 186
Camden, C., 49 n., 101 n., 103 n., 215 n.
Camden, W., 103, 132 n., 179
Camerarius, J., 66
Campanella, T., 52
Canterbury, 200
Carafa, Cardinal, 22
Cardan, G., 52, 79, 81-82, 86, 88, 98,
    103, 122; *De libris propriis*, 81;
    Libelli quinque, 81, 98
Carion, J., 53 n.
Carleton, G., 126, 135, 139-143; *Astrol-
ogomania*, 139
Cartagensis, A., *Liber de peste*, 250
Cartari, V., 48
Cassel, Provost of, 101
Cassirer, E., 6
Catholic Church, 48
Catholicism, 139
Catherine, Queen of France, 51, 52
Cato, 44-45, 237
Caton, J., 34
Cause, 44; particular, 27, 83, 119; uni-
versal, 27, 113
Cavalcanti, G., 12, 13 n., 14
Chaldean, 32, 33, 34, 47, 57, 68, 72,
    94, 113, 136, 150, 151, 208
Chamber, J., 102, 126-129, 130, 131,
    132, 133, 134, 135, 139, 169, 207,
    223; *A Treatise*, 126; *Astronomiae
encomium*, 126; "A Confutation,"
    126
Chapman, G., 157 n., 165, 168, 180 n.,
    191 n.; *Ovid's Banquet*, 159; *Androm-
eda*, 175; *Byron's Conspiracie*, 184
Character of a Quake Astrologer, 243
Charlemagne, 74, 85
Charles V, 84, 86

Charles of Burgundy, 95-96
Chaucer, G., 127, 128, 223
Chiromancy, 67
Chorlton, G., 224
Chrisogonus Jadertinus, F., *De modo
collegiandi*, 248
Cicero, 23, 167; *De divinatione*, 47
Ciceronian, 78
Cirvelo, P., 249; *Apotelesmata*, 56
Clement VII, 51
Climacteric year, 30, 129
Clocks, 50, 119
Collier, J. P., 219; *A Bibliographical
Account*, 233
Cologne, 253
Color of Planets, 33
Combustion, 30, 120, 177, 197, 202
Comets, 13 n., 74, 87, 99, 107, 115, 154;
    in literature, 178-181
Complexions and Humors, 7, 26, 36 n.,
    44, 56, 63, 66, 68, 72, 90, 92, 132,
    140, 160, 247, 253
Conception, 29, 72
Conjunctions, 12, 29, 56, 60, 64, 66, 73,
    74, 80, 91, 115, 121, 125, 174, 177,
    225, 247; and religion, 30
Constable, H., *Diana*, 159, 176
Constantine, 73
Constantinople, 110, 198
Contareni, G., *De elementis*, 68 n.
Conti, N., 48
Contingency, 132, 141
Copernicus, N., 50, 124, 155, 169, 179
Coppinger, F., 227
Cortese, P., 39
Coxe, F., 198; *Short Treatise*, 112
Crabbe, J., 94
Critical day, 68, 250
Cuningham, W., 104, 108, 109, 110,
    196
Cunning Man, The, 137
Curiosity, 47, 67, 71, 76, 87, 108, 113,
    143, 214
Curry, W. C., 150 n.
Custom, 23, 62, 68, 91
Cyrus, 236

D., T., *Bloody Banquet*, 181 n.
Dade, J., 117 n., 198, 202, 203-204
D'Ailly, P., 24, 25, 29, 30
Daniel, prophet, 72
Daniel, S., 161 n.

Da Parma, B., 156
Dariot, C., *Ad astrorum judicia*, 170
David, King, 85
Davies, Sir John, 208
Davies of Hereford, J., 208
Da Viterbo, E., 43
Death of Robert, Earl of Huntington, 181 n.
De Chasseneaux, B., 53 n., 61 n.
Dee, J., 53, 104, 105, 182, 186
Defrance, E., 50, 52 n.
Degli Angeli, A., 96-99; *In astrologos*, 96
De Hayn, J., 55-56; *Introductiones*, 55, 170
Dekker, T., 156 n., 157, 161 n., 163 n., 225, 227, 233; *Bell-man*, 233; *Dead Term*, 239; *Lanthorne*, 171, 233; *News from Hell*, 224; *Raven's Almanacke*, 229-232, 233, 239, 241; *Shoemakers*, 175; *Wonderful Year*, 224
De Lacy, H., 169 n.
Delcourt, M., 102 n.
Delle Torre, A., 4
Delphi, 78
Delrio, M., 82
De' Medici, C., 3, 4
De' Medici, G., 51
De' Medici, L., 12, 13, 21
Democritus, 23, 85
De Monantheuil, H., *Ludus iatro mathematicus*, 253
De Montaiglon, A., 212, 214
De Savoie, L., 51
De Savoie, P., 19 n.
Descartes, R., 244
Des Periers, B., *Prognostication*, 214
Desvernay, F., 247 n.
De Tyard, P., 78-81; *Mantice*, 78, 85
Deucalion, 50
Devereaux, R., Earl of Leicester, 103, 200
Dick, H., 116, 118, 169 n.
Di Fonti, A., 59 n., 172 n., 173 n., 175 n.
Digges, L., 103
Digges, T., *A Prognostication*, 103, 117 n., 210
Divination, 66-67, 113, 150
Doctor Dodypoll, 156 n.
Dominical Letter, 193, 197
Donne, J., 153, 154, 188-189

Drayton, M., 161 n., 163 n., 164 n., 168, 173, 174, 176 n., 180, 181; *Endimion*, 160, 171; *Ideas Mirrour*, 159; *Shepherd's Garland*, 176
Drummond of Hawthornden, W., 187 n.
Dryden, J., 145; *Mock Astrologer*, 186,
Dürer, A., 81, 172
Du Pleix, S., 74 n., 179
Durant, G., *Stances du Zodiaque*, 159

Earth, 76, 79, 97
Eclipse, 60, 64, 71, 74, 83, 120, 125, 178, 195, 197, 201, 217
Eddy, W. O., 243 n.
Edward VI, 98, 102
Egypt, 110
Egyptian, 33, 34, 72, 73, 94, 136
Eisenmenger, S., *Oratio de methodo*, 253
Elections, 76, 120, 138, 150, 152, 162; and literature, 163-164
Elizabeth, Queen, 49, 53, 104, 125, 149, 169, 178, 179, 182, 186, 196, 197, 198, 199
Empedocles, 85
Empiricus, Sextus, 103
Endimion, 170
England's Monethly Observations, 242
Environment, 24, 28, 43, 78, 97
Erasmus, D., 52 n., 81, 223
Erra Pater, 191, 223, 224
Essler, J., *Speculum astrologicum*, 248
Estienne, H., 52
Etzler, A., *Introductorium iatromathematicum*, 255
Euclid, 54 n.
Eudoxus, 78, 128, 133
Europe, 34, 56
Evesdropper, Adam, *Platoes Cap*, 224-227, 239
Evil, problem of, 36 n., 61-62, 68, 70, 85, 92, 93, 114
Experiment, 28, 148

Faire Em, 168 n.
Falkland, E., *Mariam*, 172 n., 176 n.
Farmer, R., 145 n.
Farmers, 26, 28, 44, 63, 77, 83
Fate and Fortune, 7, 15, 63, 68, 84, 91, 95, 162; in literature, 164-165; and stars, 43, 161, 162, 166; theories of, 40-42

Fayre Weather, Ffrauncis, 218-219
Fernelius, J., 97
Ferrier, O., 52; *Les jugements*, 170
Ficino, M., 3-18, 20, 23, 36 n., 37, 38 n.,
41, 42, 45, 49, 76, 141, 147, 153,
154, 156, 163, 188, 244, 245, 250;
Apologia, 11 n.; Commentary on Plo-
tinus, 16-18; *De Sole*, 15; *Epistolae*,
7, 11-16; *Theologia Platonica*, 4, 5,
7 n., 17, 18; *De Vita*, 6, 7, 8-11, 13,
15, 36 n.
Figure, astrological, 177
Filelfo, F., 81
Firmicus Maternus, 47, 79, 171 n., 172 n.,
173, 174 n., 175 n., 176 n.
Fischart, J., *Aller Praktick Grossmutter*,
211
Fisher, J., *Fuimus Troes*, 176 n.
Fleming, A., 74 n.
Fletcher, G., *Licia*, 159
Fletcher, J., 157, 161 n., 163 n., 180 n.,
181 n.; *Bloody Brother*, 187; *Chances*,
193; *Coronation*, 168; *Loves Cure*,
184; *Noble Kinsmen*, 161; *Prophetess*,
168; *Sea Voyage*, 173; with Beau-
mont, *Maid's Tragedy*, 168; *Philaster*,
168
Fletcher, P., 161 n., 208; *Apollynists*,
176; *Purple Island*, 191
Flood, 60, 63, 66, 249
Florence, 4
Floridus, A., *Tractatus de annis climac-
tericis*, 255
Florio, J., *Second Fruits*, 219
Fontaine, J., 89-90; *Discours*, 89; *De
astrologia medica*, 89, 255
Ford, J., 160 n., 163 n., 168, 181 n.;
Witch of Edmonton, 190
Forman, S., 50, 105, 112, 137
Forster, R., 117 n., 198, 199, 200;
Ephemerides, 104
Fouleweather, Adam, *A wonderfull,
strange and miraculous Astrologicall
Prognostication*, 219-221, 222, 224-
225, 231, 236, 239, 242
Fracastoro, G., *Homocentrica*, 251, 252
France, 198, 212
Francis I, 51
Frankfort, 206
Frende, G., 117 n., 198, 199, 200, 201
Frenetius, 85

Frischlin, N., 50 n., 87-89, 92, 93; *De
astronomicae artis*, 87
Frisia, 74
Frisius, L., *Expositio*, 248; *Spiegel*, 249
Fulgentius, 48
Fulke, W., 106-112, 113, 116, 118, 139,
190; *Pleasant Prospect*, 107; *Antiprog-
nosticon*, 107
Fuller, T., *Holy State*, 116; *Abel Rede-
vivus*, 117

Galen, 28, 49, 61, 223, 250, 251, 252,
254
Gallina, T., 38
Galluci, G. P., 53 n.
Gartze, J., 53, 69, 88; *Astrologiae
methodus*, 84
Garzoni, T., *Il serraglio*, 96; *La piazza*,
237
Gasser, A., 66
Gataker, T., 145
Gaule, J., *Mag-Astro-Mancer*, 144
Gaurico, L., 47, 51-52, 54-55, 81, 86,
140; *De eclipsi*, 55; *Oratio*, 55; *Trac-
tatus*, 55; *Super diebus*, 55, 251-252
Gazolti, F., 15
Gell, R., 144 n.
Geography, 60, 70
Geomancy, 34
George of Saxony, 74
Geree, J., *Astrologo-Mastix*, 144
Gesner, C., 35
Geveren, S. a, *Of the end of this worlde*,
121
Gilpin, B., 139
Giuntini, F., 122; *De divinatione*, 85
Godfridus, *Boke of Knowledge*, 170
Göckel, R., 53 n., 94-96; *Acroteleution*,
94; *Academia*, 94; *Conciliator*, 94;
Idea, 94; *Physica*, 94; *Physiologia*, 94;
Politica, 94
Gothein, F., 39
Grant et vraye Prenostication, 213
Grande et vraye Pronostication, 212
Grau, F., 74 n.; *Of all blasing starrs*, 179
Gray, W., 198, 202, 203, 204
Greece, 4
Greek, 75
Greeks, 57
Greene, R., 158 n., 160, 161 n., 163,
171, 173, 175 n., 177 n., 180 n., 181 n.,

183, 188; *Philomela*, 191; *Planeto-machia*, 44, 169, 172; *Tullie's Love*, 168
Grierson, H. J. C., 154 n.
Grove, F., 242
Guicciardini, F., 11 n., 37
Gyraldi, L., 48

Hall, J., 188; *Characters*, 237; *Mundus*, 183, 187; *Virgidemiarum*, 187, 191
Haly, 31, 79, 223
Hamilton, Bp. of St. Andrews, 51
Harriot, T., 103, 185
Hartfelder, K., 64 n.
Hartgill, G., 198
Harvey, G., 103 n., 121, 122, 157 n., 169, 170, 196
Harvey, J., 122, 124-125; *Astrological Addition*, 122; *Discoursive Probleme*, 124
Harvey, R., 103 n., 106, 121-122, 123, 125 198; *Astrological Discourse*, 121
Hauffen, A., 210 n.
Heat, 26, 27, 79, 97, 114, 152
Hebrews, 21, 30, 57
Heidelberg, 104
Heller, J., 61, 65-66
Hellman, G., 54 n.
Hemminga, S. van, 86-87, 89, 117; *Astrologia refutata*, 86
Henrichmann, J., *Prognostica*, 211
Henry IV (France), 52, 140
Henry VII (England), 101
Henry VIII (England), 51, 74, 81, 101-102
Henry of Hess, 23, 34
Henry of Rantzau, 53; *Catalogus*, 84
Heraclitus, 85
Herbalist, 64
Herbert of Cherbury, W., *A Dialogue*, 145
Heretics, 21, 59, 65, 164
Herus, M., 249
Heth, T., 123-124; *A manifest and apparent confutation*, 123
Heydon, Sir Christopher, 129-135, 139, 140, 141, 142, 143, 155, 169, 196; *A Defence*, 126
Heywood, T., 159 n., 161 n., 163 n., 168, 180 n., 181 n., 191 n.
Hill, T., 109, 198

Hinderbach, J., 40
Hippocrates, 110, 252, 254
Hobbes, T., 243
Holland, 198
Homes, N., *Daemonologie*, 144
Hopkins, J., 199
Hordeonius, Marcus, 43
Horoscope, 16, 31, 39, 54, 55, 68, 75, 77, 80, 81, 83, 86, 87, 90, 91, 98, 127, 131, 150
Howard of Northampton, H., 112-116, 119, 123, 139, 179; *A Defensative*, 112
Hughes, T., 157 n.
Huss, J., 74
Hydromancy, 34
Hyginus, 48
Hyleg, 178

Ibn Ezra, 32
Icarus, 79
India, 94
Innocent VIII, 19 n.
Isaiah, 24, 72
Ivan IV, 198

Jack of Dover, 224
Jack Adams His Perpetual Almanack, 242
James I, 125, 139, 140, 141, 144, 149, 153, 154, 155 n., 169, 178, 186, 199, 241; *Daemonology*, 143
Jehan, astrologer, 101
Jeremiah, 92, 110
Jeronimo, 161 n.
Jerusalem, 73
Jesuit, 90
Job, 85, 142
John of Saxony, 86
John of Spain, 34
Johnson, F., 103 n.
Johnson, S., 208
Johnson, T., 205
Jonson, B., 156 n., 161 n., 163 n., 165, 170, 176 n., 177, 178, 181 n., 188, 223, 239; *Alchemist*, 186, 190, 195 n.; *Every Man in His Humour*, 192, 240 n.; *Fortunate Isles*, 187, 192; *Magnetic Lady*, 164, 187, 192; *Mercury Vindicated*, 192; *The Silent Woman*, 192

Joseph, 73
Joshua, 48
Judicial Astrology, 11, 12, 14, 70, 106
Jupiter, planet, 8, 12, 13, 30, 79, 121, 148, 163, 173, 175, 176, 197, 203, 223, 247, 248
Justinian, 24

Kelly, E., 137
Kelway, T., 170
Kendal, Sir John, 101
Kepler, J., 50, 52, 169
Kett, F., 196
Kishon, 143
Straus-Kloebe, S., 52 n.
Knobel, E. B., 101
Kochhofe, D., 66
Kollner, J., *Tractatus physicus mathematicus*, 255
Kristeller, P. O., 17 n.

Ladislaw of Bohemia, 95
Laet, A., 194
Laet, Jasper, 194, 195
Laet, Jasper II, 194
Laet, John, 194
Lambe, J., 105, 112
Laodiceans, 21
Lariviere, R., 52
Larkey, S. V., 102 n., 113
Latin, 75
Latins, 57
Leibnitz, G. W. von, 5
Lensaeus, J., *De divinatione*, 85
Leo X, 51
Leo, A, 24
Leowitz, C., 73-74, 123; *De coniunctionibus*, 74 n.
Leube, H., 6 n.
Lewes, 104
Libau, A., 93-94, 179; *De universitate*, 93
Liebler, T., 82-83, 104; *Defensio*, 82 n.
Light, 26, 27, 36 n., 64, 79, 97, 152
Lilly, W., 105 n., 145, 174 n., 242, 243; autobiography, 105 n.
Locrine, tragedy, 161 n.
Lodge, T., 161 n., 168, 177 n.; *A Fig for Momus*, 227
London, 104, 106, 108, 177, 196
Louis XIII, 52

Louis XIV, 52
Low, H., 104, 109, 117, 196, 198
Lucian, 68 n.
Ludwig of Bavaria, 74, 86
Luke, St., 203
Lust's Dominion, 181 n.
Luther, M., 55, 74, 81
Lyle, L., 229, 232
Lyly, J., *Woman in the Moon*, 159, 176-177, 183; *Galathea*, 188
Lyons, 89, 96

Machiavelli, N., 41
Machin, A., 161 n.
Mackensen, L., 210 n.
McKerrow, R. B., 219, 232
Macliviensis, 25
Magic, 66, 90, 140, 142, 143
Magini, J. A., *De astrologica ratione*, 254
Magnus, H., 49 n.
Mahomet, 85
Maiolus, S., 59 n.
Mainz, 248
Malespina, C., 59 n.
Mancini, G., 40 n.
Mandrake, 129
Manfredi, G., *Aphorismen*, 250
Manfredi, M., 37 n.
Manichees, 59
Manilius, 47; *Astronomicon*, 169
Marburg, 94
Marcham, F. G., 155 n.
Marchant, G., *Kalendrier*, 170, 210
Marescalco, F., 15
Mariners, 26, 28, 44, 83, 110
Marliani, A., 23
Marlowe, C., 185; *Faustus*, 57, 108, 138, 163 n.; *Tamburlaine*, 162, 164, 168, 174 n.
Mars, planet, 7 n., 12, 13, 33, 61, 69, 83, 94, 148, 153, 170, 173, 176, 197, 198, 202, 203, 217, 247; and literature, 174-175
Marstaller, G., 53, 61-63; *Artis divinatricis encomia*, 53 n.
Marston, J., 161 n., 176 n., 191 n.; *Dutch Courtesan*, 228; *Malcontent*, 158; *Parasitaster*, 193, 215
Martinists, 232
Mathematicians, 23

Mathematics, 100, 140
Matter, 7, 36 n.; influence of stars on, 16, 45, 68, 96, 99, 109, 131
Mary, Queen, 74, 86
Mathew, W., 202, 203, 204
Maury, L.-F. A., 3 n., 51 n., 52 n.
Medicine, 23; and astrology, 90, 203, 206, 247-255
Melanchthon, P., 55, 61, 63-65, 66, 69, 103, 122, 245
Melton, J., 135-139, 142; *Astrologaster,* 135
Mercier, C. A., 49 n.
Mercury, god, 8, 31
Mercury, planet, 163, 174 n., 176, 188, 202, 203, 217, 221, 225
Merlin, Ambrose, 124
Merlini Liberati Errata, 243
Merlinus Democritus, 243
Merry-Conceited Fortune-Teller, 242
Merry Devil of Edmonton, 158
Mery Pronosticacion, 216-218, 220
Metius, A., *Doctrina sphaerica,* 68 n.
Michael Scot, 34
Michelangelo Buonarroti, 55
Microcosm, 5, 6, 8, 20, 253
Middleton, T., 161 n., 164 n., 168 n., 174 n., 181 n., 191 n., 224, 226
Milan, 198
Milich, J., 53, 66, 69, 87, 246; *Oratio,* 66
Milton, J., 145, 243
Minerva, 132, 153
Mizauld, A., *Aesculapii et uraniae medicum,* 252; *Harmonia superioris,* 253; *Planetologia,* 252; *Secrets,* 253
Mohammedans, 21, 25, 30
Mollinet, J., *Le Kalendrier,* 213
Montaigne, M., 107, 118, 190
Montpellier, 247
Moon, 28, 44, 49, 56, 60, 64, 72, 74, 76, 79, 82, 83, 91, 92, 99, 114, 120, 125, 174, 176, 195, 197, 203, 207, 217, 230, 247; and literature, 170-172
Moore, P., *Fourtie yeres Almanacke,* 210
Moors, 57
More, H., *Enthusiasm,* 145; *Grand Mystery,* 145; *Tetractys,* 145
More, T., 22, 101-102; *Utopia,* 102
Morin, J.-B., 52
Moses, 29, 58, 73, 88, 113

Motion, of planets, 9, 26, 27, 31, 32, 57, 64, 68, 69, 71, 92, 97, 102, 114, 132, 142, 152; of soul, 5
Mounslowe, A., 198
Munday, A., 163 n.
Murner, T., 87 n.
Mythology, 48, 57

Nabode, V., 63 n.; Enarratio, 62 n.; *Astronomicarum institutionum,* 62 n.; *De coelo et terra,* 62 n.
Naples, 36, 37
Nas, J., *Pratica,* 211
Nashe, T., 121, 124, 157; *Countercuff,* 232; *Have With You,* 188; *Pierce Penniless,* 188, 219
Nativity, moment of, 16, 31, 72, 98, 127, 150
Nature, 7, 22, 42, 141
Navigation, 70
Necessity, 15 n., 27, 68, 69, 130, 132, 162
Neoperipatetic, 6
Neoplatonism, 3, 4-5
Neptune, 171
Nero, Emperor, 45, 81
Nero, B., 11 n.
Niccolini, 12
Nicholas of Cusa, 5
Nifo, A., 59, 249; *De diebus,* 247
Nile, 82
Nixon, A., *Black Year,* 227-229; *Christian Navy,* 227; *Dignitie of Man,* 227; *Scourge of Corruption,* 227; *Three English Brothers,* 227
Noah, 25, 57, 60, 127
Norton, R., 198
Nostradamus, M., 52, 108, 109, 113
Nova, 48, 90, 131
Novati, F., 40 n.
Now or Never, 242
Number, of stars, 16
Nürnberg, 65, 68

Obicius, H., *Iatrostronomicon,* 255
Obsessio, 30
Offusius, I., *De divina astrorum facultate,* 84 n.
Ogygius, 60
Olive, Master, 137
Opposition, 177

Optic glass, 50
Orbits, 69
Orlando Furioso, 124
Oresme, N., 23, 34
Origen, 137
Orion, 91
Overbury, Sir Thomas, 192, 199
Ovid, 48, 235
Owles Almanacke, 232-238, 239, 240, 241
Oxford, 104, 126, 153

Padua, 5, 6, 164, 255
Pagans, 21, 29
Painter, W., 108, 111
Palaephatus, 48
Palingenius, M., *Zodiacus vitae,* 178
Paracelsus, 49, 82, 248
Pareus, D., 71 n.
Paris, 104
Parker, M., 242
Parron, W., 194
Partridge, J., 242
Paul III, 51
Pedlar's Prophecy, 176 n., 177 n.
Peele, G., 161 n., 162, 164; *Battle of Alcazar,* 183
Penniless Parliament, 224
Peranzonus, N., 249
Percopo, E., 37 n., 40, 52 n.
Pereyra, B., 90-91, 96, 98, 128, 130, 133, 134, 246; *De communibus,* 90; *Theatrum,* 90; *De magia,* 90
Perkins, W., 116-121, 190; *Foure Great Lyers,* 116; *Reformed Catholic,* 116
Petrarch, F., 55, 81, 156, 182
Peucer, C., 53, 66-69, 84, 87; *Commentarius,* 66
Phillips, J., *Mercurius verax,* 243; *Montelion,* 243
Philologus, T., 59
Phlebotomy, 72, 197, 206, 247, 253
Phornutus, 48
Phyrronist, 85
Physicians, 26, 28, 63, 77, 83, 90, 102, 103, 110, 119, 133
Physics, 53, 84, 92, 110, 150
Piccolomini, Aeneas Sylvius, 40; *Somnium,* 41
Piccolomini, Alessandro, 70-71; *Institution,* 70; *Speculationi dei pianeti,* 70

Piccolomini, P., 71 n.
Pickering, W., 218
Pico della Mirandola, 13, 15, 16, 18, 19-35, 36, 37, 39 n., 40, 41, 44, 45, 54, 55, 56, 58, 59, 60, 61, 67 n., 79, 81, 85, 91, 92, 95, 96, 98, 99, 100, 113, 115, 116, 117, 122, 125, 128, 130, 133, 147, 148, 153, 165, 190, 244; commentary on Psalms, 21; *Disputationes,* 15; *De ente,* 21; *Heptaplus,* 21; *In orationem dominicam,* 21; *Oratio,* 19; *Regulae,* 21
Pigghe, A., 56, 249; *Adversus prognosticorum vulgus,* 50
Pirovano, G., 54
Plagues, 61, 63, 72, 97
Planets, in literature, 170-175
Platic aspect, 131, 178
Plato, 23, 28, 78, 223; dialogues, 48; *Phaedrus,* 4; *Symposium,* 6; *Timaeus,* 6, 48
Platonic, 3
Platonic year, 30, 124
Platonist, 15
Pleiades, 91
Pliny, 48
Plomer, H. R., 194 n.
Plotinus, 5, 15, 16
Poggio Bracciolini, 40, 42
Poliziano, A., 14, 15, 16, 24, 36 n., 55, 165
Pollard, A. F., 101 n.
Pond, E., 207-209, 219
Pontano, G., 36-46, 61, 65, 72, 96, 119, 132, 148, 156, 164, 165, 169, 171 n., 172 n., 175 n., 178, 179, 245; commentary on *Centiloquium,* 38; *De fortuna,* 37; *De prudentia,* 39; *De rebus,* 36
Porta, J. B., *De magia,* 142
Possidonius, 85
Practica teütsch, 211
Praktika Doctor Rossschwanz, 211
Prenostication des Laboureurs, 213
Proclean, 4
Proclus, 220
Prognostication, 73, 102, 106, 111, 117, 118, 132, 133, 141, 170, 186, 190, 249
Prometheus, 57, 235, 236
Pronostication generalle, 213

Pronostication nouvelle, 212

Prophecy, 195

Providence, 7, 14, 15, 17, 28, 41, 43, 94, 114, 118, 119, 130, 141

Prudence, 39-40, 76

Ptolemy, 24, 31, 32, 39, 47, 58, 60, 79, 81, 98, 99, 113, 172 n., 173 n., 175, 178, 216, 221, 223, 248, 252; *De praedictionibus*, 169

Purbach, G., 124; *Theoricae novae*, 69

Puritan, 106, 112, 185

Pylades, J. F. B., 48

Pythagoras, 23

Quadrants, 32, 50

Quartile, 177

Rabadus, 223

Rabelais, F., 213-214, 220, 223; *Panta-grueline prognostication*, 212

Raleigh, Sir Walter, 154; *History of the World*, 153

Ramesey, W., *Lux veritatis*, 144

Raunce, J., *A Briefe Declaration*, 144

Raymar, N., *Fundamentum astronomicum*, 53 n.

Reason, 28, 42, 45, 70, 76, 97

Recorde, R., 59 n., 104 n.

Reed, I., 219

Regiomontanus, 122, 125, 196

Regnier, astrologer, 52

Reisch, G., 59 n.; *Margarita*, 53 n.

Religion, and stars, 58, 59, 60, 80, 120

Return from Parnassus, 191

Rheinholt, E., 63 n., 69-70, 124; *Primus liber tabularum*, 69

Richard III, 74

Richmond, 180

Ringelberg, J., *Institutiones astronomicae*, 53 n.; *De ratione studii*, 211 n.

Ripley, G., 137

Roberts, J., 198, 199

Robin Goodfellow, 124

Rocha, T., *Compilatio*, 247

Röslin, E., 94

Rome, 24, 74, 251

Roper, W., 101

Rosaccio, G., *Teatro*, 71 n.

Rostock, 254

Rowland, W., *Iudicial Astrologie*, 144

Rowley, W., 191 n.; *Noble Soldier*, 181 n.

Rudd, T., 54 n.

Ruggieri, C., 52

Sacrobosco, J., 63, 223

St. Albans, 112

St. Andrews, 198

Salisbury, 104

Salutati, C., 40

Sandwich, 115

Saturn, planet, 8, 12, 13, 14, 30, 33, 60, 69, 79, 121, 153, 163, 173, 176, 197, 203, 217, 221, 247; in literature, 172-174

Saturnine, 8, 172, 173

Savonarola, G., 21, 36 n., 71, 82; *Opera singulare*, 35

Saxony, 69

Scepper, C., 59-60, 61, 249; *Adversus*, 59

Schöner, J., 64, 87, 122, 250

Scholl, J., *Astrologiae ad medicinam*, 251

Schonheintz, J., 54

Schylander, C., *Medicina astrologica*, 253

Scot, R., *Discoverie*, 102

Scotland, 74, 198

Securis, J., 104, 117, 194, 197-198

Selden, J., 103

Selimus, 180 n.

Semprini, G., 19 n., 20

Seneca, 23

Senses, 44, 45, 113, 132, 133

Sentirius, 85

Servetus, M., *Apologetica*, 60

Sextile, 177

Sforza, L., 81

Shakespeare, W., 149, 158, 181; and astrology, 165-167; *All's Well*, 158 n., 161 n., 163 n., 168 n., 175 n., 183 n., 185; *Antony*, 167 n.; *Coriolanus*, 167 n.; *Cymbeline*, 105, 167 n.; *Hamlet*, 166, 167 n., 170; I *Hen. IV*, 170, 180 n.; II *Hen. IV*, 177 n.; I *Hen. VI*, 162 n., 166, 181 n.; III *Hen. VI*, 168 n.; *Julius Caesar*, 181 n., 183; *Lear*, 157 n., 167, 178, 184; *Love's Labour's*, 193; *Macbeth*, 105, 228-229; *Measure*, 167; *Midsummer-Night's*, 159 n., 190; *Much Ado*, 163 n., 172; *Othello*, 177, 178; *Pericles*, 163 n., 180 n.; *Richard III*, 157 n., 163 n.; *Romeo*, 167; *Shrew*, 180 n.; *Sonnets*, 158, 159 n.; *Tempest*,

105, 166; *Timon,* 167, 168 n., 176 n.; *Titus Andronicus,* 176 n.; *Troilus,* 159 n., 176 n.; *Twelfth Night,* 163 n., 164 n., 167, 178; *Two Gentlemen,* 163n.; *Winter's Tale,* 158 n., 159 n., 166 n., 176 n., 188, 193
Shinkin ap Shone her Prognostication, 242
Shipton, Mother, 101
Sickingen, Franz von, 74
Sidney, Sir Philip, 159, 165; *Astrophel,* 158
Signs, 33, 114, 120, 137, 138, 150, 173; individual signs: Aquarius, 74, 157; Aries, 27, 32, 221; Cancer, 74, 158, 202, 221, 230; Capricorn, 69, 73, 158, 174, 197, 225; Gemini, 74, 197, 221, 230; Leo, 27, 74, 151, 152, 197, 203, 230; Libra, 32, 158, 197, 202, 225; Pisces, 33, 74, 151, 158, 247; Sagittarius, 73, 203, 225, 230; Scorpio, 30, 32, 158, 197, 230, 247; Taurus, 174, 178, 193, 197, 221, 230; Virgo, 74, 157, 158, 174, 197, 235; rhetorical use of, 157-158; sex of, 30, 114
Simeoni, astrologer, 52
Sirius, 154
Sisera, 3, 48, 143
Sixtus IV, 13
Skelton, J., Jests of, 128
Smel-Knave, Simon, *The Fearefull and lamentable effects,* 221-224, 225, 226, 227, 230, 231, 236
Smith, H., *God's Arrow,* 228
Smith, Sir Thomas, 103
Smith, T., 132 n.
Smith, W., *Chloris,* 159 n., 161 n.
Fell-Smith, C., 104
Soderino, P., 11 n.
Soldati, B., 37, 38 n., 39
Somnus, 237
Sondheim, M., 87 n., 165 n.
Songecreux, A., *Le Prenostication,* 213
Soul, 4, 5, 11, 18
Spain, 125
Spaniards, 127
Sparrow, J., 154 n.
Spelman, H., 103
Spenser, E., 163 n., 169, 170, 174, 175, 176 n., 178, 210; *Faerie Queene,* 70
Spheres, 7, 31, 57

Spinoza, 244
Spontaneous generation, 89
Star of Bethlehem, 29, 48
Stars, and bodily organs, 10, 33, 49, 120, 197, 202; and Christ, 25, 29-30, 58, 79, 80, 143, and herbs and gems, 9-10, 36n., 49, 57, 80, 82, 97; as agents of God, 9, 28, 43, 65, 69, 72, 83, 91, 93, 119, 130; as causes, 27, 29, 44, 62, 67, 69, 83, 90, 141, as epithets in literature, 160-161; birth stars in literature, 162-163; fixed stars, 31, 36n ., 90; influence of, 9-10, 27, 39, 62, 64, 71, 72, 79, 90, 91, 95, 109, 114, 120, 131, 138, 148, 151, 153, 159-160, 162; influence cited in literature, 176-177
Stathmion, C., 82
Sternhold, T., 199
Stoeffler, J., 63
Strange Predictions, 243
Stratford, 107
Straus, H. A., 52 n.
Stuart, 101
Stubbes, P., *Anatomie,* 186
Sudhoff, K., 49 n., 255
Sun, 12. 28, 36 n., 44, 56, 64, 74, 76, 79, 81, 83, 89, 91, 92, 94, 120, 151, 176 197, 202, 221, 225
Superstition, 6, 64, 67, 106, 112, 149
Swabians, 74
Swadlin, T., 145 n.
Swift, J., *Isaac Bickerstaff's Predictions,* 243
Sybilla Tiburtina, 124

Taisnier, J., 66 n., 253; *Astrologiae iudiciariae ysagogica,*53 n.;*Opus mathematicum,* 253
Tamburlaine, 179
Tancred and Gismunda, 183 n.
Tanner, R., *Prognosticall Iudgement,* 123; *Probable Coniectures,* 123
Tanstetter von Rain, G., *Artificium,* 249; *Libellus consolatorius,* 249
Taylor, R., 229-230
Telesio, B., *De naturalibus rebus,* 179
Tenterden, 115
Tertullian, 24
Tertullus, 43
Thales, 128, 133

Thames, 107
Theologians, 88
Theomancy, 66
Thibault, J., 50, 194
Thomas Aquinas, St., 150
Thorndike, L., 3 n., 50 n.
Thornhill, Sir Timothy, 232
Three Ladies of London, 188
Thurinus, A., *Hippocrates et Galeni defensio*, 251
Tides, 28, 60, 82, 97
Tifernas, G., 37
Tim Tell Troth, The Knavery of Astrology, 242
Toffanin, G., 37
Tollin, H., 61 n.
Tomkis, T., *Albumasar*, 186
Tommai, P., 59
Tomyris, 236
Tragedy of Tiberius, 161 n., 164, 176 n., 181 n.
Trigon, 177
Triplicity, 34, 60, 74, 174, 177
Tourneur, C., *Atheist's Tragedy*, 184; *Revenger's Tragedy*, 181
Trapezuntius, 81
Tudor, 101, 106
Tübingen, 253
Turnebé, A., 118, 190
Two Maides of More-Clacke, 156 n.
Twyne, T., 104, 117 n.

Uhl, W., 210 n.

Valori, F., 12
Vaughn, L., 108, 109, 196
Venice, 96, 177, 198, 247, 251, 254
Venus, planet, 8, 12, 148, 163, 172, 173, 176, 198, 202, 203, 248; in literature, 174-175
Vergil, 47, 238
Vespucius, B., *Sphaerae tractatus*, 68 n.
Vicary, T., 104 n.
Vienna, 206
Vignal, F. G., 19 n.
Villiers, George, Duke of Buckingham, 105
Vincenza, 255
Virdung von Hassfurt, J., 59; *Pratica*, 250; *Nova medicinae methodus*, 251
Vox Graculi, or Iacke Dawes Prognostication, 238-241

W., W., *A New and Merry Prognostication*, 218, 238
Walford, C., 216 n.
Walsingham, Sir Francis, 113
Warner, W., 103, 185
Warren, H., *Magic and Astrology*, 144
Watkins, R., 198, 199
Watson, R., 199
Weakest Goeth to the Wall, 157 n.
Webster, J., 157 n., 162 n., 163 n., 168 n., 180 n., 181 n., 187, 191; *Duchess of Malfi*, 177; *Anything for a Quiet Life*, 193
Wedel, T. O., 150 n.
Weigel, V., *Astrology Theologized*, 145, 255
Weller, E., 210 n.
Welshman's Almanack, 242
Westhawe, R., 199
Wilhelm of Bavaria, 74
Wilkins, G., *Miseries*, 176 n., 181 n.
Will, 11, 14, 17, 18, 19, 20, 22, 28, 36 n., 43, 45, 56, 58, 67, 68, 69, 71, 85-86, 91, 92, 93, 97, 99, 141, 148
Willett, A., 71 n., 155 n.
William of Auvergne, 34
Wilson, F. P., 216 n., 218, 219, 224, 226, 233, 239
Wily Beguiled, 176 n.
Windsor, 126
Winzemius, V., 87
Wit of a Woman, 157 n.
Witches, 126
Witchcraft, 130, 141
Wither, F., 170
Wittenberg, 66
Wolf, J., 74-78; *Admonitio*, 75, 84
Wonders Foretold, 242
Wood, Anthony a, 139
Woodes, N., *Conflict of Conscience*, 188
Worlds, plurality of, 79
Wright, E., 131, 132
Wright, T., *Passions of the Mind*, 227
Wright, W., 219

Xylander, G., 50 n.

York, 198

Zodiac, 15, 18 n., 27, 30, 31-32, 59, 137, 158, 177, 178, 234